"*How to Think Strategically* is without question one of the most useful books I have read. Greg talks you through the big skills and microskills of strategic thinking. He guides you toward sharpness of thought, and away from the dull and dumb. For business or your personal life, you'll find Greg leading you on a journey of well-organized thought orientations and approaches. The book is a must-read for all who wish to build their skills and expand their views beyond just creative, critical, and systems thinking.

— **Paul O'Connor**, President and CEO, The Adept Group

"A great strategist needs great strategic thinking skills. *How to Think Strategically* gets the job done. It provides all the necessary tools and insight to help you become an influential strategic thinker. A great read!"

— **Jeroen De Flander**, strategist and bestselling author of *Strategy Execution Heroes* and *The Execution Shortcut*

"In a world focused on data analytics, financial models, and ROI, the human dimension of strategic planning can be subordinated or overlooked. Githens' *How to Think Strategically* elevates the role of personal leadership and virtues in the process for wise choices, buy-in, and execution. The trait of commitment and the microskill of courage, for example, are indispensable for making hard decisions in uncertain times. Attention to this human dimension empowers complex organizations for effective planning and success."

— **Gregory P. Crawford**, professor of physics and university president

"*How to Think Strategically* will enlighten leaders throughout the organization. Githens stresses the power of an individual to find and make sense of weak signals and use them to create powerful insights. His methodology is refreshingly effective in building a coherent path to learn and enhance specific capabilities to become an effective and influential strategic thinker. It is a must read for any leader wanting to enhance their strategic thinking skills.

— **Bill Blackmore**, board member of five companies, retired CEO, business owner

"Get your hands on this book as soon as possible! It's practical. It's insightful. It's accessible to all. Githens has the courage and experience to dismantle strategy and challenge long-held orthodoxies. I plan to keep this book nearby for years to come!"

— **Mazy Gillis**, Ph.D., Vice President Global Human Resources

"I've held the positions of Chief Strategy Officer and Chief Operations Officer for the same company, so Greg's outline of the two thinking maps for strategy and operations particularly resonated with me. Both are critically important to the success of an organization, but it's equally important that you know which area you are in and not confuse the two. It would be detrimental for both strategy and operations. Furthermore, Greg's portrayal of ambiguity as a critical component of strategy development was eye-opening and truly the embodiment of what strategic thinking is all about, rather than the rush to create a strategy (as it is many times inappropriately labeled). Well done!"

— **Vincent P. DiPofi**, PE, Chief Operating Officer, SSOE Group

"Greg Githens' approach to strategic thinking offers a wealth of practical advice for the most seasoned strategist about how to reason more clearly and with greater self-awareness about the often murky and discontinuous world in which we live. Githens is such a crisp and direct writer that his insights sound like common sense you've known all your life, but don't be fooled: Nuanced and usefully counterintuitive insights are there in abundance for the careful reader. Soak in recommendations to learn, for instance, the 'micro skill of conceptual mapping' or how to 'devalorize' management orthodoxies in order to better understand them. While the ultimate target of strategy itself is the organization, the value of this book lies in the effort to empower individuals – that is, each of us – to be braver, more exploratory, and more confident in initiating change when it is often a fearful and daunting task."

— **Amy Zaltman**, Ph.D., CEO, Prescient (formerly the Strategic Narrative Institute)

HOW TO **THINK**
STRATEGICALLY

HOW TO **THINK**
STRATEGICALLY

Sharpen Your Mind
Develop Your Competency
Contribute to Success

Greg Githens

MAVEN HOUSE

Published by Maven House Press, 4 Snead Ct., Palmyra, VA 22963;
610.883.7988; www.mavenhousepress.com; info@mavenhousepress.com

Special discounts on bulk quantities of Maven House Press books are available
to corporations, professional associations, and other organizations. For details
contact the publisher.

While this publication is designed to provide accurate and authoritative
information in regard to the subject matter covered, it is sold with the
understanding that the publisher is not engaged in rendering legal, accounting,
or other professional service. If legal advice or other expert assistance is
required, the services of a competent professional person should be sought.
— From the Declaration of Principles jointly adopted by a Committee of the
American Bar Association and a Committee of Publishers and Associations

Quotes from pp. 2, 46, 57, 61, 107, 115, 119, 121, 123, 127, 129–130, 153, 175,
212, 214, 223, and 257 from *Who Says Elephants Can't Dance?: Inside IBM's
Historic Turnaround* by Louis V. Gerstner. Copyright © 2002 by Louis V.
Gerstner Jr. Reprinted by permission of HarperCollins Publishers.

Library of Congress Control Number: 2018967236

Paperback ISBN: 9781938548901
E-book ISBN: 9781938548918

Printed in the United States of America.

CONTENTS

DEDICATION

For my wife, Helen, and my mother, Juanita

FIGURES

ACRONYMS

CapEx – Capital Expenses

CtB – Change the Business

DICE - Drive, Insight, Chance, Emergence

H1 – Horizon 1, the near-term future

H2 – Horizon 2, the intermediate-term future

H3 – Horizon 3, the distant-term future

IBM – International Business Machines Corporation (discussed in Chapters 8, 9, and elsewhere)

OpEx – Operational Expenses

RtB – Run the Business

RWE – RWE AG is a German electric utility company (described in Chapter 11)

PoF – Pockets of the Future (in the present moment)

STF – The initials of a non-profit community organization (discussed in Chapter 10)

VUCA – Volatility, Uncertainty, Complexity, Ambiguity

PREFACE

*In the case of good books, the point is not to see
how many of them you can get through, but rather
how many of them get through to you.*

— Morton J. Adler

The Big Idea

STRATEGIC THINKING IS AN INDIVIDUAL COMPETENCY – that's this book's big idea. A competent individual is one who understands the situation and acts reasonably. She is sharp: she applies effort to discern relevant nuance, generate options, and uses evidence in her reasoning.* She is skeptical of conformity, orthodoxy, and predictions.

The benefits of being a competent strategic thinker are significant: you can contribute to the success of an existing organization, foster new endeavors, and empower your success. I tell entrepreneurs, "Strategic thinking will determine whether you make it through those first lean years." I tell executives of nonprofit and charitable organizations, "Strategic thinking will determine the amount of impact and good you can do." I tell middle managers, "Strategic thinking can get you promoted!" When you show others that you are a competent strategic thinker, they will reward you with respect and growth.

Everyone wants to be regarded as competent and would feel embarrassed if labeled incompetent. Because labeling someone as incompetent is a bit blunt and insulting, I suggest the best contrast with

---

* I will use the pronoun *she* throughout the book as a convention when referring to the individual. Although there are mostly males in my examples, I sincerely believe that women are fully capable of achieving excellence in strategic thinking.

competency is mediocrity. A mediocre strategic thinker settles for too-narrow understandings of the situation, prefers simple problems and obvious answers, relies on instinct and intuition, is willing to accept the first reasonable answer that presents itself, and tolerates the excuse, "I'm too busy to think about that."

Anticipating New Futures

Good individual strategic thinking is a direct and proximate cause of good strategy. Each uptick in the quality and quantity of strategic thinkers brings benefits to the organization and its stakeholders.

Strategy is an important topic that's relevant for institutions, ventures, and enterprises of any size or mission: large and small businesses, the military, government agencies, nonprofits, churches, schools, charitable organizations, and startups.

Risk is everywhere, and I like to remind people that the Chinese character for risk is a combination of the symbols for threat and for opportunity. The future is certain to be different from today. No matter the place or time, a strategic thinker accepts the potential for disruption and the benefits of emergent opportunity.

Strategic Thinking Is Rare and Valuable

There are thousands of jobs posted on career search sites that explicitly require strategic thinking. Organizations clearly value individuals who can think strategically and want them on the front line of management as well as in the executive suite and board room.

Competent strategic thinkers are exceptions from the norm. For that reason, they are rare. One challenge of organizational development is in recognizing that prevailing culture often discourages deviation from the norm. Hence the cliché, *the nail that sticks up gets hammered down.*

You need to think strategically about how you develop and practice your strategic thinking. Many people find comfort in this statement: *No one needs to know that you're thinking strategically.* You can attend to your daily responsibilities while simultaneously researching the situation, anticipating the future, and exercising your imagination.

Meaningful Learning

To experience the joy of a book "getting through to you," you must read the book. Many people succumb to *Tsundoku*, a Japanese word describing the practice of collecting books and not reading them. A book that *gets through to you* is one that challenges and changes your worldview.

The premise of meaningful learning is that individuals come to situations with an existing baseline of knowledge. Learning occurs when the learner adds new pieces of knowledge to that baseline or when she edits or reorganizes her mental scaffold of concepts.

Here is an example. While driving a car in traffic, you have anticipated obstacles and anticipated the intentions of other drivers. That real-world experience gives you a baseline of relevant knowledge. This book will introduce strategic thinking concepts such as sharpness, anticipation, and empathy, which some would treat as isolated abstractions. Meaningful learning is simply the task of creating relevance by connecting your baseline to the introduced concepts.

Returning to the driving example, recall your feelings when another driver cut you off or made a rude gesture. Hopefully, you kept your emotions in check and focused on your responsibility to be safe and courteous. Similarly, a strategic thinker needs to be able to sidestep anger and other mind states that can corrupt her ability to make good decisions.

Here is a short list of other real-world-concepts that have analogies in strategic thinking:

- You have experienced well-designed and poorly-designed buildings, products, and experiences.
- You've expressed skepticism about the trustworthiness of overconfident, impulsive people.

- You've established goals and worked toward goals and objectives established by others.

- You know that scientists and journalists put much effort into discovering new truths.

- You have made plans and later revised them due to changed circumstances.

- You have applied for jobs and promotions and hired and promoted others.

- You have observed and participated in games and competitions.

- You have assessed situations while making decisions.

- You've read or listened to prognostications.

- You've made bets and investments.

- You've visited museums.

- You know stories.

None of the above are *exactly* strategic thinking, but each of them provides a useful analogy to its practice.

Learning is not solely the acquisition of new knowledge but is also the expulsion of misconceptions. Often, the biggest challenge for meaningful learners is unlearning invalid rules, tools, and assumptions. Watch for the discussion of the confusion of goal setting and strategy, as an example.

Take your time with this book. Find the personal relevance in the examples and questions. You will be rewarded with a personal competency and mastery that will benefit you in all areas of your life.

What to Anticipate

I intend this book to strike a balance between examples and application versus principles and theory. I've kept each chapter short, aimed to use familiar terms and examples, and used graphics to illustrate concepts.

The "How to" in the title of this book is not a promise of a prescriptive, step-by-step methodology. Rather, I instruct by using frameworks and examples, knowing that your application of meaningful learning will shape your use of the tools.

The book has two parts. Part I is titled "The Nature, Purpose, and Scope of Strategic Thinking." Its nine chapters establish foundational concepts and principles, supported by real-world examples.

Part II is titled "Personal and Interpersonal Mastery." Its four chapters will help you mature your perspective and talents. The issues addressed include trust in self and others, confidence, regulating your thoughts and behaviors, influencing others, high-quality conversations, and the courage of leadership.

The book contains six appendices. In each, you'll find useful supplemental information, including unified lists of key concepts like microskills and strategic thinking landmarks.

About the Author...and His Perspective

In the spirit of applying unorthodox ideas, I write this biography in the first person. I write with the purpose of *engaging*, rather than *impressing* the reader. I hope that you can detect authenticity in this nontraditional approach.

I've had the good fortune to work, as an employee and as a consultant, for a diverse array of organizations: fast-growing entrepreneurial companies, family businesses, large businesses, government agencies, military, universities, and nonprofit community and professional organizations. I've worked with those at the top of the organization and those on the front line.

The role of an explainer and a coach has been my most-rewarding professional activity. Like other teachers, I gain great satisfaction when the student applies her learning to make a positive impact on the world.

One of the more interesting influences on my strategic thinking is my regular participation in financial markets as a trader of options (more specifically buying and selling puts and calls). Most of those trades have been profitable, but some have not. My most important lesson has been in managing my own habits of mind.

It's also customary, with book bios, to list the author's previous publications. It's a fact that I have been published before. The most important learning to offer is that good, insightful writing reflects good, insightful thinking. If you want to improve your strategic thinking, share your ideas: write more, speak in public more, and use social media.

Greg Githens
Lakewood Ranch, Florida, USA
email: GregoryDGithens@cs.com
Follow: Twitter: @GregGithens
Follow: LinkedIn.com/in/greggithens/

The Nature, Purpose, and Scope of Strategic Thinking

PART I DESCRIBES the nature, purpose, and scope of strategic thinking. You will learn that strategic thinking is not a system of subsystems but rather a loosely integrated cluster of concepts. I suggest reading the nine chapters in order, since early chapters establish principles and examples that are further developed in subsequent chapters.

Chapter 1 (Are You Strategic?) introduces ambiguity as a fundamental challenge that is usually neglected in the work to craft strategy. I introduce the strategic-thinking narrative technique and apply it to Billy Beane and the Moneyball strategy. The narrative reveals the importance of confronting the reality of a dire situation, of being curious in seeking new strategic logics, and of coordinating the organization during implementation. The chapter concludes by encouraging readers to adopt the beginner's mind.

Chapter 2 (Cleverness) shows that using adjectives like *good* or *clever* allow you to better characterize the quality of a strategy. I return to the Billy Beane Moneyball story to show that it was clever because a relatively weak organization was able to accomplish brilliant results. I introduce one of the most popular and effective tools in the book, the five-part template for writing strategy.

Chapter 3 (Big Ideas) uses the Christopher Columbus strategic-thinking narrative to reveal essential principles of competent strategic thinking. This includes a four-pillar definition of strategic thinking, the four X-factors, and six important lessons for Columbus's success with his big idea.

Chapter 4 (Twelve Microskills of Strategic Thinking) introduces a set of specific conceptual skills. As you make the microskills of strategic thinking a habit of mind, you will improve your capacity for thinking strategically. If you adopt only one thing from this book, I recommend practicing the Ben Franklin technique to highlight and practice one microskill each week.

Chapter 5 (Why Strategic Thinking is Rare) explains that strategic thinking is rare because individuals tend to pay attention to the map of operational thinking. The prevailing culture enhances that attention. The consequence is that operational thinking tends to crowd aside strategic thinking. The path to better strategic thinking is to orient yourself toward the navigational beacons of the core challenge, the future, and insights. This chapter introduces the microskills of devalorization and contrarianism to help you distance yourself from the map of operational thinking.

Chapter 6 (The Fuzzy Front End of Strategy) introduces the strategy funnel, which is a three-phase framework. The first of the three phases is the fuzzy front end of strategy. It involves sensing and interpreting weak signals. The strategist then practices sensemaking and synthesis, resulting in a set of beliefs about the situation. The second phase is the structured back end. It's here that the strategist identifies a core challenge, the dominating ideas of strategy, and makes strategic decisions. The third phase involves programming. It is the application of resources and methods to address that core challenge. This chapter introduces the microskills of high-quality questions and abductive reasoning.

Chapter 7 (Pockets of the Future) introduces the idea that you can find weak signals in the present that have significant implications for the future. Things that we presently consider curiosities can become dominant in future systems. You will find useful the three horizons framework for describing the dynamics of qualitative change in future systems. This chapter introduces the microskill of anticipation. Strategic thinkers must be oriented toward the future and consider their anticipatory assumptions.

Both Chapter 8 (Strategic Decisions) and Chapter 9 (The Spark of Insight) feature the strategic-thinking narrative of Lou Gerstner and his time as CEO of IBM, when he led the company's turnaround and transformation. Chapter 8 explains the criteria for strategic decisions and tactical decisions, using Gerstner's decision to keep IBM together as an example of a strategic decision. The chapter also provides another example of written strategy using the five-part model similar to that provided in Chapter 2. Insights are the secret sauce of strategy, and Chapter 9 unpacks its mechanisms. The chapter introduces the microskill of reframing and suggests techniques for increasing the quantity and quality of insights.

CHAPTER 1

Are You Strategic?

An Introduction to the Nature, Purpose, and Scope of Strategic Thinking

The most important thing is to find out
what is the most important thing.

— Shunryu Suzuki

Q: What is one characteristic of strategy that is essential to
  understand, yet is mostly overlooked, even by expert strategists?

A: Ambiguity

THE LATIN ROOTS of the word *ambiguity* suggest wandering, uncertainty, and multiple meanings. An example of ambiguity is found in Figure 1-1, a graphic that many know as "the young lady and the old lady." It is one of many examples of a quaint form of graphic design known as pictorial ambiguity. Some people can only see the old lady, and some can only see the young lady. (Hints: The young lady is looking away from you, and the old lady is looking downward. The young lady's chin is the tip of the old lady's nose.) It takes an effort to resolve ambiguity.

Another example of ambiguity is multiple definitions of words. For example, the three-letter words *run* and *set* have meanings that can only be understood by placing the words in sentences or paragraphs. The word *strategy* itself is ambiguous. Many people define its meaning in partial ways: as the opposite of a tactic, as another name for a goal, as the steps to reach a goal, as a process tied to the organization's calendar, as a plan, as a methodology, etc.

Ambiguity is inherent to strategy. From an entrepreneur's perspective, ambiguity is the source of opportunity and competitive advantage.

Figure 1-1. An example of pictorial ambiguity. Can you see the two faces?

An example is a young Steve Jobs visiting Xerox Corporation's Palo Alto lab in California There, he was shown prototypes of the now familiar computer mouse and graphical interface. Recognizing the potential of the technology, Jobs incorporated the ideas into Apple's new line of computers.

People get signals from all directions but don't know whether to ignore them or to attach great significance to them. Is the data in the government's report on the economy a signal that a trend is starting or ending? Is a new technology going to fizzle or disrupt? Are the signals a threat, an opportunity, or both? Will the new CEO use the same approach as she used at her previous company?

Sometimes people take time from their busy lives to consider questions like those just posed. However, most people find it more comfortable to pay attention to those things that are simple, immediate, and unambiguous. Stated differently, most individuals (managers and executives included) cope with ambiguity by neglecting it most of the time. The reason for the neglect is obvious: ambiguity mentally taxes a person. Consider your reaction to Figure 1-1. If you're like most, once you saw one of the faces, you allowed your attention to shift to something else.

Returning to the Steve Jobs example, the top Xerox executives in headquarters could have chosen to exploit these inventions but instead focused on their existing operations. They didn't see the potential. Maybe the Xerox executives only saw one of the faces in Figure 1-1, and Jobs saw both?

Volatility, uncertainty, complexity, and ambiguity (VUCA) is a common framework used to describe the indeterminant and dynamic nature of strategic situations. (You can learn more about VUCA in Appendix A.) The strategist must consider VUCA and be able to distinguish it from conventional, goal-oriented planning.

One technique for resolving ambiguity is the straightforward practice of defining terms. Accordingly, I must next explain the meanings of two essential concepts of strategic thinking, which are the words *competence* and *strategy*.

Competence

This book's big idea is that individuals are the sole practitioners of strategic thinking, and each person practices it in a way that can be judged as competent or not. *Competent individuals have the capacity and ability to understand a situation and act reasonably.* Let's unpack the three main components.

Individual capacity. Stating the obvious, individuals are unique. Each person has her life experiences, formal education, and own stylistic approach to dealing with people and situations. People vary in the degree to which they are curious, analytical, open-minded, creative, and disciplined. Strategic thinking is a habit of mind, a mental stance reflecting the individual's perspective.

> *Competent individuals have the capacity and ability to understand a situation and act reasonably.*

Competent strategic thinking is a personal characteristic that is independent of a person's rank in an organization. This is an empowering concept where every person in the organization can develop their habits of mind and contribute in small and large ways to the organization's strategy and operations.

The obstacles to competent strategic thinking are generally twofold: the individual's natural inclinations for mental ease coupled with the smothering effects of the prevailing culture. The neglect of ambiguity is one example of mental ease. Organizational culture is a powerful force for the status quo and a restraining force for individual initiative. It takes considerable effort to overcome orthodoxy, dogma, and mediocrity. Any individual who shows herself contrary to the norms might be subject to teasing, shaming, or ostracism.

Fortunately for the promotion of strategic thinking, progressive organizations value leadership, innovation, diversity, sound judgment, collaboration, and empowerment. Unfortunately, the traditional organization-as-machine and institutional concepts retain much power in many ongoing narratives.

Understanding the situation. The jargon phrases *tunnel vision, lost in the weeds*, and *silo mentality* are common in most organizations, especially larger ones. Many managers are unwittingly committed to inertia, doing things the same way that they've always been done, through habits of mind reinforced by the organization's culture. People may understand their local situation but often have an incomplete understanding of the organization's place in a more extensive ecosystem of relationships.

Acting reasonably. Figure 1-2 lists some criteria useful for determining the reasonableness of actions. A reasonable person can justify her beliefs and actions. Importantly, not everyone has the same concept of reasonableness, since ambiguity can lead to different interpretations. One person may look at a situation and arrive at a conclusion that's different from that of others. If 99 percent of people see only the face of the old lady, it doesn't mean that the 1 percent who see the young lady are wrong.

For a given situation, a reasonable person would *strive* to:

☑ Be deliberate and not impulsive

☑ Consider all relevant facts and circumstances

☑ Identify the advantages and disadvantages of policy choices, listening to the questions and comments of stakeholders

☑ Not enrich herself at the expense of others or breach fiduciary or other ethical responsibilities

☑ Explain the rationale for their decisions and actions to another reasonable person, if requested

☑ Avoid mistakes such as overconfidence and magical thinking

☑ Show proactive rather than reactive behaviors

Figure 1-2. Characteristics of a reasonable person.

Strategy

Asking "What is strategy?" will provoke many answers among academics and practitioners.* The idea of sustainable competitive advantage, a dominating idea of for-profit organizational strategy, is of little relevance for a startup entrepreneur, a school principal, a military field commander, a county commissioner, a pastor, or a middle manager. The template-driven practices of long-range planning used in many bureaucratic institutions is a time waster for a company operating in a VUCA world of continually-emerging opportunities.

Here is the definition of *strategy* that guides our understanding of the nature, purpose, and scope of strategic thinking:

> Strategy is a specialized tool used to advance the interests of the organization by managing issues that have a broad and long-term impact.

---

* There are many schools of thought on strategy. This definition of strategy is consistent throughout the book and coherently supports a model of strategic thinking as an individual competency.

This definition of *strategy* is broadly applicable to any organization: big and small business, the military, the government, nonprofits, political campaigns. It's appropriate for bureaucracies and for entrepreneurs. It's relevant to explaining the actions of any organization throughout history.

The following four main ideas characterize strategy:

- The first main idea is that strategy is a specialized tool. As a specialized tool, strategy is appropriate for some situations and not for others. Strategy's primary concern is fitting the internal resources to the situation of emerging, significant opportunities and threats. The need for strategy arises from dynamic change in the external environment.

- The second main idea is the premise that all organizations (businesses, governments, nonprofits, militaries, charities, churches, schools, etc.) have interests. For example, a school's interests could include educating its students and fostering a more productive and civil community. Many businesses have obligations to shareholders but also intend to contribute to society's interests. Interests can and do change, sometimes deliberately, but sometimes they drift in a new direction on their own, unrecognized by stakeholders.

Strategy is practiced to advance the interests of the organization.

- The third main idea is that managers must confront issues in order to advance the organization's interests. The concept of an issue can include exploiting opportunities as well as mitigating threats. An essential task is to scan for weak signals and determine the need for further action. The issues may be present-moment battles, or things that loom with future significance. After the issue is identified, it's characterized, prioritized, and resolved by making decisions and applying resources.

This focus on confronting issues and advancing interests is usefully reinforced by this simple, powerful concept of strategy taught in the U.S. Army War College:

Conceptually, we define strategy as the relationship among ends, ways, and means. Ends are the objectives or goals sought. Means are the resources available to pursue the objectives. And ways or methods are how one organizes and applies the resources. Each of these components suggests a related question. What do we want to pursue (ends)? With what (means)? How (ways)?

> *Strategy is a relationship among ends, ways, and means.*

In the next chapter, I apply these concepts of issues and interests and their relationships with ends, ways, and means and show how to write strategy.

- The fourth main idea characterizing strategy is that some organizational issues have broad and long-term impacts and other issues don't. This fourth main idea reinforces the first, that strategy is a specialized tool. The issues that are narrower in scope and more day-to-day are usually better handled through operations management, as discussed in the next paragraphs.

Run the business or change the business? I earlier wrote that strategy was a specialized tool for appropriate situations. The inappropriate situations for using strategy are ongoing operations.

A person working in operations is *operating* a system to deliver results to its customers. A person with an operational focus typically attends to short-term, narrow issues and relies on the managerial tools of goal setting, budgeting, delegation, prioritization, benchmarking, and continuous incremental improvement. Productivity, optimization, and stability are salient values.

In contrast to operations and its emphasis on "running the business," strategy focuses on "changing the business." Stated differently, operations involves working "in" the organization whereas strategy involves working "on" the organization's fit with the external environment.

11

Balancing action and conceptualization. You can easily find, especially in entrenched operations, people who are openly dismissive of abstract concepts such as the future, competitive fit, or insight. Jerry Rhodes observes, "There is a die-hard attitude that still survives in many managers that thinking smells of the abstract and must be the enemy of action." They are the people who buy and gift things such as the coffee mug in Figure 1-3 that boldly pronounces, "We have a strategic plan. It's called doing things." They are the same people who will say, as an excuse for narrow framing and a short-term orientation, "I'm too busy to think about anything other than what's right in front of me."

Figure 1-3. An example of celebrating action over thoughtfulness.

There are undoubtedly good reasons for valuing action, practicality, and simplicity. However, some managers are impulsive, dogmatic, stubborn, and lazy. There must be a role for thoughtfulness and nuance, and elevating these values enhances the cultural embrace of strategic thinking.

Setting the agenda. Numerous broad and long-term strategic issues originate externally to the organization. There are also issues related to the internal capabilities, resources, and aspirations of the organization. Which issues are worthy of being placed on the organization's agenda for action?

Top management has essential responsibilities for shaping the strategic agenda. One responsibility is to participate in, champion, and sponsor the search for weak signals. Ideally, all members of the organization are encouraged to be curious. With more eyes engaged in scanning the internal and external environment, the organization has available more potentially useful information for its strategy. Ideally, each person also understands the issues and how her contributions align with strategy and with operations. When it's time to launch a new strategy, people are better able to understand the rationale for the strategy.

A second responsibility is to determine the organization's core challenge and help stakeholders understand that core challenge.

Third, top management must make the essential decisions about where to focus scarce resources. With this responsibility, top management also has a critical governance function to help guide the decentralized execution of its policy decisions.

While strategy requires a certain amount of centralization in decision making, strategic thinking is not the exclusive responsibility of a "strategic level." Anyone can think strategically, and if empowered, anyone can act strategically, too. And, as part of a virtuous loop, strategic thinking increases individual empowerment, and empowered individuals are more apt to want to think strategically.

Strategy and Strategic Thinking in Action

Good examples of strategic thinking are easy to find in popular media, history, sports, political campaigns, and elsewhere. The movie and book *Moneyball* is a story about a brilliant strategy developed by an unorthodox leader willing to challenge conventional beliefs. The movie opens with a challenge to Billy Beane, the general manager of the Oakland A's professional baseball team. The team is under new ownership, and the new owners are unwilling to continue absorbing financial losses. The owners tell Beane to reduce his payroll.[†] But he must also find a way to field a winning team.

[†] The movie captures the essential narrative of the use of Moneyball as a strategy, although it does deviate from the book in many important ways. My paraphrasing combines the events from the movie and the book.

Since some readers may not know (or care) much about the business model of American professional baseball, a little background will help to explain why Beane innovated the Moneyball strategy. The essence of the game is a contest between the pitcher and the batter. The pitcher throws a ball to a target with velocity and curving movement and the batter swings to hit the pitched ball. If the batter successfully makes contact and places the ball into the field of play, the defensive players attempt to execute a play to keep the batter from taking a position on the base. Each pitch, each swing of the bat, and each struck ball influence the outcome of the game.

The game has many traditions. Since the game's origination in the 19th century, scorers have constructed a set of metrics, such as runs batted in (RBI). Those indicators became part of the lore of the game and a basis for making business decisions in negotiating contracts. Management pays high salaries to players with high RBIs.

There is a significant disparity between the financial resources of each professional team. This is because some owners have more financial wealth than others, some local markets are more loyal than others, and some teams have a national following as well as a local market. A few so-called superstar players can negotiate and receive extraordinarily high salaries, many multiples better than average players. If the rich teams overpay, they seem not to care; they're rich.

Given the new owners' budget restrictions, the Oakland A's were unable to compete in the marketplace for superstar talent. Their best players obtained lucrative contracts with richer teams such as the New York Yankees or the Boston Red Sox.

Billy Beane believed that his rivals were not valuing talent correctly, and that he could exploit his better knowledge. A growing body of evidence showed that traditional indicators, such as RBI, overvalued the contribution of the hitter and undervalued luck and other factors beyond the hitter's control. His insight was that conventional indicators influenced teams to overpay their talent. In other words, the marketplace for baseball talent was inefficient. Beane wanted to exploit his rivals' ignorance (or their complacency; it's hard to tell the difference). His policy was to secure the contracts of undervalued players and deal away overvalued players.

Oakland's Moneyball strategy was effective and produced an exceptional result: over a multiple-year period, Oakland won more regular season games than any other team (except the Atlanta Braves) and reached the playoffs several years in a row. They did this with the lowest payroll in the industry.

The strategic-thinking narrative for Billy Beane and the Oakland A's organization reveals several lessons for good strategy, which are applicable to many other situations and organizations. Here are seven:

- **They recognized the reality of their situation.** Their rivals had comparatively immense resources. If the Oakland A's used conventional thinking, they would have little chance of being successful. A line from the movie captures the requirement for unconventional (strategic) thinking, "If we think like the Yankees in here [referring to a competitor and the criteria for drafting players], we will lose to the Yankees out there [on the playing field]."

- **They found and applied insights.** Building off the hypothesis that the marketplace for baseball talent is inefficient, Oakland expanded the use of sabermetrics, the empirical analysis of in-game activity in baseball. Sabermetrics originated with a group of hobbyists who played fantasy baseball (also called Rotisserie leagues). The owners of these fantasy teams would compose teams based on actual players, and then compete based on the real players' actual performance on the field. Sabermetrics, with 20 years of publications, was not a secret weapon. Any of Oakland's rivals could have exploited it.

  This outside-the-mainstream innovation provided specific, actionable insights that allowed Oakland to construct a new competitive logic.

- **They developed a new set of dominating ideas.** Some ideas are more important than others, and a new strategy is a configuration of elements. For Oakland, the dominating ideas included these: nontraditional statistics could model a player's performance, the average player usually performed to his statistical average, the market for talent was inefficient in that rivals were willing to overspend for performance, and shrewd negotiation could acquire undervalued talent.

The logic of baseball offense is straightforward: the presence of a runner on base increases the likelihood of scoring runs, and the more runs scored, the more games won. Oakland's strategic logic emphasized getting the maximum offensive productivity possible for the minimum payroll dollar. Their premise was that getting runners on base was the key to winning games. In their model for the 2002 season, they estimated that scoring 800 to 820 runs would allow them to win between 93 and 97 games. To achieve this offensive productivity, they emphasized finding and coaching players to get on base and score runs. The most straightforward means to this strategy was to find players with high on-base percentages, subject to a design constraint of payroll affordability.

A new strategy has a new dominating idea that organizes its logic.

The dominating ideas of the Moneyball strategy stand in contrast to the traditional approaches: scouts assess the talent, managers organize the players on the roster, a player's salary reflects his productivity.

The emergence of new dominating ideas implies that any given strategy may have a short shelf-life. Conditions change, causing misfit, and internal capabilities develop to yield new advantages.

- **They decided what they were going to do and, importantly, not do.** Oakland decided that they were not going to contract highly-paid superstar players and would instead apply their limited payroll to undervalued hitters. A strategy's power comes from coherent design: it's the focus on certain

16

leverage points and the willingness to stop doing traditional activities that don't support the new strategy. A good strategy is a systematic, orchestrated, coherent effort by the entire organization.

- **They used data to suppress cognitive bias.** The prevailing system in Major League Baseball placed much power in the ability of professional scouts to judge the potential of a prospective player. Most scouts worked intuitively, many of them holding to the illusion that physical appearance is predictive of the player's ability. Oakland's strategy included a belief that empiricism was a better predictor of performance than subjective intuition.

- **They placed smart bets.** A good strategy is a bet or a series of bets. Some bets may pay off, and some may not.

  Each of Oakland's unconventional trades was a bet, testing the idea that a team could measure productivity as a function of payroll expense and configure a productive offense at minimum cost. Many of those resource-configuration bets were failures, but some paid off spectacularly.

  The Moneyball strategy itself was a bet that a new dominating idea could prevail. Over time, and with continuous experimentation, Oakland improved its understanding of performance and gained an advantage.

- **The strategy was novel.** The Moneyball strategy did not emerge from writing statements of mission, vision, and values. The strategy didn't originate with facilitated organizational retreats, budgeting, and SWOT‡ brainstorming or other so-called best practices of strategic planning.

  One lesson of this strategic-thinking narrative is the unique perspective of an individual. Billy Beane was not from an elite educational background (he skipped college to accept

---

‡ SWOT stands for Strengths, Weaknesses, Opportunities, and Threats.

a professional baseball contract). His success came from sound principles: he confronted the reality of his situation, he was curious and opportunistic, he developed a unique commonsense, he looked outside of conventions for new ideas, and he leveraged his resources and his know-how.

The Moneyball story is well known. Many writers commonly use it as an example of the potential of technology: big data, data mining, and analytics. The strategic-thinking narrative is an alternative theme, which is that a good strategy's roots are with individuals who perceive the situation more accurately than others. Good strategy has its origins in the fairly prosaic activities of scanning the environment, noticing curiosities, analyzing with a skeptical eye, deliberating with others on the situation, and designing a path forward. However, it's also a matter of luck and placing yourself where you can benefit from the emergence of opportunity.

Good strategic thinkers are skeptical of conventional management wisdom, borrow external ideas and innovations, and construct new strategic logics. I regularly hear people who exalt the idea of leadership vision, and cite as examples the genius of Steve Jobs and more contemporary business leaders such as Mary Barra, Elon Musk, and Jeff Bezos. There's much to admire about these people, but they're not freaks of nature. They're not seers who predict the future, nor are they wizards who magically create it. A more accurate story is that they're reasonably intelligent people who are open to novel ideas, are opportunistic, and focus on the essential actions needed for future success.

The worlds of strategy and leadership have many tropes,[§] and it's important to be skeptical of them. Conventional thinkers prefer neat, compact stories. They like to attribute outcomes to a person's character or as a supernatural gift of vision. The hard work of analysis and reframing are much better explanations for the sources of good strategic thinking.

[§] We use the word *trope* in the sense of a common and over-used theme or tool of rhetoric.

You'll see other examples of strategic thinkers in this book, and I encourage you to search for them in movies, books, and your own life. An individual who holds a nuanced understanding of the situation and is willing to make tough choices about focus is more likely to craft good strategy.

How to Construct a Strategic-Thinking Narrative

The strategic-thinking narrative is a useful tool for understanding the creation of strategy as a competent response to a situation. The idea is straightforward. First, find a real-world example of organizational success or failure. Questions like this can help you identify the main elements:

- Who are the main and supporting characters?
- What is the context for the story?
- What is the core challenge they face?
- What are the tensions?
- What insights did the characters acquire?
- What decisions did they make?
- How did they experiment and adapt?

Answers to these questions provide a useful deepening of understanding about the source of the strategy. For example, the Moneyball strategy did not spring into Billy Beane's mind fully formed. Billy Beane was exposed to sabermetrics ideas years earlier by his predecessor general manager at Oakland, Sandy Alderson. Going back further in time, sabermetrics approaches predated the events in the movie by at least 20 years. If Billy Beane was the father of the Moneyball strategy, Alderson was its grandfather. Bill James, who started writing about baseball statistics in the 1970s, was its great-grandfather. Like many other innovations, much time passes between the initial development of a good idea and that idea's fully realized benefits.

You can discover a narrative of strategy in every story of success or of failure.

Are You Strategic?

Many people have been told in their performance reviews, "You need to be more strategic." With a definite tone of frustration in their voices, they ask, "What do you mean *be more strategic?*"

The phrase *be more strategic* likely was not meant to invite the person to participate in developing enterprise strategy. The speaker more likely intended it as an instruction to enlarge one's perspective, to be less absorbed in their specialized daily work, and to coordinate their efforts with the efforts of others, including sacrificing their personal efficiency to serve the broader interests of the organization.

Strategic things ought to be connected to strategy and not status.

In this sense, a person who is more strategic holds a more systematic view of the organization and its fit with the external environment. She has learned the structures and disciplines that characterize her organization and its context of stakeholders, suppliers, regulators, and the like. With this knowledge, she is able to more adroitly coordinate her activities with others.

As an adjective, the word *strategic* is often used as a decoration – for example, strategic leadership, strategic plans, strategic decisions, and strategic markets. Mostly, when people use *strategic* as an adjective, they are signaling their opinion of the importance of the noun being modified. Used this way, the adjective strategic is self-indulgent, and many people use it to advance their personal status within the organization.

Most organizations have too many strategic things, a cacophony of goals and aspirations in competition with each other. The indiscriminate use of the adjective *strategic* adds to the ambiguity and doesn't reduce it. Ideally, the adjective *strategic* should link to the organization's strategy, and ideally the organization's strategy should be good and not bad.

Emptying the Mind of Preconceptions

The knowledge and experience that have served you well in the past might anchor you to no-longer-relevant stories and conventions, causing you to neglect new learnings. Your intuition might make you complacent.

Adopt the ideas of Shoshin as a preferred approach to learning to think strategically. Shoshin is the Zen Buddhism concept of encouraging a beginner's mind, which is a mindset that resembles a child who is discovering something for the first time. Your beginner's mind is enhanced when you:

- Let go of rigid distinctions of what is right and wrong
- Eliminate expectations of what will happen
- Fill yourself with curiosity to understand more deeply
- Open yourself to new possibilities
- Ask simple questions
- Are open to possibilities

To learn to think strategically is not an exercise in rote memorization. It's not stuffing your memory with a stack of facts about strategic frameworks and best practices. Instead, you cultivate an enthusiasm for the undiscovered and novel. You're optimistic that someone can find a better way of doing things, and you know that step jumps can be better than incremental improvement. Start by emptying your mind of preconceptions and recognize the presence of ambiguity.

This chapter has introduced you to several important ideas about the nature, purpose, and scope of strategic thinking. It started with the underappreciated presence of ambiguity and concluded with a call for Shoshin. Along the way, I defined several essential concepts relating to competent strategic thinking.

In the next chapter, I more closely examine ambiguity as it affects strategy, goals, and plans. I take Chapter 1's explanation of strategy as the inter-relationship of ends, ways, and means and use that to explain cleverness and to distinguish goals and plans from strategy. Finally, I examine the crafting of strategy and review a written statement of Oakland's Moneyball strategy.

CHAPTER 2

Cleverness

Strategy is a Crafted Approach of Fitting Resources to the Nuances of a Situation

Hope is not a strategy.

— Vince Lombardi

IT'S NATURAL TO SAY, "This is a clever child," and less natural to say, "This is a clever adult." The word *clever* implies that a person is creatively leveraging her resources to gain an advantage over a rival. With that characterization in mind, consider these three statements:

- The Oakland A's had a clever strategy.
- The Oakland A's had a clever goal.
- The Oakland A's had a clever plan.

To what extent does each statement make sense to you? For me, the first statement is perfectly sensible because Oakland's players were undervalued by others, yet they were configured in a way that led to sustained high performance. On paper, Oakland's team was unexceptional. But despite their apparent weakness, they generated a superior record of competitive performance.

The second statement associating cleverness with goals seems odd, maybe nonsensical. This reveals a profound obstacle to good strategy and competent strategic thinking, which is people's tendency to confuse goals and strategy.

The third statement is subject to the ambiguity of the word *plan*, which people often use to mean a coordinated approach to the challenge. The strategic-thinking narrative of Billy Beane reveals that he was curious about the potential of sabermetrics, skeptical of the intuitions and habits of baseball scouts, and willing to experiment to discover better methods of acquiring and using resources. Considering those elements, it's appropriate to declare that Oakland had a deliberately conceived, clever plan.

> *A strategy can be good and clever, or bad and stupid.*

People sometimes use the word *plan* in the literal sense of a document. Many strategic plans are wish lists of the organization's goals and objectives. The authors often add graphics of favorable trends and pictures of smiling people and soaring eagles to create an illusion of achievement. Too often, they neglect the essential issues and choices for the organization.

Cleverness as the Integration of Ways, Means, and Ends

In Chapter 1, I shared the U.S. Army's definition of strategy as a relationship between ways, means, and ends. It's an excellent framework for helping people find a useful amount of rigor about what strategy is and how it works. The word *relationship* is the most important concept, because *it is the relationship between ways, means, and ends that gives strategy its power.*

A strategy has a less-powerful punch when it's disintegrated. Many managers overlook the word *relationship* and focus on one of the elements. For examples of disintegration, some will tell you that strategy is a statement of vision (they're focusing on the *ends* statement). Others will tell you that strategy consists of the steps toward the goal (they're focusing on the *ways* statement). Yet others regard strategy as a matter of budgeting resources during an annual planning cycle (they're focusing on the *means*).

Here are two examples of the incomplete view:

- **Top executives.** The typical pattern for top executives is to exchange the word *strategy* for *goals*, such as, "Our strategy is to internationalize," or "Our strategy is to cut costs," or "Our strategy is to be the industry leader." Statements like these focus on the ends of strategy and ignore the ways and means.

    Many people like to include visioning and vision statements in their strategy work. Many subscribe to the value of a "visionary leader" who describes a future state. These are simple and attractive ideas because the vision can establish a direction and motivate people to apply extra effort.

    For contrast, former IBM CEO Lou Gerstner declares that, "in and of themselves, [vision statements] are useless in terms of pointing out how the institution is going to turn an aspirational goal into a reality." He even goes so far as to criticize vision statements as "truly dangerous" because they create a comfort and confidence that's not backed up by a commitment of resources and a logic for making progress. (Gerstner has the experience of being a CEO of several organizations. We examine his time at IBM in Chapters 9 and 10.)

    I emphasized the word *how* in the preceding paragraph to stress that a strategy is hollow if it doesn't identify the resources, commit those resources, and provide guidance for configuring those resources to pursue that strategy. Resources are finite. Managers must make difficult decisions about what the organization is going to stop doing or which opportunities it can't afford to pursue. Strategy is more than declaring goals and setting a vision.

- **Project managers.** Managers who are assigned goals often use the word *strategy* to mean the steps (the ways) to achieve the top manager's vision (the ends). Their goal is to determine the optimal sequence of actions to accomplish that goal.

When I hear *strategy* defined as the steps to get to a goal, I'm reminded of standing in the checkout aisle at the grocery store perusing the covers of magazines that have teaser headlines such as, "Five strategies to get a flat belly," or "So-and so's strategies for sinking long putts." The articles describe techniques, tips, and hacks.

Use the word goal when you are referring to a targeted outcome. A good strategy is not a goal, nor is it the steps to reach a goal.

I prefer to use the word *programming* (and not *strategizing*) to describe the activity of combining techniques with resources for the purpose of accomplishing goals. I also find it helpful to keep this question in mind: What if the assigned goal is illegal, impossible, or poorly thought out?

It's an unfortunate shortcut when people oversimplify to define strategy as a target (the ends), or in other cases, the steps (the ways) Figure 2-1 provides a general template, structured to describe the organization's beliefs, choices, and adaptations. There are five numbered statements that serve as a preamble for introducing each part.

1. **The collective interests.** Oakland's interests could be stated this way (the first preamble):

   > Our interests, as the Oakland organization, include…fielding a successful team and supporting our community. Our owners are important stakeholders and have established budget constraints that limit our ability to outbid our wealthier competitors for baseball talent.

   It's worth noting that an organization's interests can change with the arrival of new ownership, new management, new governance, new rivals, new regulations, and changes in technology and social trends. Too, events can overtake the organization. As an example, during the time I was writing this book there were weekly controversies involving firearms rights, sexual harassment, and race relations in the United States. High-profile organizations found themselves making important choices and pronouncements clarifying their interests and policies. It was common to hear executives,

Beliefs

 1. Our interests, as an organization, are the following...
 2. Given our interests and circumstances, we believe...
 3. The core challenge for our organization is...

Choices

 4. Given our interests and diagnosis of the situation, we choose to...

Adaptations

 5. Given our centralized choices about the direction and focus of the organization, our decentralized execution involves...

Figure 2-1. A five-part template for writing strategy, originating from collective beliefs, choices, and adaptations.

as well as politicians, say, "My thinking on this matter has evolved."

The identification of interests provides an opportunity to challenge assumptions about fundamental values and the organization's place in a larger network of stakeholders.

2. **The collective beliefs about the context, situation, and issues.** The next part of writing strategy describes the context for the strategy and the group's underlying justified knowledge.

    Given our interests and circumstances, we believe that:

    • We are at a competitive disadvantage to our rivals.

    • The talent market may be inefficient. We believe that we have advantages over rivals in evaluating talent.

The above is not a comprehensive list. Further, it isn't likely that there would be a widespread agreement with the "we believe" part of the preamble. Gaining agreement is one of the tough challenges of strategy and is a topic we'll explore in Chapter 12.

Much of the development of good strategy involves testing beliefs. More specifically, the strategist will develop a hypothesis, collect data, and evaluate the data. For the Oakland example, if the market is inefficient, then the organization's challenge is to discover methods to exploit that inefficiency.

3. **The collective beliefs about the core challenge.** A core challenge is the biggest issue (threat or opportunity) facing the organization. It's the stimulus for undertaking the development of strategy. I state the core challenge for Oakland as follows (the third preamble):

> The core challenge for our organization is…that we are in a weak position, compared to rivals, because we are a small-market team with a constrained budget for resources. The presence of inefficiencies in the market for baseball talent provides us an opportunity to recruit affordable talent, enabling us to field a winning team.

The recognition of a core challenge is a crucial element of strategy. Since strategy is defined as a specialized tool for issues management, the crucial task for the strategist is to articulate the specific nature of the opportunity or threat facing the organization. I explain more about the core challenge in Chapter 6.

4. **Choosing the ways to configure the means.** Strategy involves a stream of aligned, reinforcing decisions through the organization. I use the phrase *we choose* to qualify each object.

It's helpful to understand those choices regarding the previously used concept of strategy as an integration of the ways, means, and ends. I have indicated the ways and/or means in brackets to help clarify the impact of the decisions.

Here is the fourth preamble applied to Oakland:

Given our interests and diagnosis of the situation, we choose to:

- Emphasize offensive performance over defensive performance [ways].

- Emphasize a logic of high on-base percentage leading to a targeted number of runs leading to a targeted number of wins [ways].

- Recruit talent based on our forecast of their performance and their affordability [ways and means].

- Not recruit highly-paid free agents [ways and means].

I made a simplifying assumption that Oakland's goal was to win as many baseball games as possible. Accordingly, I identified the ways and means but not the ends. As you give thought to your own situation you should consider the broadest set of success criteria, including examining the ends statement.

Note that the fourth bullet point is an exclusionary statement. Limited resources (means) are a fact of life. Managers need to make choices (ways) about what to do and not do. A good strategy is one that focuses resources on the essential levers of power. A bad strategy is one that is unfocused and fails to address the real world of limited resources.

5. **State the adaptation of the organization.** The fifth preamble for writing strategy is this:

Given our centralized choices about direction and focus, our decentralized execution involves:

- Focusing research on college players rather than high school players.

- Positioning players in the lineup to maximize each player's probability of getting on base.

- Experimenting with reassigning players from one position to another in order to leverage the player's hitting prowess (for example, training a catcher to play first base.

This fifth part of the template helps us to understand that strategy involves policy choices that shape decisions made at the front lines of the organization.

In contrast to establishing and communicating goals, executives provide policy guidance in combination with resources. A good strategy recognizes that front-line managers have more expertise in some specific part of the organization. Empowered lower-level managers make better choices if they understand the interests and beliefs that frame the strategy.

Sometimes the top managers must use formal power associated with their position to compel others to act against narrower, personal interests. An example is the diminished decision-making prerogatives of Oakland's field manager.

Crafting Strategy

If *clever* is an appropriate adjective for describing how strategy functions, the word *crafted* is a good verb for characterizing the act of developing it. Picture a woodworker crafting a table or a potter crafting a vase. She balances two guiding ideas in her mind: the general shape of the goal (e.g., table or vase) and the properties of her materials. She does not exclusively fixate on the goal, nor does she exclusively focus on her materials. She imagines a combination, a fit, of the function of the object and the properties of the materials. She iterates and experiments.

It is better to say that "strategy is crafted," rather than "strategy is planned."

Billy Beane's multiyear work with the Moneyball strategy shows many parallels with the crafting analogy. The early Moneyball practices were simple. They evolved, with experimentation, into a more-refined and sophisticated strategy.

Another example of craftsmanship in strategy is the development of 3M's Post-it Notes. The story starts with a researcher, Spence Silver, who developed a substance that he called microspheres. These microspheres had unique physical properties (they were weak adhesives). Silver's genius was in noticing the interesting properties of the microspheres and in his drive to search for a potential application. Silver persevered even when his bosses discouraged him. Success came years later when Silver's colleague Art Fry made an insightful connection that the microspheres could be coated onto paper and used as a placeholder in documents.

There are three more essential points in this strategy-as-craft analogy. First, strategy has raw materials: beliefs, bets, dominating ideas, insights, strategic resources, actions, and choices. Second, just as a vase functions as a container, strategy functions to advance the interests of the organization and manage issues. Third, strategy evolves from simple experiments to more-elaborate programs, just as techniques of craftsmanship evolve from crude to sophisticated.

The Sharpness Theorem

"The real challenge in crafting strategy," writes Henry Mintzberg, "lies in detecting the subtle discontinuities that may undermine a business in the future. And for that," he continues, "there is no technique, no program, just a sharp mind in touch with the situation." Mintzberg's idea of "a sharp mind in touch with the situation" echoes my assertion that a competent person is one who understands the situation and acts reasonably.

A competent strategic thinker is a sharp mind in touch with the situation.

Let's unpack three important ideas.

Organizations will be undermined in the future. Very few established organizations sustain their power and leadership. Evidence of undermining is easily found in business, such as the turnover of membership on the Fortune magazine list of largest corporations. Moreover, loss of relevance can also be seen in schools, churches, communities, and not-for-profit organizations that were once vibrant and are now shuttered or are making little impact.

External environments are always in flux, and leaders of these declining organizations find it easier to focus on operations (that is neglect the ambiguity of the situation) and their personal aspirations. We can confidently predict that the future of today's successful organizations is to face significantly different conditions. We can also predict that some institutions will fail to effectively respond and will lose power and relevance.

Detecting subtle discontinuities is the *real challenge* of strategy. A discontinuity is a deviation from expectations. It's a weak signal that may (or may not) grow into a force that alters the future of an organization.

Specific discontinuities are not predictable. One may emerge at a specific time and place. Or it may not. Once a discontinuity emerges, there is no way to know whether there will be a significant impact or not. This is true whether we're considering an economic bubble, new technology, or legislation. Some individuals sense the implications of the discontinuities and some do not.

Figure 2-2 presents a general model of the life cycle of a discontinuity. Imagine an offshore earthquake as an example of a discontinuity. The average person is unlikely to notice a subtle occurrence. Perhaps the earthquake causes a disruptive tsunami, but perhaps it has no effect. Let's assume that it causes a tsunami and that the tsunami crashes into a populated area and disrupts normal life. Chaos ensues. What new norm will appear in the reconfigured system?

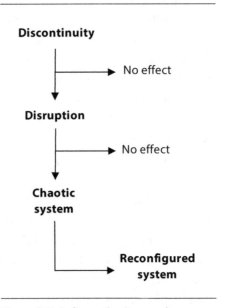

Figure 2-2. A discontinuity may (or may not) trigger a chaotic, large-scale effect.

Disruptions seldom destroy systems. For example, even though both World War I and World War II were devastating, new political and economic orders emerged that retained certain legacy elements of the incumbent systems and added innovations. Systems have various degrees of brittleness or resilience. When the system is disrupted, the emerging replacement can be quite different, such as when mammals became the largest land animals after the mass extinction of dinosaurs.

It's worthwhile to note that an earthquake doesn't instantly cause a tsunami, nor does a tsunami immediately cause destruction. Delays characterize any dynamic system. Further, the impacts might be severe, or the impacts might be insignificant.

Avoiding idealized best practices and methodology. Mintzberg asserts that "there is no technique and no program" for detecting discontinuities. This third part of the sharpness theorem contrasts with the preferences of many linear thinkers. It serves as a warning to strategic thinkers to avoid reflexive desires for methodology, such as using a formal set of strategic-planning templates.

The metaphor of organization-as-machine is longstanding, but it is also obsolete. There's not one best way to approach an ill-defined issue in a dynamic environment.

Best practices are not suitable for uncertain environments.

Instead, the best approach for crafting strategy is a sharp mind in touch with the situation. It echoes this book's big idea about the importance of individual competency in strategic thinking.

How Does Dullness Arise?

Oakland's Moneyball strategy was the result of a sharp mind in touch with the situation. Consider, though, that its rivals could have independently developed and tested the hypothesis that the market was inefficient. Stated differently, why were Oakland's competitors dull, and what lessons does the answer offer?

The answer is that individual managers of Oakland's competition were subject to their own minds' predispositions for mental economy and ease. Oakland's competitors had access to the same sabermetrics methods and data. They were lax, whereas Billy Beane felt the insight borne of creative desperation.

There are at least three tendencies that foster dull strategic thinking.

People are dulled by their routines. Karl Weick and Kathleen Sutcliffe's excellent book, *Managing the Unexpected*, explains how organizational routine dulls people's ability to notice warning signs and changes in context. They explain that people operate on mental autopilot. In this condition of mindlessness, they see the familiar rather than the unfamiliar, and they categorize events with old labels. They are out of touch with their situation, yet their intuition gives them a false sense of security. They become overconfident and lax.

People build stories out of events. Most people tend to interpret their experience as a series of events. Consider this daily-life example: You see a broken window, a ball lying on the ground below it, and a group of children playing nearby. Your mind naturally tends to associate things that are proximate with each other (broken window, ball, children) and construct a plausible story: The children threw the ball that broke the window. People easily generate explanations and have confidence in those explanations. They don't need all the facts. The story can change with new information (the neighborhood has had a series of burglaries, or an earthquake recently struck the area). However, people are reluctant to alter already-developed stories.

Murphy's Law is a call for alertness, not a dour expectation of dystopia.

Event-oriented thinking (or linear thinking) reflects the mind's tendency to create simple stories of proximate causes and effects. When people pass around stories that are simple explanations of "who did what to whom" or "sales are down, so we lowered prices," they are practicing event-oriented thinking.

People, managers included, tend to react superficially to events instead of having a more subtle, nuanced understanding of systems behaviors over long periods of time. Most people remember the famous Murphy's law this way: *If it can go wrong, it will.* The source is Edward A. Murphy, an engineer tasked with improving airplane cockpits. Many people tend to see Murphy's Law in a pessimistic way.

In systems language, an airplane cockpit is a loosely-coupled system with multiple interactions between elements, such as the delay between cause and effect. It requires effort and expertise to understand complicated and non-linear systems. Murphy's law is not a dour and cynical view of the future. Ed Murphy was advising us to be alert for the early, weak signals of discontinuities that might lead to threat or might lead to opportunity. The better lesson is that when you find yourself in a complex situation, mentally process it this way: *If something can happen, sooner or later, it will.*

Aspirations drive goal setting. Goal setting is typically a form of event-oriented thinking where a person's aspirations become her most-salient mental anchors.

Imagine a typical, busy manager reviewing a forecast of the next month's revenues. She concludes, quickly and without deep thought, that the organization can do better. Her quick mental comparison of the situation and aspirations yields her goal.

Figure 2-3 illustrates how event-oriented thinking guides goal setting. The manager feels the pressure of limited time. Her mind *easily perceives* two things: her readily available data and her aspirations. The mind prefers information that is readily available and then makes the best use of it that it can. (This mental action will be explained in more detail in Chapter 11 as the *availability heuristic.*)

For contrast, strategic thinkers practice broad framing, which is the search for and consideration of additional information. This can include general economic conditions, existing and emergent competition, social trends, technology, and natural events. Sometimes those signals increase in salience and contribute to disruption. Sometimes not. Certainly, the effort to broad frame can consume too much time

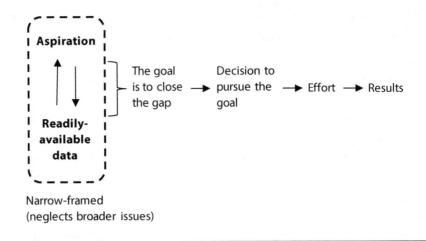

Narrow-framed
(neglects broader issues)

Figure 2-3. Many people tend to narrow frame and set goals.

for people who already feel the pressures of the day-to-day. On the other hand, to neglect weak signals is to risk increased exposure to an emerging threat or miss an emerging opportunity.

Advice for Clarifying Goals and Strategy

A competent strategic thinker is curious and asks questions. She is alert for the mistaken substitution of goals for strategy. Here's an example of how a more junior person could interact with a more senior person:

> Top executive: "Our strategy is to launch 20 new products in the coming year."
>
> Project manager: "That's a very interesting goal. What's the thought process behind the establishment of that goal?"

The project manager's response is subtle. She hasn't compounded the mistake of substituting goals for strategy and has correctly recognized that a goal is another name for a target or end.

Her question avoids a confrontation over the semantics of definitions of *goal* and *strategy*. Also, it creates an opportunity for a more-productive discourse about the organization's strategy. (Strategy-as-conversation is a topic for Chapter 12, and the courage to confront reality is a topic of Chapter 13.) That discourse might include discussing questions such as the following:

- Are the ends reasonable, given the means available?
- Given the means available to us, if we were clever, what ends might we be able to achieve?
- What are the tradeoffs?
- How might a competitor use cleverness to gain an advantage over us?
- Have our organizational interests changed?
- What issues are we trying to address?

Rather than focusing on goal setting, a competent strategic thinker looks more broadly and deeply for meaningful signals. Strategy, as defined in Chapter 1, is a broadly applicable construct that fits government, business, and charities. The search for good strategy encourages us to answer this question: What are the potential combinations of ends, means, and ways to advance our interests?

Adjectives tell you something important about strategy. I encourage you always to have an adjective to associate with the word *strategy*. For example, use the adjective *clever* to describe a configuration of ways and means of strategy (a clever strategy) that results in a relatively weak competitor gaining the advantage.

Another example is the use of the adjective *good*, which is explained in Richard Rumelt's excellent book, *Good Strategy, Bad Strategy: The Difference and Why it Matters*. Good strategy has three distinguishing characteristics: a diagnosis of the situation, a set of essential choices (called guiding policy), and coherent action in the organization to pursue those essential choices. Good strategy is mostly the hard work of identifying and solving problems and exploiting opportunities. Rumelt explains that a bad strategy is one that's all about desired performance outcomes. Bad strategy is "a stretch goal, a budget, or a list of things you wish would happen."

Everyone wants to have a strategy that's clever or powerful or good or effective or brilliant or nuanced. Similarly, no one would be satisfied if her strategy was labeled stupid, weak, bad, ineffective, dull, or generic.

Adjectives also tell you something about strategic thinking, which is why I've chosen to associate the word *competent* with the individual strategic thinker. I encourage you to assess the individuals around you: Are they sharp minds in touch with the situation? Are they acting reasonably?

A competent strategic thinker is more likely to craft good strategy. An incompetent strategic thinker is more likely to craft bad strategy.

Strategic Thinking's Three Literacies

We would expect a literate person be able to read and write and to have a working knowledge of the use of verbs, nouns, adjectives, adverbs, and so forth. We would also expect her to be able to distinguish broader concepts, such as the difference between a book of fiction and a book of nonfiction; within those categories, a literate person could recognize a science fiction adventure from a romance novel and a history of civilization from natural history.

When addressing specialized topics, we expect a practitioner to be literate with the theory and application of her domain, such as a physician using professionally correct terms to describe the human anatomy and an accountant being able to distinguish a balance sheet from an income statement.

A competent strategic thinker is literate in three areas: strategy, judgment, and futures.

Literacy with strategy. There are thousands of articles and books published on strategy every year. Because strategy is an ambiguous concept, people pick up small pieces of good thought (the importance of planning, for example) and hold incomplete understandings of the principles of good strategy. The specialized language of strategy includes concepts such as the organization of resources, power, statements of the core challenge, and weak signals. As I've discussed, strategies are not synonymous with goals, nor are goals the steps to achieve a strategy.

Grand strategy is a term used by the military to describe the interests of a nation and its use of political, military, and economic power. The acronym VUCA originated with the U.S. military as a concept for showing the limitations of master planning and for encouraging agility.

In the for-profit business environment, the phrases *corporate strategy*, *business strategy*, and *functional strategy* have specific meanings. Corporate strategy is concerned with the question: What businesses do we want to participate in? General Electric's famous approach to its portfolios of business is an example. GE wanted to be number one or a strong number two in each of its businesses and divested its businesses that couldn't meet that criteria.

Business strategy is concerned with developing and sustaining a winning value proposition. Oakland's Moneyball strategy is an example of a business strategy.

Functional strategy is associated with departments within the organization, examples being marketing strategy, or IT strategy. Upon closer inspection, functional strategy is typically practiced as programming. The department has a set of goals to achieve, and it is programming the implementation of its resources to meet those goals. In some cases, the department is nurturing some capability (such as a technology or a talent development program) that may bring unique competitive advantage to the business.

A literate strategic thinker will also recognize the distinctions of emergent versus deliberate strategy. Deliberate strategy is traditional, institutionalized strategic planning where management establishes a long-range vision and then directs the organization to implement actions to move toward espoused goals. Emergent strategy is entrepreneurial, flexible, and opportunity seeking.

Judgment literacy. An individual with judgment literacy is aware of the presence of cognitive biases and the possibility that individuals may make decisions that are not in their own best interests.

Daniel Kahneman was awarded the Nobel Prize for his contributions to a better understanding of decision making. Kahneman's excellent book, *Thinking Fast and Slow*, provides an excellent and detailed description of topics that are relevant to strategic thinking: perceptions, memories, and decisions. Kahneman states, in the introduction to the book, that his goal is to "improve the ability to identify and understand errors of judgment and choice, in others and eventually in ourselves, by providing a richer and more precise language to discuss them." This precise language includes the terms *fallacies*, *illusions*, and *neglects* (such as the previously described neglect of ambiguity).

People want to be systematic, rational, and deliberate in their strategizing. A fundamental task for a competent strategic thinker is to override, when appropriate, her intuitions, habits, impulses and inclinations.

Chapter 11 provides more on the role of judgment literacy and Chapter 12 describes how better conversation can help avoid mistakes in strategic judgment.

Futures literacy. One common way of anticipating the future is to rely on extrapolated trends or forecasts of a "projected future" or "predicted future." Another kind of future is the "preferred future," where leaders establish some wished-for outcome. Planning is done by backcasting to envision the steps to the goal.

A strategic thinker often uses a third discovery-oriented approach. She wants to see things that she couldn't see before. She notices weak signals and explores their implications. She wants to fully grasp the potential of the future rather than be locked into a particular view.

Futures literacy is not the ability to make better predictions. Its purpose is to examine the anticipatory assumptions that connect present-day choices to their future effects. With an increased understanding of futures concepts and tools, strategic thinkers can make more-proactive decisions and can sidestep unintended consequences.

Futures literacy is probably the least-well-known of any of the three strategic thinking literacies. Fortunately, the mainstream of strategic management thought is embracing it. You will learn more about the tools of futures literacy in Chapter 7.

Nuance Matters

The text of Oakland's Moneyball strategy contains many words because situations are unique and the response must match it. Like the words *clever, powerful, effective,* or *good,* the word *nuanced* is also a suitable adjective for characterizing a strategy. A nuanced strategy is desirable, and a generic strategy is not.

Given knowledge of the detail of a situation, we can see that a good strategy is understandable and commonsensical. Notice that I didn't need pretentious words or complicated graphics to describe the Moneyball strategy.

In Chapter 1, I discussed Shoshin, the beginner's mind. The beginner's mind is appreciative of detail. A learner with a beginner's mind embraces nuance because it can reveal the logic of a particular good strategy.

The next chapter describes the strategic-thinking narrative for Christopher Columbus. It will help you deepen your understanding of the purpose, nature, and scope of strategic thinking. Two highlights are the four pillars and the four X-factors of strategic thinking. These concepts provide an essential framework for defining and applying strategic thinking.

CHAPTER 3

Big Ideas

The Four Pillars of Strategic Thinking and DICE

It is always because of one person that all of the changes that matter come about. So be that one person.

— Buckminster Fuller

Y OU MIGHT NOT REMEMBER much more than the rhyme *in 1492 Columbus sailed the ocean blue,* but you probably know that Christopher Columbus is one of the most significant people in the history of humankind, bringing the lands that are now called the Americas to Europe's attention. This chapter uses the Columbus strategic-thinking narrative to reveal more about the nature of strategic thinking.

Christopher Columbus was born in the Italian city-state of Genoa in 1450 or 1451. Columbus spent much of his early life on the Mediterranean Sea learning the basics of seamanship. He later ventured north and south on the "Great Ocean," as the Atlantic was then called. He acquired the idea of finding a trade route to Asia by sailing west. He approached Portugal for sponsorship but was rejected, eventually securing three ships from Spain. In October 1492, he landed on an island in the Bahamas, believing he had reached islands off the eastern coast of Asia. He returned to Spain and secured resources to make three more trips to the west. On the second trip, his party discovered

Cuba and Hispaniola. The third voyage was especially significant because he encountered the large freshwater flows of the Orinoco River in South America, signaling the presence of a continental landmass.

He held a big (transformative) idea. The fact that the Earth was round was not in dispute among educated Europeans. Columbus's big idea of sailing west probably originated early in his sailing career.

We don't know the source of his big idea. We do know, from studying his journals, that he was curious and had an eye for details. Imagine Columbus spending hours in conversation with fellow sailors at sea or in port, trading stories of the mundane and the fantastic. Perhaps when Columbus was in the British Isles (and possibly Iceland), he may have heard stories related to centuries-earlier Viking settlements in lands to the west. Regardless, the big idea of sailing west captured Columbus's attention and organized his thinking and energy.

He held specialist knowledge. Columbus had practical, applied knowledge of sailing. His know-how included navigation, ship construction, and the operational details of sailing. Important, too, was his experience as a merchant trader. This knowledge was valuable for advancing the interests of the Spanish Crown and his other investors. His mapmaker experience supplemented his navigational expertise, giving him both a global perspective and knowledge of details. Finally, he understood political power and developed influencing skills.

Big ideas often originate in small details gathered over an extended period.

He spent significant time in an innovation hub, exposing him to emerging technological and social trends. The 30-year span from 1462 to 1492 was a time of considerable development in sailing and exploration. Innovations in design and construction of ships improved their performance on long trips over the stormy waters of the Great Ocean. With the ability for longer-range travel, merchants could open new markets and establish new trading business models.

Columbus's time in Lisbon (1477 to 1485) is crucial to the narrative. Lisbon was one of the wealthiest and most cosmopolitan cities in the world. For part of that time he worked with his brother Bartholomew in a business that produced and sold maps, keeping him attuned to emerging knowledge in geography. Imagine Columbus finding himself in energetic discussions of what lay over the western horizon. This debate would have stimulated the integration of ideas, sharpened his arguments, and subsequently built his confidence to promote the idea to sponsors. It was in Lisbon that Columbus acquired a map made by Florentine thinker Paolo Dal Pozzo Toscanelli that showed a westward route across the Great Ocean to Asia. Columbus was inspired and carried a copy of the map with him on his voyage, a signal of its significance to him. Some scholars refer to Columbus's voyage as the Toscanelli project.

He had a valuable insight. An insight reorganizes our understanding of the situation and contributes to a strategic logic. Here is my conjecture of the events of one week. Watch for the spark of insight.

It's the year 1485. Columbus is at the mapmaking shop with his brother Bartholomew. On a Monday, the brothers complete a chart of wind patterns of the Iberian Peninsula. They talk about prevailing westerly winds, making small jokes about reasons for the wind's directions that prohibit sailors from sailing into the sunset. That conversation sparks a memory by Bartholomew of the Toscanelli map, which Christopher had inherited from his father-in-law. The next day, Bartholomew asks Christopher if he still has his copy of Toscanelli's map. He retrieves it from a box, and they have a lengthy discussion about traveling to Asia by sailing west. This conversation between the two brothers causes Christopher to recall years-earlier shipboard discussions and conjecture about lands to the west of the Great Ocean.

The next morning, Wednesday, Columbus returns to examine Toscanelli's map more closely. He notices the notation that one could get to Asia by sailing west. His thoughts are interrupted when another customer enters the shop with a request for charts showing wind patterns on the coast of western Africa. During this conversation,

Columbus recalls his experiences sailing off the West African coast, where the winds blew toward the west and northwest. His customer information matches his experience that winds were out of the east.

That night Columbus awakens with the insight that will unify and integrate his history-making project. Biographer Eugene Lyon declared that it was Columbus's most important insight: the secret to a round trip to the west of the ocean sea was to "drop down south to go westward with the trade winds, and return at a higher latitude with the westerlies." The insight gave him a powerful advantage compared to the traditional notions of sailing into the westerly headwinds.

On Thursday, Christopher Columbus writes a letter to the court of King John II of Portugal, petitioning him for resources to make a voyage west.

He secured resources. I've previously explained that strategy is characterized by an interrelationship of ends, ways, and means. The means of strategy, the resources put at risk, are essential elements. Columbus had a big idea, but he needed resources. He undoubtedly found it logical to begin with a request for sponsorship from King John II of Portugal because Columbus had contacts within the Court. Columbus also smartly developed a relationship with the Spanish royalty, who eventually provided him with the resources needed for his project.

He adapted to change in the situation. Here are two examples of how adaptability contributed to Columbus's success.

Columbus had placed an initial bet on securing the sponsorship of Portugal's King John. When Portuguese explorer Bartolomeu Dias crossed the Cape of Good Hope, he established the potential for a southern trade route to the Indian Ocean, and eventually the Orient. Portugal now shifted toward leveraging Dias's accomplishment.

Columbus's initial bet on Portugal's sponsorship had failed. Wisely, he had hedged that bet by cultivating a relationship with Spain. Columbus pivoted to Ferdinand and Isabella of Spain, who were receptive when he most needed their sponsorship.

Columbus pivoted again on his later voyages to the New World. He began his voyages expecting to find large and sophisticated trading centers, drawing on his experience in Europe and what he had learned from those who had been to Asia. He never found those cities, so he switched tactics, approaching trade as he had experienced it in Africa, moving from small port to small port conducting smaller deals.

A good strategy adapts to changing information about the situation.

These elements of the Columbus strategic-thinking narrative offer many useful lessons for strategic thinking. He was trying to advance his interests (self, family, business, and political) as well as those of his patrons.

With Columbus as an example, I'll describe strategic thinking's four pillars and four X-factors.

The Four Pillars of Strategic Thinking

The narrative of Christopher Columbus gives us a better understanding of the nature of strategic thinking. The four pillars model as shown in Figure 3-1 offers a complete definition of strategic thinking.

I'll start with Pillar IV for a commonsense reason: people remember outcomes, and often neglect the causes of those outcomes. We'll focus on the outcome that everyone wants from strategy, which is Pillar IV. We'll then work back to Pillars I, II, and III.

Pillar IV – Success in the future. Naturally, people want to be successful, and a person will define success in a multifaceted way. How do you define success? is not a trivial question. We can identify some of Columbus's criteria through his demands to the Spanish Crown: He would be knighted, appointed Admiral of the Ocean Sea, made the viceroy of any new lands, and awarded ten percent of any new wealth.

The phrase *in the future* is a landmark of strategic thinking. A competent strategic thinker seeks to understand the potential future situations and act proactively.

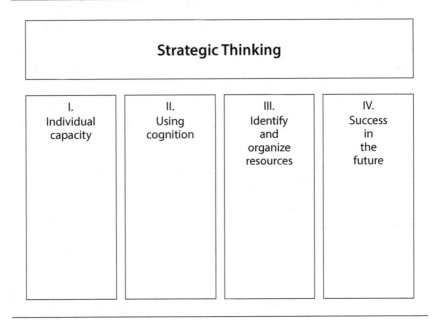

Figure 3-1. The four pillars of strategic thinking.

Pillar III – Identify and organize resources. Columbus combined his know-how and insight with the tangible assets provided by the Spanish Crown: ships, crew, provisions, and goods for trading. He deliberately configured those assets to maximize success.

The game of chess is often used as the symbol for strategy. The movement of chess pieces is a Pillar III activity, where the strategist configures chess pieces (the strategic resources) to respond to issues and create issues for the opponent. For organizations, the strategic resources include capabilities, financial assets, intellectual property, and know-how. The player wins or loses the match (Pillar IV) based on the positioning and movement of the pieces (Pillar III) according to the mental approach (Pillar II) of the player (Pillar I).

Any move of a chess piece is deliberate. This principle is an essential tool for the strategic-thinking narrative in that one can infer reasons for a past choice by asking, *Why was this resource used this way?* Similarly, in considering a prospective configuration of resources, the why question can provide focus and logic for strategy.

Pillar II – Using cognition. Columbus's curiosity and other habits of mind are consistent with the concept of higher-level thinking. It's the intelligence of recognizing things, remembering things, imagining things, and applying reasoning. Reasoning includes activities such as analysis, synthesis, and imagination. In strategic thinking, cognition is explicitly the mechanism that perceives weak signals, makes sense of those signals, and makes decisions.

We all like to believe that we're in control of our decisions and behaviors. Science has shown that much of the mind's cognition is in the subconscious. The argument includes an observation that the human brain evolved over thousands of years in a harsh environment much different from that of present times. The brain's cognitive functioning, in many ways, is locked into specific patterns that work well for us most of the time yet leave us vulnerable at other times. We must not overlook the presence, when crafting strategy, of the "reptile brain" that causes people to get angry, get frustrated, withdraw, and oversimplify. The modern-day result is that people, including managers, often make decisions that are not factually grounded, not logical, and not in their self-interests. The idea of a consistently rational person is no longer accepted.

The mind prefers simplicity and certainty. It is quite adept at neglecting complexity, ambiguity, and other features of the strategic situation. Managers convince themselves that they know more than they really do, they uncritically trust conventional explanations, and they trust experts in areas where the experts are guessing. Categories and stories dominate their mental life, and then they find themselves surprised by fast-moving events.

Sometimes thinking is delusional. For example, John Nash made many original contributions to economics and game theory, resulting in him sharing a Nobel Prize in 1994. Nash also had a history of mental illness, such as believing that men who wore red ties were part of a conspiracy against him. Nash claimed that the same place in his brain that was the source of his most significant contributions to scholarship was also the source of his delusions. Insights are powerful but so is delusional thinking, and there may be a thin line between the two. Columbus wrongly insisted that the distance to Japan was about one-sixth of the actual distance. Perhaps Columbus was delusional, but maybe he was like a modern entrepreneur, Steve Jobs of Apple Computer, with a mental "reality distortion engine" that he used to influence the adoption of his ideas.

Pillar IV of strategic thinking is a focus on success in the future, and the continual change in the world around you (in general) and technology (in particular) introduces a set of challenges that will only increase the "struggle against the limitations of our intelligence."

A competent strategic thinker doesn't necessarily have a higher IQ than anyone else, nor is she necessarily better educated. Instead, she is more aware of what she knows and doesn't know. She is skeptical about reliance on intuition, whether it be her own or that of others. She is resolved and determined to pursue betterment for herself and her stakeholders.

It's tempting to conflate strategic thinking with critical thinking, creative thinking, and systems thinking. Figure 3-2 provides selected similarities and differences that will help you understand that the nature, purpose, and scope of strategic thinking are distinct. Strategic thinking is explicitly concerned with strategy, including an orientation toward the future. When appropriate, strategic thinking incorporates the other styles of thinking.

Pillar I – Individual capacity. Although Columbus needed the help of many other people, his individual experiences, insights, and effort are at the center of the story. He understood the situation, adapted to it, and formulated a reasonable approach to advance his interests and the interests of his sponsors.

The emphasis on the individual also points out an interesting challenge for organizational development. Organizational culture is the reflection of individual values and preferences. It establishes and reflects conventions, however, that can suppress the genius of the individual, leading to dullness and mediocrity.

Organizations need competent individual strategic thinkers at all levels. Everyone has the capacity to detect weak signals, to make sense of them, and to design and implement reasonable actions.

	In common with strategic thinking	Differs from strategic thinking
Critical thinking	Concerned with discovering objective truth Accuracy Questions, logic Establishing hypotheses and experiments	Strategic thinking is concerned with exploring the implications of the future for potential opportunities and threats. Extrapolation has value limited to the short and intermediate terms. We can't accurately predict the long-term future. There may be no logic to it at all. Linear and deductive analyses don't find these future implications.
Creative thinking	Expanding boundaries Challenging and changing the status quo Encouraging cleverness and unconventionality Perceiving novelty, interestingness Self-expression, a personal statement of one's values and aesthetics Betterment-oriented Creative thinking tools such as brainstorming and analogy can be used in some elements of strategy work Craft and design	Strategic thinking is concerned with the crafting of good strategy for specific challenges in specific situations. Strategic thinking is more explicitly focused on the use of imagination in a purposeful way. An emphasis on creativity is helpful, but it can be distracting. Sometimes people become preoccupied with visionary dreaming and fail to face up to the challenges that their organizations face.
Systems thinking	Understanding the consequences (intended and unintended) of policy Attempting to understand, through models, the current situation and to anticipate the change of that system	Strategic thinking is a more qualitative approach with a focus on insights and the shapes of the future. Also, it's more associated with leadership as a tool for creating betterment.

Figure 3-2. Strategic thinking shares some but not all characteristics with other styles of thinking.

Strategic Thinking Defined

The four pillars suggest a concise definition of strategic thinking:

> Strategic thinking is the individual's capacity for – and practice of – using cognition to identify and organize factors that increase the probability of success in the future.

The four pillars also present a simple model of strategic thinking. As described in Chapter 4, the model provides a baseline for contrasting operational thinking and strategic thinking and thus gives us a useful tool to recognize what strategic thinking is and when it applies. As a learner, your challenge is to internalize this and adapt it to your own experience. How does each pillar appear in your personal strategic-thinking narrative?

The Four X-factors of Strategic Thinking

An X-factor is a variable that has a significant impact. In Figure 3-3, I show the four X-factors of strategic thinking and their approximate relationship to the four pillars. X-factors 1 and 2 affect the crafting of strategy, whereas X-factors 3 and 4 are situational characteristics. This acronym can help you remember the four X-factors: DICE.

X-factor #1 – Drive. This X-factor is associated with a person's motivation, energy, ambition, and courage. Some people have drive and will do the things that conventional people will not do: immerse themselves in the details longer, persevere on goals, and take risks. Others simply don't have the energy.

Christopher Columbus's survival of a deadly pirate attack and shipwreck in 1476 is a turning point in his narrative. Near-death experiences can provide people with a compelling sense of clarity and perspective.

In a survey of 250 CEOs of companies with revenue of $50 million or more, management consultant Grant Thornton reported that 22 percent said that they had had an experience when they believed they would die and, of those, 61 percent said that it changed their long-term perspective on life or career. The experience led 41 percent

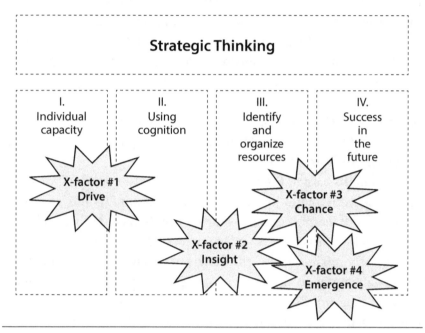

Figure 3-3. The four X-factors of strategic thinking.

of them to say that it made them more compassionate leaders; 16 percent said that it made them more ambitious; 14 percent said that it made them less ambitious. Maybe Columbus shrugged off his brush with death, but maybe it profoundly affected him. Did surviving the attack enhance his ambition and grit, changing him from an ordinary, unremarkable, seafaring merchant to one with the drive to act on his big idea?

X-factor #2 – Insight. Columbus noticed the pattern of the prevailing winds (east to west off the coast of Africa), which stood in contrast to the westerlies that prevailed on Portugal's coast. This insight became the basis of his strategic logic, providing a solution to the problem of sailing west and returning.

Insights are the secret sauce of strategy.

Insights are the *secret sauce* of strategy making; they're a proprietary kind of information that strategists use to their advantage. As I develop a strategic-thinking narrative,

I always look for insights and search for their origination. Much of the power of the Moneyball strategy comes from capturing and exploiting insights. I explain insights in more detail in Chapter 9 using the example of IBM's transformation from a product-centric to a services-centric business.

X-factor #3 – Chance. Imagine yourself in 1492 watching three small ships leave the harbor in Palos de la Frontera, Spain. You don't expect to ever see or hear from Columbus again.

Columbus earned his place in history due to a series of fortunate events, culminating in his excellent luck of bumping into a small island of the Bahamas. Other fortunate events include these: He survived a vicious pirate attack and shipwreck. He lived in the innovation hub of Lisbon. He married the daughter of a middle-class merchant with connections to the royal court. The King and Queen of Spain changed their minds about sponsoring him. Spain's possession of the Canary Islands was good luck because the winds there are especially favorable for the westward voyage, compared to Portugal's Madeira Islands and the Azores. He sailed through a dangerous stretch of water at the peak time for hurricane spawning. Had his luck been bad instead of good, another adventurer would have introduced the western hemisphere to Europe.*

The presence of chance highlights a connection between Pillar III (organization of resources) and Pillar IV (success in the future). The better approach is to configure resources with the intention of favorably tilting the odds. Success is merely a possibility and is not guaranteed.

Another confirmation of the importance of chance appears in the writing of the book *Moneyball*. Its author, Michael Lewis, originally planned to write a magazine article on the Oakland A's. During his reporting Lewis observed a contentious meeting on drafting players. He saw a richness of content that convinced him to write a book rather

---

* Let's assume that there was a 50 percent chance that each of those five events was favorable for Columbus's discovery of the New World. The math shows that the probability of success was low: $0.5^5 = 0.03125$.

than a magazine article. Paul DePodesta of the A's, who was present at that meeting, recalled the meeting as atypical and one of the most drama-filled of his career. Had it been a typical meeting, Michael Lewis may not have written the book. Absent the book, Hollywood wouldn't have made the movie. Without the film, there would have been little awareness of Moneyball in popular and business culture. We can extend the role of luck even further back. Michael Lewis became a best-selling author because of his talent but also because of his good luck. As a recent college graduate, he attended a dinner party. A woman struck up a conversation with him, asking about his plans. Lewis replied that he didn't know. The woman promptly introduced Lewis to her husband, an executive in a Wall Street trading firm, and told him to hire Lewis. Lewis was placed on a trading desk, where he observed a fraudulent system at work. He wrote of his experiences, and it became the bestselling book *Liar's Poker*.

One of the first questions I ask in evaluating a strategic-thinking narrative is this: "What is the role of chance in this story? Did the strategy embrace the role of randomness and chance?"

A theme emerges: history turns on small events that are random, unpredictable, and thus non-linear. The X-factor of chance reinforces this comment from Daniel Kahneman: "Luck plays a large role in every story of success; it is almost always easy to identify a small change in the story that would have turned a remarkable achievement into a mediocre outcome."

There's an interesting connection between the X-factor of chance with Pillar II of cognition. Most people tend to attribute their success to their talent. They recall their hard work, and they see that hard work as a cause of the success. That's a simple and memorable story. The story is strengthened be-

Chance plays a vital role in every strategy.

cause the same person will overlook the times that she worked hard and failed. Similarly, her mind will neglect the times that she didn't work hard but had good fortune. She remembers (easily) that hard work leads to success. It requires more mental energy to find counterexamples to the hard-work-leads-to-success narrative.

It's no secret and no surprise that managers are overconfident, and this overconfidence can be a reason for many disastrous strategies. People can easily believe themselves to be exceptional, can easily neglect the intentions of rivals, and can easily disregard chance events.

X-factor #4 – Emergence. Emergence is "the arising of novel and coherent structures, patterns, and properties during the process of self-organization in complex systems." Consider two examples of emergences associated with the opening of the Americas to Europe. The first is the eventual discovery of new food crops such as corn, cocoa, and potatoes. These new crops offered Europeans many new nutritional possibilities. The second is the introduction of European diseases and enslavement, which profoundly changed the aboriginal societies of the New World.

You've probably heard the speculation that a tornado in North America could have been triggered by the flap of a butterfly's wing in the Amazon rain forests. That flap established a small wind current, which was further amplified by other forces. The emergence (the tornado) is the result of causes and effects. It theoretically could be modeled.

However, the occurrence of a tornado is unpredictable. Because a butterfly *might* spark the emergence of a tornado doesn't mean that a butterfly has ever caused a tornado. Moreover, it doesn't mean that a butterfly hasn't indirectly caused a tornado.

Those wing flaps are unnoticed weak signals. We can't predict the emergence of a tornado (or any other given phenomenon). A strategic thinker is ready to notice the weak signals and accept the plausibility of discontinuity and disruption.

To summarize, the four X-factors provide a guiding message for strategic thinking. You should emphasize:

- Drive instead of complacency
- Insight instead of intuition
- Chance instead of certainty
- Emergence instead of master planning

Closing Thoughts:
Historical Thinking and the Future

You can identify a strategic-thinking narrative for any historical person or event and find useful lessons within that narrative. There are conventional accounts of what happened and why, but there are insights to be gathered from reexamining evidence to craft alternative narratives of cause and effect.

This pattern is characteristic of a strategic-thinking narrative: a curious individual scans the world around her for interesting signals. As part of the scanning, she evaluates her existing resources and emerging technology for underappreciated potential. Eventually she realizes a big idea and an insight. She experiments and organizes her resources to improve the fit of her resources to the situation.

A strategic thinker appreciates the value of historical thinking.

Let's imagine that we could time-transport Christopher Columbus from the 15th century into the contemporary milieu with his X-factor of drive intact. Would he be successful? This conjecture might help us understand factors that are relevant to our situation. Context influences the answer. Moreover, it raises more questions: Would he have acquired a different knowledge of technologies that are cutting edge for our times (for example, advanced materials, mapping, management, navigation, and artificial intelligence)? What is the nature of his network with other innovators?

The four pillars and four X-factors of strategic thinking provide a useful model for speculating about individuals in situations that call for good strategy. The exercise offers a lens for identifying plausible new states of the world and actions to advance our interests. We can't predict what would happen to Columbus in the modern day, but we can identify some forces that might shape the search for opportunity.

The blue oceans of opportunity today are not the same as in Columbus's time. The technologies are different. But the Columbuses of today are just as curious, observant, and thoughtful.

I've heard people criticize Columbus for not knowing where he was going, not knowing where he was when he got there, and not knowing where he had been when he returned to Europe. From a perspective of strategy, this is unfair and ignores the roles of ambiguity and emergence.

Students of strategy should recognize that an expeditionary mindset is valuable. The world is one of complex and emergent systems that seldom bend to the elitist notion of a strong-willed visionary genius. Paul Graham, a venture capitalist, writes, "Neither Bill Gates nor Mark Zuckerberg knew at first how big their companies were going to get. All they knew was that they were onto something." We don't know when Christopher Columbus realized that he was "onto something." Although he was probably a narcissist and possibly delusional, he learned and adapted to changing situations.

The Christopher Columbus strategic-thinking narrative reinforces the importance of a sharp mind in touch with the situation. Columbus discovered an insight that any other competitor could have exploited. He persevered and maintained his focus on gaining strategic resources.

One of the most empowering aspects of competent strategic thinking is the realization that ordinary people can do great things. Your challenge is to sense the details of your situation and craft an effective response.

The next chapter describes a major feature of this book, the microskills of strategic thinking. Microskills help to emphasize Pillar II of our strategic thinking model. I describe 12 of them and suggest a five-minute-a-day practice to improve your capacity to think strategically.

CHAPTER 4

Twelve Microskills of Strategic Thinking

Essential Practices That Will Enhance Your Competency

Knowledge is of no value unless you can put it into practice.
— Anton Chekhov

A PROFICIENT AUTOMOBILE DRIVER uses microskills such as accelerating, braking, changing lanes, turning, passing, and parking. Similarly, strategic thinking is a macro ability composed of several distinctive, developable microskills. Microskills of strategic thinking are a key feature of this book. They enhance the idea of Pillar II of the strategic thinking model (the use of the mind and cognition) and are helpful for crafting coherent (Pillar III) responses. The microskills apply whether one is discussing military strategy, stock market investing, or governance of a philanthropic organization. This chapter introduces you to 12 of them. There are an additional 8 described in subsequent chapters. (Appendix B provides brief definitions of all 20.)

The Microskill of Curiosity

Curiosity is perhaps the most familiar of the strategic thinking microskills and perhaps the easiest to incorporate into a busy daily routine.

One tip for keeping curiosity in operation is to monitor your thinking, asking yourself this question: "Am I in learning mode?"

Many people, in their formal schooling, lose their creativity. They are given standardized tests and they habitually ask, "Is this going to be on the test?" As I discuss throughout the book, strategy involves a search for weak signals. A curious person will ask, "What's interesting about this object, idea, or person?"

Curiosity is a distinguishing characteristic of top executives. One observer (Adam Bryant of the *New York Times*) has interviewed over 5,000 chief executives, noting a pattern: "They tend to question everything. They want to know how things work and wonder how they can be made to work better. They're curious about people and their back stories."

One crucial element of strategy work is that of probing and experimenting in unfamiliar domains. You want your curiosity to take you to the point where references and experts can no longer provide you with answers. You must venture outward and discover the answers through observation and empirical testing. As we'll discuss, your goal is not a perfect understanding of the world but instead a seizing of the unknowns and future opportunities.

Organizational culture often tends to suppress curiosity, discouraging individuals from asking profound questions. A cultural emphasis on curiosity will promote strategic thinking, and vice versa.

Here's a tip: Find people whose points of view are the opposite of yours. Rather than try to change their minds, learn why they hold that point of view and how they arrived at it.

The Microskill of Pragmatism

Pragmatism is a person's concern for how the world works and a desire to use that understanding to advance her interests. It reinforces the definition of *competency* provided in Chapter 1: the ability of a person to understand a situation and act reasonably.

I often rename this microskill "pragmatic curiosity" to reinforce the notion of understanding the factors that underlie current and emerging real-world problems. Pragmatism isn't a rejection of art and theory. Pragmatists recognize that art and theory are useful rather than frivolous.

The opposite of pragmatism is quixotism or utopism. The dictionary defines *quixotism* as "impracticality in pursuit of ideas, especially those manifested by rash, lofty, and romantic ideas or extravagantly chivalrous." A utopian is one who advocates for impossibly idealistic schemes of social perfection.

The word *pragmatic* is often confused with the word *practical*. A practical person is concerned with what's real. This reality is often the concrete and tangible nature of the present situation. A practical person would see imagination and speculation as entertainment or danger. On the other hand, a pragmatic person would see imagination and speculation as tools, because they allow the pragmatist to evaluate the possible future effects of present decisions.

> *Action without thought is impulsiveness, and thought without action is procrastination.*

Pragmatism is a balance between action and contemplation. Action without thought is impulsiveness, and thought without action is procrastination.

The Microskill of Ambition

I use the term *ambition* to suggest one's personal drive (X-factor #1) and one's resolve to contribute to the interests of her organization (and of society). I don't mean ambition exclusively as a self-centered and narcissistic drive for personal glory.

The concept of mastery is useful in clarifying the value of ambition. Mastery means the capacity to produce results with a deep and intuitive understanding of the principles that underly those results. Compared to the overconfidence of novices, masters have a better understanding of the nuances of the system in which they're working.

I find that people need to be reminded to think strategically about their careers. An ambitious person is alert for personal growth opportunities. That might mean taking on a new project, making a lateral transfer to a new position, pursuing a promotion, or representing the community in a civic organization. She should also evaluate the opportunities and threats of pursuing employment outside of her current organization.

The word *politics* has a bad connotation for many people in organizations, and for many it becomes a reason to not show leadership. Politics is about the acquisition and use of power. That power can be applied for beneficial purposes or it can be used selfishly. The choice of *how* to use power is one that's shaped by one's ethical reasoning.

The presence of ambition explains why some people prevail and others don't. Ambition reflects a desire to express oneself, to achieve, to see reality clearly, to influence others, to persevere, to win, to prevail, to make an impact, to serve others, and to pursue excellence.

Appendix F provides some additional thoughts on personal branding as a competent strategic thinker.

The Microskill of Sharpness

I unpacked the sharpness theorem in Chapter 2, emphasizing that a strategic thinker has a sharp mind in touch with the situation. The microskill of sharpness is one of being attentive to weak signals, which may appear as emerging trends, patterns, and anomalies.

In Chapter 6, I discuss how strategic thinking has a fuzzy front end. It's here that sharpness is particularly crucial for sensing weak signals. As you might surmise, sharpness overlaps with the microskill of curiosity. A curious person can get distracted, whereas a sharp person takes more care in their sensemaking and judgment. Sharpness brings an extra edge, encouraging you to distinguish a useful signal from a false positive (a signal that seems relevant but isn't). A sharp person balances sensitivity to weak signals with the judgment and determination to respond to critical signals.

Pay attention to weak signals, emerging trends, patterns, and anomalies.

The Microskill of Analogous Reasoning

Children start to use analogy at an early age, and it's one of the most common ways of grappling with abstract concepts. The strategic-thinking narratives of Billy Beane and Christopher Columbus show that there are useful similarities between two men who lived 500 years apart. The comparison reveals that individual strategic thinkers are sensitive to their situation and search for new ideas from outside the mainstream. Each was sensitive to the limitations of his resources and deliberate in focusing his available resources.

By use of analogous reasoning, you could apply those same learnings to other situations in domains far removed from exploring the world or running a professional baseball team. Using analogy, you could imagine those principles in application in military units, churches, philanthropies, and start-up businesses.

However, analogies have limitations. While it's true that business strategy and military strategy have similarities, businesses don't achieve success by destroying their competitors' resources.

The Microskill of Storytelling

Stories and storytelling are among the most powerful tools of human culture. People remember stories. Our religions, our national identities, and our corporate cultures all have within them stories that are told and retold. Those stories provide cohesion for people, giving them shared values and a common explanation of their origins.

The strategic thinking microskill of storytelling is a natural capacity. People understand the basics of stories: characters, tensions, actions, and resolutions. A typical story recounts events that have already happened. One can draw powerful lessons about the dos and don'ts of the culture. They explain an organization's current position in society and its relationship to its rivals. Undoubtedly, these retrospective stories have merit.

I steer people toward a different kind of story that I call a prospective story, which is a story that involves the organization and its people in a new, different, future state. In telling a prospective story, your goal is to construct a plausible logic for the audience. The story needs to be expansive in scope to acknowledge the potential of the future. It doesn't need to "be true" (because there's no certainty that any given future state will occur), but it needs to "feel true" to the audience. Although the future is unfamiliar, people need to feel that the story is credible. A cognitive bias works in favor of the storyteller: people can easily construct a coherent story with only a few hints and patterns. This bias can work against us, too. The mind can easily believe a story that feels true even if there are few facts to support that story.

Strategy must rank as one of the most prominent, influential, and costly stories told in organizations.

Speaking of patterns, a strategic thinker has a good archetype for considering strategic thinking. I find the heroic-quest archetype to be influential in organizing my prospective story and helpful for others who want to improve their strategic thinking. It has a significant advantage because it's a familiar pattern found in Hollywood blockbuster movies as well as in other stories of popular western culture such as personal memoirs and religion. Films such as *Star Wars* or *The Lord of the Rings* are excellent examples. The heroic-quest archetype follows this pattern:

> In Act One, the protagonist (imagine Luke Skywalker or Frodo Baggins) finds himself in a world that is familiar, normal, comfortable, and ordinary. The story builds in tension as he experiences a discontinuity or its disruptive effects. A quest beckons, but he's often reluctant to leave. A mentor-like figure appears (imagine Obi-Wan Kenobi or Gandalf) and nudges the protagonist to leave the ordinary world. This crisis is called "crossing the threshold."
>
> In Act Two, the protagonist finds himself in the special world where "he faces tests, battles enemies, questions the loyalty of friends and allies, withstands a climactic ordeal, teeters on the brink of failure or death," and eventually resolves the fundamental mission of the quest.
>
> In Act Three, the protagonist returns to the ordinary world. He has been victorious, and he returns with an elixir, something that

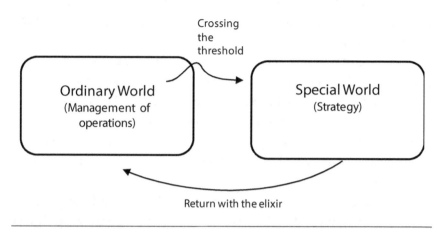

Figure 4-1. The quest narrative archetype is one where the protagonist leaves the ordinary to enter the special world.

> brings benefit to the ordinary world. His experience in the special
> world has transformed him in some important way.

The hero (the protagonist) of this narrative archetype has a specialized function:

> The hero functions to serve others; that is, to put the needs of
> others ahead of her comforts.

I use the term *hero* with an apprehension that some might misinterpret it as a male warrior stereotype (a focus on aggression and physical strength). But other cultures don't share the American view of heroes, and I recognize that females have a unique story involving different strengths and conflicts.

The heroic-quest archetype is useful in distinguishing operations from strategy. Let's examine more closely the two worlds, as illustrated in Figure 4-1. The hero's ordinary world is the daily work of the existing organizational model. She leaves it to journey into the special world of strategy, where she will be tested by circumstances and by others.

The ordinary world is comfortable and familiar. The hero typically finds it difficult to leave, and this is known as the crossing-the-threshold crisis. The contemporary experience in strategy is that people have many good excuses to not invest their time in strategic thinking, chief among them the assertion that they are busy with their day-to-day work.

The role of a mentor is also familiar in the quest narrative. In organizations, a mentor might be a member of the board of directors or an external consultant who helps leaders to recognize discontinuities and the potential for disruption. My role, as the author of this book, is to challenge you to leave your comfort zone and take on the heroic role, helping your organization achieve excellence in strategy. I serve as a mentor.

In Figure 4-1 there's an arrow marked "Return with the elixir." In the quest archetype, the elixir is something of value to the ordinary world. In the movie Star Wars, the hero provides a rendering of the construction of the Death Star, allowing his comrades to identify an exploitable weakness. In the movie *Raiders of the Lost Ark*, the Ark is an artifact with the power to destroy one's enemies. The elixir, in the analogy for strategic thinking, is a piece of information, an insight, a new-and-better dominant idea, or possibly a completely articulated strategy. The strategy-as-elixir transforms the organization of resources in the ordinary world of operations.

Strategy is a battle with ambiguity. The most significant challenges are those that are within you and the ways that culture has shaped your habits of mind. The hero serves the collective good by doing things that others are unwilling to do. Frequently the protagonist is tricked by characters known as shapeshifters and shadows. The analogy for strategy is that ambiguity often is a force that deceives managers into overconfidence or tricks them into maintaining the status quo.

Another part of the strategy-as-story analogy concerns itself with the hero's gifts and special powers. In *Star Wars*, we learn of a gift called The Force, and in *The Lord of the Rings*, the gift is a ring that makes the holder invisible. From the earlier strategic-thinking narratives, Billy Beane's mentor, Sandy Alderson, introduced him to the writings of Bill James and sparked Beane's desire to explore sabermetrics as a tool for professional baseball strategy. Columbus was inspired and reliant on Toscanelli's map. Likewise, you have many personal gifts that are resources for your time in the special world. If you develop your microskills of strategic thinking, you will have developed a gift that will be valued by your stakeholders.

People often fail to recognize the gifts they have. Earlier I wrote about 3M's experience with Post-it Notes, and how the microspheres that were key to the product languished for years because the inventor couldn't find a viable commercial use. People need to search internally as well as externally for resources and the potential for value.

Those gifts stimulated the X-factors of insight. As I discuss in Chapter 9, an insight is a reframing of a mediocre story to make it a better story. If story is strategy (and vice versa), then I make the claim that mediocre strategies and mediocre stories are cut from the same cloth. The ordinary world is often dominated by stories that block out the unfamiliar and reinforce the status quo. Throughout this book, I argue that an important strategic thinking task and leadership task is confronting the reality and helping others to replace mediocre stories and strategies with better ones.

"Strategy must rank as one of the most prominent, influential, and costly stories told in organizations," state David Barry and Michael Elmes. The microskill of storytelling offers many benefits to the strategic thinker and her organization. A story can help others make sense of ambiguity, help people adopt new beliefs, and organize their actions.

The Microskill of Open Mental Stance

In sports, stance refers to the physical posture of the athlete and is typically the first thing that's taught to a beginner. A proper stance, being "in position," enables the athlete to respond to the evolving game quickly. Sports coaches often call the ideal physical stance the "ready position."

By analogy, the mental stance for strategic thinking has a ready position: alert for weak signals of emerging opportunities and threats.

Like a physical stance, the person is calm and not agitated. When a person detects a signal, she is ready to respond with appropriate action.

A person with an open mental stance is receptive to new information and able to mentally play with new ideas and patterns. She's prepared for novelty and assumes that the situation is different from other prior experiences.

Avoid the stubborn and overconfident belief that your worldview is correct (this is called ontological arrogance).

Recall that an essential concern of strategy is ambiguity. Having an open mental stance is useful for searching out multiple explanations and frameworks for knowing what's true. With an open mental stance, you question your questions.

There's some jargon that I will periodically use in this book to reinforce our understanding of the microskill of open mental stance:

- **Steamrolling** – This is the practice of ignoring information that's not consistent with your existing knowledge and worldview. It's another word for confirmation bias.

- **Solutioneering** – This refers to the tendency of people to focus mental energy on promoting a solution rather than fully understanding the strategic context.

- **Backcasting** – This is the planning technique of identifying a vision and working backward to the steps needed to achieve the outcome. It can be an acceptable approach for planning, but it has an assumption that limits people's ability to imagine the potential of the future fully.

- **Ontological humility** – This is the attitude that there's much that you don't know. It's a counterweight to steamrolling and a reinforcement of the beginner's mind. It contrasts with ontological arrogance, the stubborn and overconfident belief that your worldview is the only correct worldview.

The Microskill of Skepticism

The first goal of skepticism is to protect you from the faulty claims of others. In the Moneyball example, the illusion that scouts could predict a player's on-field performance was a faulty claim. Billy Beane's practice of skepticism helped him to be an independent thinker and free of the orthodoxy.

Just because someone in authority claims to know something doesn't mean that the knowledge is valid. Many organizations are structured in traditional bureaucracies, where one's position in the hierarchy explains one's authority and power. Often the organizational culture conflates knowledge, position, and authority. In many organizations, privilege and power determine the knowledge that counts for making decisions. This creates a problem for strategy in that "the power of

A competent strategic thinker pursues the truth because it leads to principled success.

authoritative knowledge is not that it is correct, it is that it counts." A skeptic doesn't automatically assume that a person has correct knowledge.

The second goal of skepticism is to search for novelty, with the intention of adapting our worldview to those new facts.

Skepticism is different from cynicism and dogmatism. Cynicism is a suspicion of the motives of others, a prejudice about a person's character. A skeptic will modify her beliefs to align with data, whereas a cynic might believe that others have maliciously contaminated the data. If cynicism is the unwillingness to believe, dogma is the unwillingness to doubt. A dogmatist will not consider questions that call into doubt her established beliefs. One of the reasons for the success of upstart entrepreneurs is that incumbents are mired in dogma and slow to respond to changes in their situation.

Skepticism, like pragmatism, is concerned with the pursuit of truth because correct understandings of the situation are more useful than invalid beliefs. *A competent strategic thinker pursues the truth because it leads to principled success.* Likewise, the pursuit of success leads one to search for fundamental truths about the world. Billy

Beane had a healthy skepticism of conventional baseball wisdom. The Moneyball strategy reflected a search for a more accurate model of baseball team productivity.

Many times, people see skepticism as permission to analyze and find fault with others. Unfortunately, they *only* find fault. I encourage people, when practicing the microskill of skepticism, to be optimistic and hold the idea that finding better truths involves turning toward excellence and away from mediocrity.

The Microskill of Reflection

The microskill of reflection is sharpness applied to oneself. Your goal is to develop a constantly improving understanding of what is important to you and your organization. Those important things can include interests, values, ambitions, strengths and weaknesses, experiences, passions, mistakes, and ethics. The microskill of reflection unifies a person's learning journey.

Reflection is facilitated by freeing yourself from distractions. I call it productive solitude, and you can perform it while driving alone, shoveling snow, or taking a walk. This respite is not an escape from unpleasantness. It's an opportunity to detach from the urgently felt impulse to act. Productive solitude provides the opportunity for you to test your inclinations and deepen your understanding of the nature of your present reality and the possibilities of the future.

Reflection takes time and is uncomfortable because it doesn't result in a neat and tidy product. The effort of reflection is one additional reason that strategic thinking is valuable and rare.

Figure 4-2 shows my adaptation of Will Taylor's model of learning. At the core of the model is the microskill of reflection. Notice the arrow labeled "Start with the beginner's mind," a suggestion I made in Chapter 1. Beginners follow a general flow in learning. They begin in a state of naïveté, and they don't know what they don't know (they are unconsciously incompetent). They progress in their learning so that what they know is second nature (they are unconsciously competent).

People learn from experience. When a person reflects upon her experience, she gains a more powerful conceptual knowledge. Was

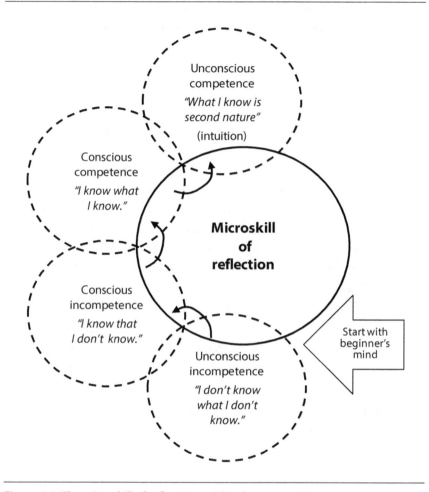

Figure 4-2. The microskill of reflection guides the progression to competence and mastery.

her experience part of a pattern? What characterizes the pattern? Where are the anomalies?

We saw the importance of accumulated learning in the Billy Beane and Christopher Columbus strategic-thinking narratives. A core idea of strategy is that strategy is a form of organizational learning about the organization's current and future environments. Individuals make up organizations, so individuals accrue information and internalize knowledge. Reflection is a key to unlocking this resource.

Several years ago, I interviewed the CEO and several other top executives of Domino's Pizza about their experiences with a successful strategic initiative. As our meeting ended, the executives remarked about how valuable it was to refresh their memories about the initiative and to draw lessons from their experience. As happens with others, the urgency of the present had distracted their strategic thinking. You will always find value when you reflect on the past and anticipate the future.

In a similar vein, I've worked with senior executives and middle managers who can benefit from reflecting on their careers and their personal brands. Their resumes are typically litanies of positions held, contributions to projects, and responsibilities. I encourage them to write about their experiences, using complete sentences rather than bullet points. I encourage them to reflect on and identify their "proud moments," which are accomplishments and benefits. I want them to tell a story of how they faced obstacles and overcame them. Solving problems and grasping opportunity are the essence of strategy, after all.

Reflection is complementary to the microskills of storytelling and ambition. Questions like these help you to develop a clearer idea of your perspective and value:

- Where have I been and what have I learned?
- Where am I now?
- Where am I going?

The Microskill of Empathy

Empathy is a person's ability to discern the mental state of others: their emotions, their logic, and their intentions. History records many problems when someone misreads another's reactions and intentions. Saddam Hussein famously misread a meeting with the U.S. Ambassador to Iraq, thinking that the United States wasn't concerned about Iraq's territorial disputes with Kuwait. Hussein subsequently invaded Kuwait and found himself facing an angry response from the United States and its allies. Psychologists call the capacity to anticipate the intentions and reactions of other actors in any strategic situation *theory of mind.* Empathy is central to many decisions where there is potential for conflict.

An empathetic person is also sensitive to the context of the situation and its influences on strategy. One of the biggest business blunders of all time was the Coca-Cola Company's misreading of consumers' reactions to New Coke. Taste tests proved that people preferred New Coke's flavoring, but the research didn't account for all the intangible benefits represented by the existing Coke brand.

I include the ability to listen well as a sub-microskill of empathy. Managers spend too much energy telling and explaining solutions and not enough energy understanding the interests and needs of stakeholders. You want to consider the words and actions of others in the context of their own culture, rather than in the flavoring of your culture.

Moreover, an empathetic person is sensitive to the inherent ambiguity of strategy and the strategic situation. Perhaps people are ready for a blunt warts-and-all assessment of the situation, but maybe they need a deliberate and carefully worded presentation of data, premises, and conclusions. Your empathy will help you to recognize the presence of discomfort in the discussions of strategy and to prepare for the appearance of anger and various forms of passive aggressiveness.

Earlier we considered goal setting as an activity that's distinct from strategy. One reason that goal setting is inadequate is that it lacks empathy for the situation, such as ignoring the response of a competitor. If you decide to lower your price to gain market share, your competitor will react and change the business environment.

The microskill of empathy reinforces many other microskills. Of note is its relationship with the microskill of storytelling, because other actors, as well as the audience for a story, have existing stories that they're telling themselves. If you're not aware of those current stories, or if you don't try to be sharp and perceive them, you'll be at a disadvantage.

Another interesting overlap of empathy is with the microskill of ambition. A person's (and an organization's) motivation and volition build and decay over time. An important task of strategic thinking is assessing the willingness of both friends and foes to persevere in a contested situation. For foes, you need to evaluate their attempts to disguise their intentions, what they might be doing to weaken your volition, and what you can do to cause the decay of their volition.

The Microskill of Personal Resilience

Let's continue with the idea that VUCA characteristics of strategy (ambiguity in particular) are a source of pain and anxiety for people. Individuals respond to adversity in different ways. Some people are knocked down and deflated. Others return stronger and more effective.

Personal resilience, sometimes called grit, enables individuals to overcome adversity. A resilient person confronts the messiness of the world, challenging themselves to better their situation.

The strategic-thinking narratives of Billy Beane and Christopher Columbus show evidence that various events in their earlier lives tested them. They met resistance to their ideas, which tested their convictions. Both persevered, and their successes were the results of years of sustained effort rather than quick-fix impulses. From their strategic-thinking narratives, we find two essential characteristics of personal resiliency:

Two essential characteristics of personal resilience are inventiveness and innovativeness.

- **A resilient person is inventive.** She faces up to the challenges and goes to work to develop solutions to them. To do that, she's optimistic that she can create betterment and can improve upon an existing practice. She's not satisfied with mediocrity.

- **A resilient person is innovative.** She develops a support network of people to share information. She tests new ideas out with them and solicits feedback. She strives to hold the big picture while working in the details.

Here's a suggestion for your personal development: Find an opportunity to work in a "crew" setting, a small group of people available for rapid response. There are many volunteer groups (fire departments, church groups, Red Cross, and the like) who help others who have had their lives disrupted by external events. Most businesses and institutions have business continuity programs in place with teams available to respond to interruptions of operations.

Crew-work exposes you to the unpredictability and messiness of a world that doesn't respond to conventional, linear, strategic planning. It gives you a better understanding of your own capacities and capabilities and how they contribute to the crew's agility. Also, you will experience the value of honest communications and trust.

In Chapter 9, I briefly explore the related concept of system resilience, which describes the capability of a system to reconfigure itself, such as the emergence of new plant and animal life after a forest fire. If the future holds the potential for disruptive changes, then one of the pre-eminent goals for any organization is to improve its capacity for resilience.

The Microskill of Conceptual Mapping

A person feels anxiety when she is disoriented. A map lessens that anxiety by helping you to orient yourself. It's an inconvenient truth that many executives are lost, unable to grasp the essential concepts of strategy, crafting it, or conveying it to others. In addition to orientation, maps help you frame and answer questions like these:

- Where could I go?

- Where should I go?

I like to use the analogy of comparing conceptual maps with conventional (spatially-organized) maps. Both can be used for orientation (knowing where you are) and navigation (knowing where you could go or where you should go). Any mental map can be normative (describing what should be) or descriptive (representing what is).

Landmarks are salient features, and the concept of landmarks-as-navigational-beacons is a fundamental message of this book. A landmark that gives you a broader reference, such as a lighthouse marking the entrance to a harbor, is a navigational beacon in the physical world. As I discuss in the next chapter, an operational thinking map has a set of landmarks (that is, navigational beacons) that are distinct from the landmarks of strategic thinking.

Besides navigational beacons, three other mapping concepts enhance the analogy of a physical map and conceptual map. They are the presence of orientation cues (helping you know where you are), associative cues (helping you know if there are other nearby points of interest), and boundaries (helping you recognize your frame of reference).

Individuals have multiple maps, and they organize their maps differently. Since organizations are collections of individuals, they likely have numerous individual mental maps. Organizational culture will encourage consistency in an individual's mental map. However, the organization's culture is also a force of conformity that suppresses weak signals of discontinuities.

With the idea of multiple maps, you can pose questions that inform your strategic thinking:

- What are the boundaries of the map?
- What are the salient features on the map?
- What maps are others using?
- How do I know when to change maps?

Strategic thinking benefits from collaboration. The practice of conceptual mapmaking can help generate better understandings of the situation and the logic for improving the organization.

In Chapter 2, I discussed the distinctions of corporate strategy, business strategy, functional strategy, and programming-as-strategy. Each of these probably deserves a different map.

Ben Franklin's Learning Technique

Every learner is concerned with turning the abstract into application. This adaptation of Ben Franklin's wisdom works well for internalizing the microskills of strategic thinking.

Benjamin Franklin (1706–1790) is one of the most respected of the founding fathers of the United States. In the pursuit of his personal development, Franklin identified 13 virtues that would help him in the perfection of his life. His technique was to spend a full week on each virtue and then switch to the next attribute. Since there are four sets of 13 weeks, he would practice each of them four times per year.

Franklin wrote his autobiography a few years before his death. In discussing his technique of focusing on virtues, he declared that he never achieved perfection, yet concluded that the method made him a better and happier man.

You can develop your strategic thinking microskills using a similar approach. I recommend devoting Week 1 to the practice of the microskill of curiosity. It could be as simple as reading an article (there are thousands to choose from). If you work in X (for example, healthcare or manufacturing or chemistry), search on the terms *curiosity and X*. You'll find that the microskills mutually reinforce each other.

Here is an example: During my focus on pragmatism one week, I searched on the words *strategy* and *pragmatism* and came up with some interesting writings on strategic pragmatism, pragmatic analysis, and pragmatic competence. Each of those topics gave me useful new strategic thinking ideas.

I recommend that you devote Week 2 to the microskill of ambition. You could take a fresh look at your resume and personal brand. You could consider the kinds of positive impacts that you want to make on your community. Continue practicing each microskill for one week and reflect on what you learn. Franklin discovered a way to be a better and happier person – you can learn to become a natural strategic thinker.

Another tip for enhancing the development of microskills is to compliment others when you notice them using one. "Muriel, I really like the way that you showed a healthy skepticism of the data. You helped all of us get a better understanding of the situation." Alternatively, "Thanks, Jim, for being open-minded about our proposal. Your curiosity helped to sharpen our value proposition."

In addition to the 12 listed in this chapter, 8 additional microskills are listed in Figure 4-3 that I introduce in later chapters. I practice them in a 20-week repeating cycle.

Regardless of how busy you are, you'll find that regularly practicing the microskills will significantly enhance your strategic thinking competency.

◆ ◆ ◆

You're probably familiar with most of the dozen microskills of strategic thinking described in this chapter. You should practice them and develop them. As they become a more prominent part of your perspective, you'll find that you have increased your sensitivity to the weak signals of discontinuity. You'll be more imaginative in the crafting of strategy.

The next chapter continues to advance your understanding of the purpose, nature, and scope of strategic thinking. It introduces a map of operational thinking that contrasts with that of strategic thinking. You enhance your strategic thinking competency when you focus on the landmarks of the strategic thinking map. That strategic-operational distinction is one of the foundational ideas of this book.

Curiosity
Pragmatism
Ambition
Sharpness
Analogous reasoning
Storytelling
Open mental stance
Skepticism
Reflection
Empathy
Personal resilience
Conceptual mapping

Devalorization
Contrarianism
High-quality questions
Abductive reasoning
Anticipation
Reframing
Metacognition
Courage

Figure 4-3. The microskills of strategic thinking. The last eight are introduced in later chapters.

CHAPTER 5

Why Strategic Thinking Is Rare

When You Have the Wrong Map, Its Accuracy Doesn't Matter

There is a fundamental difference between operational effectiveness and strategy.

— Michael Porter

THE SIMPLEST EXPLANATION for why strategic thinking is rare in larger organizations is that most people in most organizations function comfortably with an alternative. That alternative is operational thinking, which is a manifestation of their experiences with the day-to-day, get-things-done pressures of managing the organization.

I've heard many times people say, "I'm too busy to think strategically."

The goal of any manager should be to balance her allocation of mental energy between strategic thinking and operational thinking, shifting back and forth as appropriate for the situation. She needs to know the essential components of each as foundational knowledge. That knowledge provides her the ability to distinguish the two styles. In the distinction, we discover why strategic thinking is rare.

In this chapter, I introduce two additional microskills of strategic thinking, devalorization and contrarianism, that can help you to shift mental energy toward strategic thinking.

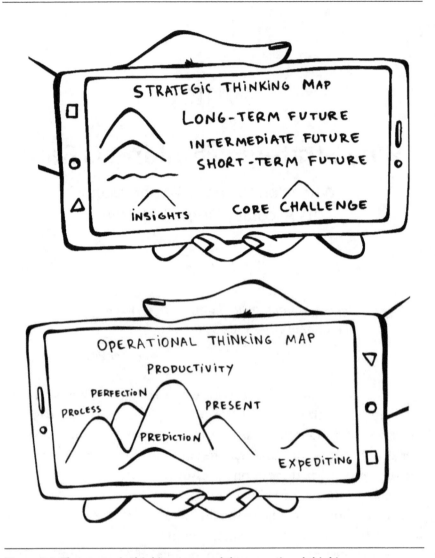

Figure 5-1. The strategic thinking map and the operational thinking map.

Landmarks of Operations and of Strategy

Imagine that you're holding two maps, each of which has prominent landmarks as illustrated in Figure 5-1.

Let's begin with the strategic thinking map. The future is a salient landmark that serves as a navigational beacon. When in doubt about where to direct mental energy, a competent strategic thinker orients herself toward the future.

The strategic thinking map also has landmarks for the core challenge and for insights, which I introduced in Chapter 2 and will discuss more in Chapters 6–9.

Also, note the three peaks of the future associated with the short-term future, the intermediate-term future, and the long-term future. (I discuss them in more detail in Chapter 7, using the respective labels of Horizon 1, Horizon 2, and Horizon 3.)

When in doubt about what to do, remember that a strategic thinker chooses to focus on success in the future (Pillar IV).

Appendix D provides an expanded list of navigational beacons found on the map of strategic thinking.

The operational thinking map is a separate map dominated by the landmark of productivity and four other words beginning with the letter *P*. These concepts should be familiar to anyone in a larger organization.

The maps indicate two distinct but complementary realities for organizations: operations are real (and necessary), but so is strategy. If you want to improve the operational environment, you focus on the 5Ps. If you want to craft strategy, you want to set aside the operational thinking map and instead find and explore the landmarks on the strategic thinking map.

The Five Ps of Operational Thinking

The five Ps of operational thinking collectively help to explain why operational thinking dominates a manager's mental energies. It reflects three aspirations of the individual: her desire to be productive, her desire for perfection, and her desire for predictability.

Productivity. The source of operational thinking originates with an organization's *raison d'être*, its fundamental mission. Armies exist to fight or deter land battles. Philanthropies exist to advance culture and society. Business exists to deliver products and services to customers. Schools exist to educate students. All organizations exist to produce something.

You can learn much about an organization by identifying its most prominent metrics. To achieve the overarching goal of efficient output, operational thinkers naturally prefer concrete, quantitative measures. They readily find value in common artifacts of report cards, dashboards, and Kanban. A person pays attention to that which is measured and that which the organization links to an incentive.

A focus on production creates a day-to-day operating rhythm for the organization, which people adopt and internalize into their behavior. Do you know a person who has a to-do list and is fond of "checking off the boxes?" That person is showing a preference for this operational thinking landmark.

Perfection. An operations environment is one that is orderly, tidy, and neat. People desire to minimize disorder, using the assumption that reducing errors (deviations from a standard) will improve performance. Perfection is a good thing if people interpret it as a call to strive for excellence. However, many people understand perfection in its literal sense and reduce the system to constituent factors and study them. They gain great specialist expertise at the expense of a broader awareness of the strategic context.

Standards and categories facilitate more-efficient mental processing. It's easier for people to match the category and respond with standard practice. While this is a benefit for operations, this is a problem for strategy because anomalies, curiosities, and other weak signals of discontinuities are swept into the standard categories and masked by them. I know of several entrepreneurs who created unique businesses by ignoring conventional categorizations of market segments.

Predictability. People like routine and they like predictable environments. Their mental energy isn't taxed, and they can maintain a sense of ease.

Predictability often reflects the metaphor of the organization as a machine that follows rigid rules. The word *determinism* is similar. There is no room for randomness, discontinuity, and disruption. Every cause has an effect, and every effect has a cause.

The organizational tool of budgeting reflects an aspiration for predictability. Most organizations find that their cash flows and cost structures vary little from year to year. Cost is more predictable than the organization's revenue stream, which can be affected by the general economy, political trends, and competitive actions. However, the size, mix, and rate of revenues probably have a greater longer-term impact on the organization.

Because budgets are essential to the organization and are a kind of plan, it's easy to attach the adjective *strategic* and misname it the strategic plan. A budget may be a kind of plan but it's a mistake to consider it a strategy. A good strategy addresses the core challenge.

Process. An assembly line is a convenient example of a process. A process is a mechanism that functions to synchronize and coordinate production. Smaller organizations invest in process because it enables them to scale up to a larger size and find cost efficiencies. Larger organizations invest in process and continuous improvement because it creates efficiencies that strengthen their power and impact.

Process is a logical consequence of aspirations for productivity, perfection, and prediction. Process reinforces the coherence of the aspirations and results in a predilection for the present (the fifth P). You can examine the logic of this in Figure 5-2.

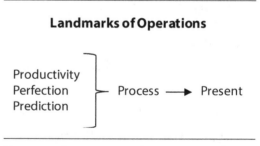

Landmarks of Operations

Productivity
Perfection   — Process ⟶ Present
Prediction

Figure 5-2. Process strengthens operational aspirations and enhances focus on the present.

The effect of process and the attendant specialization of people in it creates a barrier between an organization's day-to-day work and the ambiguity of its external environment. The elimination of ambiguity also removes a source of anxiety and distraction. Unfortunately for strategic thinking, process can mask weak signals of discontinuity and discourage people from taking initiative when facing non-standard events.

Present. I was once told about an operations manager in a large aerospace company, a company that requires years to bring a new product to market, who was asked to contribute to a long-range plan. In refusing the request, the manager proudly declared, "I never look further out than 90 days into the future." Operational managers can find the future orientation of strategy irrelevant, and they can be dismissive.

Many people focus on the short term because an organization's cadence imposes constraints upon their work, because of culture, and because their available mental energy is absorbed. The fifth P is a consequence of the four previously described Ps: the more a person concentrates on productivity (or process or prediction or perfection or predictability), the more she will find that the day-to-day work of the organization consumes her mental energy.

Moving from the Operational Thinking Map to the Strategic Thinking Map

Operational thinking is a coherent worldview that reflects the power of culture. In the next sections of this chapter I describe three general approaches to embracing the strategic thinking map. The first approach involves using landmarks that are common to both maps as a bridge. The second is to approach the process landmark with more finesse. The third, most-radical approach, is to dismiss the operational thinking map, arguing that it holds no value.

Transitioning by Finding Common Landmarks

You can develop your ability to think strategically by finding landmarks common to both maps and use them as a bridge that conceptually unites the operational thinking map and the strategic thinking map. You can use the bridge to cross from one side to the other and back. Figure 5-3 illustrates five landmarks.

Time. On the operational thinking map, people mark time with increments such as days, months, or years. An operational thinker is

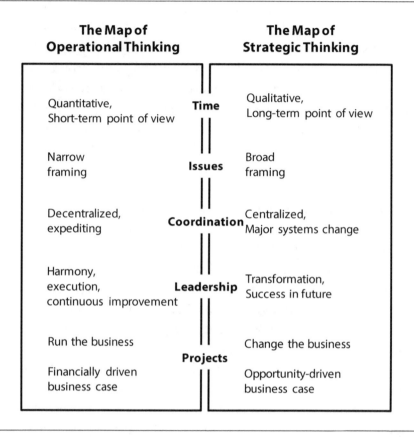

Figure 5-3. Find shared landmarks and use them as a bridge from the operations thinking map to the strategic thinking map.

naturally inclined to retain the quantitative mindset and substitute the concept of long-range planning for strategy.

Instead of time as a measurement, a competent strategic thinker considers qualitatively different systems. Time is not a unit of measure, but a place to find opportunity. The distant future is one with new dominating ideas: different assumptions, different flows of value, different resources, and new possibilities.

Issues. Issues management is a straightforward management activity. It begins with scanning, noticing, and announcing the presence of some problem, opportunity, or concern that requires managerial attention. Many people record those issues on a continually updated issues log, where the issue is assigned a status of open or closed. The essential task is to close issues, using analysis, decision making, and resourcing.

On the operations side of the bridge, the issues are shorter term and more narrowly framed than those on the strategy side, reflecting the definition of strategy as specialized for those kinds of issues. In the next chapter I introduce several tools and concepts to help you scan for strategic issues and manage them.

Coordination of resources. Notice the smaller landmark of expediting (near productivity) on the operational thinking map in Figure 5-1. Expediting is the day-to-day coordination of resources and priorities to meet production goals. Its strategic-thinking-map complement is restructuring, a more significant coordination of the organization's processes and its tangible and intangible resources. An example of coordination in strategy is the aligning processes or combination of resources between firms in a joint venture.

Coordination has a cost, regardless of whether it's on the operational thinking map or the strategic thinking map. Expediting's cost appears in the wages of specialized expeditors or in the cost of interrupting a lower-priority project with a higher-priority project. Given the importance of productivity, expediting becomes a routine budgeted expense.

Coordination is more severe and costly in strategy. A strategic decision might involve a policy choice to terminate a product line or abandon a group of customers. It might mean terminating employment for a long-term, valuable person for the simple reason that their expertise is less relevant for the new direction. It might mean deferring a dividend to fund an increase in the Research & Development budget.

I previously discussed budgets as tools of prediction. They are also tools of coordination. Two important accounting concepts are OpEx and CapEx, which refer to operating expenses and capital expenses. Operating expenses are those expenses that are needed to run the business, to integrate many other organizational activities such as production plans, hiring plans, and financing plans. Capital expenses are for those resources that are depreciable according to accounting rules. Sometimes CapEx investments are associated with transforming business models or adopting new ones and may provide insights to an organization's strategy.

Leadership. Leadership is an individual competency that involves two inter-related choices. The first choice is the leader's focus on the collective betterment of the group (rather than her comforts). The second choice is her willingness to use influencing skills (instead of exerting formal organizational power or administrative technique).

The operational thinking map is dominated by the aspirations for productivity, perfection, and predictability. There we would expect a leader to influence others to pursue excellence in execution, harmony with others, perseverance, and incremental continuous improvement. Leadership complements the ordinary managerial functions of planning, controlling, and administering.

Leadership on the strategic thinking map involves helping others align their efforts toward the navigational beacon of success in the future, discerning discontinuities and other difficult truths, searching for and recognizing insights, and generating new narratives (and reconciling or discarding competing narratives).

Projects. Projects and project management are tools useful for both operations and for strategy. Operational projects are focused on the betterment of the existing systems, such as quality or process improvement. Project managers hold optimization as a dominant idea and seek quantitative metrics, often containing a financial component such as return on investment or payback time. Managers carefully vet these projects for their economic benefits and prioritize them to maximize financial returns. People often assume that all relevant information is available at chartering. I call these kinds of projects run-the-business projects and use the acronym RtB to designate them.

Another kind of project is a change-the-business project, designated by the acronym CtB. These projects are transformational in nature, and they often affect the organizational status quo in small and large ways. Quantitative financial metrics are of lesser importance for CtB projects because it's difficult to measure the fit of the organizational model with its environment. Sometimes the overall improvement of the enterprise requires some parts of the organization to sacrifice local, short-term performance.

One of the challenges for any organization is to achieve a balance between the RtB and CtB portfolios of projects. Specifically, the goal is to assure that sufficient resources are invested in CtB projects, even if the natures of the CtB projects are ambiguous and may not have the strongest financial case.

It's the nature of operations that many RtB issues have an immediate and urgent nature. They are safer investments than the CtB projects.

In Chapter 1, I noted that many managers use a rhetorical trick of labeling their projects as "strategic" to obtain funding and prioritization. I remind the reader to recognize and avoid that designation. Instead, I find it better to identify those projects that are aligned with strategy and designate them as CtB projects.

Recognizing Strategy as an Art (Not as a Process)

One of the ways to distinguish operational thinking from strategic thinking is to develop a more-nuanced understanding of three organizational activitities: process, practice, and art. With a correct use of the definitions, I argue that strategy is never a process and most commonly an art.

It's common to find the word *process* incorporated into people's titles, into department names, and associated with functions (e.g., engineering processes, or human resources processes, or sales processes). The word *process* implies a managed flow of work that can be made more efficient. A narrow definition of a process is one where software and mechanical devices automate the work, eliminating the need for human involvement in the work. Most mature organizations can point toward dozens of examples of work that were once entirely performed by people and are now completely automated.

An art is characterized in its essence by personal preferences. Most managers don't like using the term *art*, the exception being an organization that's inherently creative (an advertising agency or a movie studio). For the operational thinking mindset, the term *art* implies activities that are inconsistent, performed by opinionated people with subjective information. It implies something that is out of control.

Regardless of the preferences of managers, a strategy is best described as an art. Other examples of art would be crafting a complicated sales proposal or merging two organizations. Art is characterized by differing inputs and differing outputs, for which people hold subjective views about what is acceptable quality.

I have found that this strategy-as-art assertion brings consternation to those who prefer the organization-as-machine metaphor: objectivity is good and subjectivity is bad, quantitative measurements are good and qualitative metrics are bad, control is good and chaos is bad. Risk is to be avoided. Stated differently, these people have mindsets that value productivity, predictability, and perfection.

In some organizations, the phrases *strategic planning process*, *strategic management process*, and *strategy process* are common. But they are misnomers and don't meet the above criteria for distinguishing a process. Further, in strictly applying the criteria of automated software and hardware, strategy is unlikely to ever be a process. It's best to recognize that the word *art* is the most appropriate designation of the fundamental nature of strategy because its result depends upon individual skills and attitudes.

An interesting middle ground between process and art is occupied by practice. A practice allows individuals to use their style and judgment to achieve a commonly agreed-upon output. Most standardized plans and reports are the results of practice. There is a generally agreed-upon format for the document, but the author of the document uses her judgment to determine what content needs to be highlighted and uses her personal preferences in writing it.

An organization could mature strategy-as-art to strategy-as-practice. The organization would need to standardize its criteria for the outputs and inputs of strategy. The organization would need to agree on definitions of terms for inputs to strategy: *weak signals*, *beliefs*, *core challenges*, and *assumptions*. Similarly, it would need common definitions for the outputs, particularly adjectives such as *strong*, *good*, *clever*, and *powerful*. The standard format for writing strategy, such as the examples provided in Chapters 2 and 8, provides a useful template.

The Microskill of Devalorization

This chapter introduce 2 more microskills of strategic thinking to add to the 12 presented in the previous chapter.

Devalorization is a French word that means to devalue or diminish something that the culture venerates. The technique is simple: you take something that the prevailing culture considers important, and you imagine the opposite. You develop arguments that justify this unorthodox view. You then explore the implications.

Devalorizing productivity. As an example, let's develop the premise that productivity is a useless and valueless aspiration. In devalorizing, I imagine that a person should be unproductive. It makes sense when you think about the advice offered to many workers: get more sleep, take a vacation, follow your religion's traditions by having a day of rest, invest in your social relationships, invest in learning new skills.

Additional arguments against productivity include the side effects of industrialization (which is a manifestation of productivity): environmental degradation, product safety, exploitation of child labor, and dehumanizing work environments. Indeed, these are frequent topics of corporate statements of social responsibility.

Most modern enterprises are not solely interested in productivity and understand the benefits for balancing productivity with interests like social justice, environmental responsibility, and human dignity. These interests – beyond productivity – reinforce this book's definition of strategy and the template from Chapter 2 for writing strategy.

Extending the practice. I encourage you to develop devalorized arguments for other concepts on the operational thinking map. Here are some answers that will help you confirm that you understand devalorization for the other four Ps of predictability, perfection, process, and present. Instead of valuing prediction, you appreciate spontaneity and serendipity. Instead of valuing process as a way of accomplishing work, you emphasize the creative aspects (the artfulness) of the work. Instead of valuing perfection, you value discovering opportunities, which happen to be easiest to find in the messiness of the VUCA environment. Instead of focusing on the busy-ness of the present you value the certainty that the future will be different.

Profanity as a tool of devalorization. Profane language is profane because it's not part of the norms of society. It's often used to shock people. It's a useful tool of strategic thinking in that, by making accepted norms problematic, the person opens herself to ideas that might be novel and lead to a breakthrough and intellectual revolution.

The word *gay* provides an example of profanity. A hundred years ago, saying "You're gay" to a person would be understood by most to mean "You're in good spirits." A few decades later, people used the word *gay* as a slur – a profanity – to reference a person's sexual orientation. The profanity has diminished in recent times. Most of the contemporary culture accepts non-traditional orientations, and some parts of the culture even celebrate it.

Here are a few words and phrases that are worthy of considering as profane: *religiosity, family connections, education, liberalism, conservatism, nationalism, institutionalism, socialism,* and *capitalism.*

Revolutionary ideas can come from embracing abnormal perspectives.

By contemplating profanity, you raise questions of social and cultural power. Certain classes of people gain the power to author the accepted norms, values, and behaviors. They determine what is sacred and what is profane. But people don't stay in power forever, and one can gain insights into the future by contemplating the changes in the balance of power.

As an alternative to the word *profanity* (some people find it too radical and too unconventional), consider the word *iconoclast*, which means "smasher of icons." An iconoclast is a person who assertively rejects cherished beliefs and institutions or values and practices. Many well-known entrepreneurs have been called iconoclasts.

Another way to practice devalorization is to imagine yourself as a refugee fleeing your home because of the danger there. To develop your strategic thinking, imagine you're fleeing the status quo of operations. When you return home, you return with knowledge of a different world. By understanding both maps, you have enhanced and matured your values and perspective.

Imagine that you're a brand-new member of a group, an outsider, and imagine those things that an outsider would determine to be unconventional, unorthodox, crazy, irrelevant, abnormal, nonsensical, and heretical. This activity may cause you discomfort, but find solace in the observation that other competent strategic thinkers have been called strange, quirky, weird, stupid, and dangerous.

No one needs to know you are thinking strategically.

Although devalorization might provoke discomfort, the feeling need not manifest itself into observable behavior. This discomfort is simply a troublesome and temporary state of mind that you can manage.

Nobody needs to know that you're thinking strategically. You need not share your ideas with anyone you don't trust.

Manifestos. I encourage you to organize your opinions and write a manifesto as a tool for developing a strategic perspective. Appendix C provides an example of a Strategic Thinking Manifesto, along with some tips for writing a radical manifesto.

The Microskill of Contrarianism

Whereas devalorization is a microskill of imagination, contrarianism is an observable action. Both offer benefits by separating you from conventionality and orthodoxy. Contrarianism is zigging when others zag. It recognizes that routines, habits, and herd behaviors often have side effects that lead to complacency, laxity, and inattention. Some people are temperamentally contrarians and practice it naturally. They deliberately dress differently, or argue any point, or try to shock others.

One tip for practicing and demonstrating contrarianism is to sign your name and then sign it again with your nondominant hand. Your nondominant hand can accomplish the task, but it feels awkward. Contrarianism augments the microskill of personal resilience, allowing for new methods of functioning in changed situations.

Contrarianism increases flexibility and learning. By routinely doing things differently, you act your way into a new way of thinking. As your habits change, you enlarge your comfort zone to embrace novelty and increase your ability to think strategically.

Shifting Mental Energy to Strategic Thinking

It's easy to be preoccupied with the operational thinking map and neglect the landmarks on the strategic thinking map. Managers find that it's tough to carve out time for strategic thinking. Managing their attention is their fundamental priority, not managing time. A manager who claims "she is too busy to think strategically" is really saying that "strategy is not a priority at this moment." A day is the same length for highly accomplished people, serene people, and stressed-out people. As the cliché goes, life isn't about how much time you have, it's about what you do with the time that you do have.

Operational thinking and strategic thinking aren't mutually exclusive. Ideally, you develop balance in your thinking styles and switch emphasis from one to the other based on the situation. We discuss the microskill of metacognition, the ability to recognize and regulate your behavior, in Chapter 11.

In the meantime, I offer you this tip: Whenever you notice yourself making the excuse that you're busy, donate to charity.

Culture is Learned (and Unlearned)

Culture is a broad topic that is relevant to both strategy and operations. Most agree that culture includes a set of shared values (about what is good and bad), beliefs (about the relationships of cause and effect), and assumptions (about the things that can be taken for granted).

Ideally, operational thinking and strategic thinking are equally well developed and complementary to each other.

As a simple working definition, *culture* means the "shared learning of a group of people." Their shared learnings are about their originations, their strengths, and their future. Indeed, our families, churches, schools, and organizations go to great lengths to imbue members with shared values and beliefs.

Organizational culture imprints on new entrants and influences their behavior. Anyone who has spent time in a large organization has interacted with new hires and their enthusiasm and fresh ideas. Unfortunately, the drive and fresh ideas diminish over time as they become immersed in operational specializations, bureaucratic rules, and processes. Not to be overlooked are the erosive pressures of day-to-day problem solving and the energy-suck of political infighting. Jerry Weinberg explains that the individual is more likely to sop up the values and quirks of culture than a culture is to be changed by the actions of an individual: "The cucumber gets pickled more than the brine gets cucumbered."

Organizations hold deeply embedded values for productivity, prediction, and perfection. The organization's culture of operations is the brine that pickles a person's inclination to think strategically.

Advantage Entrepreneurs?

A strong operational culture is an organizational asset that enables a group of individuals to achieve economies of scale and impact.

With few exceptions, operational culture is a force for the status quo. It brings with it the hazard of collective blind spots, causing individuals to overlook discontinuities (both opportunities and threats) that might disrupt the future.

The external environment is continually changing. A reading of history shows a pattern of emerging organizations replacing sclerotic institutions. Joseph Schumpeter coined the phrase *creative destruction* to describe the phenomenon of "industrial mutation that incessantly revolutionizes the economic structure from within, incessantly destroying the old one, incessantly creating a new one." There are persuasive arguments that the unconventional and strategic thinking of entrepreneurs is a source of economic vigor. Perhaps government policy should encourage disruption and chaos in incumbent organizations and likewise encourage entrepreneurs.

Why Strategic Thinking Is Rare

Competent strategic thinking is rare for many reasons. There are potent implications in this widely known quote, attributed to Peter Drucker: "Culture eats strategy for breakfast." I rephrase it with this more-nuanced statement: Operational culture supports a style of thinking that crowds aside strategic thinking. Because the mind has a finite capacity for paying attention, and because habits and heuristics are ingrained in the mental machinery, operations absorb most of a person's available mental energy.

Operational thinking is important. But so is strategic thinking. Your personal development task is to gain fluency with both concepts. Assuming that most people spend most of their time on operational thinking, your task is to carve out some time for practicing strategic thinking.

Operational culture tends to foster a style of thinking that crowds aside strategic thinking.

If culture is the shared learning of people, then a strategic thinking culture will emerge proportional to the increase in numbers of competent individual strategic thinkers. An ongoing threat to increasing the number and effectiveness of strategic thinkers comes from powerful operational thinkers who are wedded to the concept of process management and best practices.

◆ ◆ ◆

In this chapter, I began with the familiar and ventured into the unorthodox. In the next chapter, I use a similar technique. I begin with the familiar concept of formally initiating a project (the charter) and move toward exploring the landmarks on the fuzzy front end of strategy. I explain strategic thinking as the intent to sense weak signals, make sense of those signals, articulate a core challenge, develop a logic for strategy, and then program that strategy with structured actions and implementation.

CHAPTER 6

The Fuzzy Front End
of Strategy

Turning Weak Signals into Actionable Initiatives

*I have always been driven to buck the system, to
innovate, to take things beyond where they've been.*

— Sam Walton

PROJECTS ARE FAMILIAR ORGANIZATIONAL LANDMARKS. In theory, all projects start with a charter, which is a formal commitment by the organization to invest resources and leadership in the pursuit of valued organizational outcomes. Typically, the charter identifies the project team, the project manager, and the scope of the project. This information becomes the input for project planning and execution. Next, the project team plans its work and works its plan. Projects are closed with verification of requirements or when management decides to transfer resources elsewhere.

A fair question for a project manager to ask is: "What happens before an organization charters a strategic project?" The answer is that the organization synthesizes (crafts) a strategy, based on an identified core challenge. Before the organization determines the core challenge, individuals must sense and make sense of weak signals in the internal and external environments.

A Key Landmark on the Strategic Thinking Map:
The Core Challenge

All organizations have numerous interests, issues, stakeholders, and performance gaps. To determine the core challenge, individuals must agree on the following critical question: What is the biggest challenge that this organization faces that we can do something about?

Knowledge of the core challenge can help answer questions such as these:

- Which of many interests and issues are most important to the organization's long-term success?

One essential task in crafting strategy is to determine and state the core challenge for your organization's situation.

- Which projects and programs align with strategy and which align with operations?

- Should the organization ignore the sunk cost of its prior commitments to operations?

- How much of the organization's funding should be allocated to the portfolio of run-the-business projects versus change-the-business projects?

- Will the organization need to acquire more funds to pursue new investment opportunities?

- Should the organization choose to pursue opportunities outside of its existing business model?

The answers can help the organization focus on those interests and issues that affect its future success.

The name *core challenge* has some important semantic nuances. The adjective *core* encourages attention to an essential set of concerns. Since a core is at the center of something, it implies the need for *centralized* decisions, which are those made by a headquarters function, typically located at the center of the organization. The word *decentralized* refers to decisions that are made by people who are closer to the local issues of the organization.

A Map of Crafting Strategy

Figure 6-1 intends to help develop a fuller description of strategic thinking and strategy crafting. It's a beginning-to-end, front-to-back, open-to-closed depiction of the flow of ideas into strategy and into projects. Note the funnel shape, more open on the left and narrower on the right. The right-hand side depicts the chartering milestone and the associated project planning and implementing. The core challenge is located near the center of the figure.

Figure 6-1 describes the crafting of strategy as three phases: the fuzzy front end of strategy, the structured back end of strategy, and the programming of

> *The work of strategy involves individual and collective beliefs about the nature of the reality facing the organization.*

strategy. Note the quoted phrases "We believe," "We choose," and "We adapt." These three phrases link to the writing-strategy technique of Chapter 2.

The fuzzy front end of strategy. The most nebulous, ambiguous concepts of strategy are found in the fuzzy front end of strategy. VUCA is most apparent there. A person's cognitive approach on the open end is more qualitative and nonlinear than on the narrowed end.

The primary activity in the fuzzy front end is sensing, an act of noticing the emergent indicators (the weak signals) of discontinuities that affect the interests of the organization. Other appropriate terms are *scanning, exploring, searching, researching, foraging,* and *curating information*. The individual is noticing interesting things, such as patterns, trends, coincidences, curiosities, and anomalies. This activity can be done informally, such as by reading a newspaper or talking to a colleague, or it can include more formal research projects.

In this phase, the individual develops beliefs about the nature of reality, both internal and external to the organization. As we discuss in Chapter 12, an important task of strategy is to reconcile individual beliefs through conversations in which individuals articulate, discuss, and test their beliefs and advance to a common understanding.

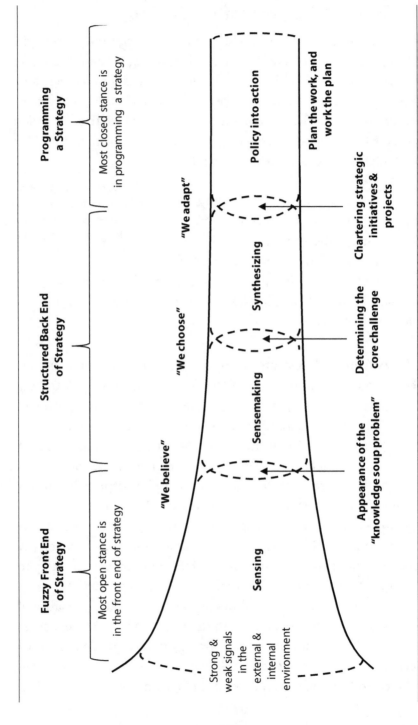

Figure 6-1. A depiction of strategy from the fuzzy front end into action. *Hint: Read this from right (relatively familiar) to left (unfamiliar).*

The hard work of crafting strategy includes developing a collective agreement about the nature of the situation.

The structured back end of strategy. Whereas the fuzzy front end emphasizes divergent thinking, the structured back end involves convergence toward a collective understanding of the situation. Here, the strategic thinker is sensemaking and synthesizing.

Sensemaking is the mental process by which a person interprets signals and ascribes meaning to them. Those meanings are described by a set of assumptions about the realities of the present, the possibilities of the future, and an assessment of the fit of the organization's resources with the environment.

Many individuals find it risky to express a belief to others. Imagine a businessperson enthusiastically stating, "I believe that some new competitor is going to arrive and steal all of our business!" It wouldn't be hard to imagine the passion of someone who has a spiritual epiphany responding, "Oh Lord. Yes!"

While passion is an admirable quality, sometimes passion is based on weak data or it overstates a reality. For contrast, imagine the same person saying in a matter-of-fact tone, "I doubt that we'll continue to hold our market share in the future." This doubt-centric view would probably be easier to support with data and hypotheses.

People use maps to represent their views of reality. Sometimes people mistake the map for the terrain and lose sight of the source of their mental maps. As an example, there are countless individual financial traders, who make countless decisions each day about buying and selling financial contracts. They chart price-trend data over time, looking for patterns and breakouts from patterns. But they often see the chart *as the market*, rather than see the chart *as a model of the market*. Van K. Tharp advises financial traders to distinguish their beliefs from reality. He warns, "You don't trade markets. You can only trade your beliefs [about their nature and direction] in markets."

Mental synthesis, as a neurological phenomenon, involves a specific neuron that fires only when a particular object is shown or imagined. Synthesis is the matching of mental concepts. Suppose you had a specific neuron for mothers and another specific one for pills. When these neurons synchronize, you imagine mothers taking pills.

Similarly, suppose you had a neuron for core challenge and another one for innovation. When the firings of these two neurons are synchronized, you might invent a new problem-solving idea or borrow an idea in use elsewhere.

Continuing with this mental-concepts matching, consider this list for strategy: the strategic power of the organization's resources, the constraints of the situation, preferences, obstacles to progress, benefits, costs, sacrifices, tradeoffs, beliefs, bets, dominating ideas, insights, actions, and choices.

Finally, one of the essential ideas of synthesizing is that strategies involve policies concerning choices. People in bureaucratic organizations often see the word *policy* as interchangeable with written procedures or instructions. In organizational strategy, a policy is a pattern of decisions directed toward achieving desired outcomes. Policy helps to answer the questions:

- What are the desired essential outcomes?
- What is to be avoided?
- What is the range of possible configurations of ways, means, and ends?
- What should be done?

As the sensemaking and synthesizing activities close, information becomes more concrete, clear, and actionable. In writing strategy, "We choose" is the group's collective synthesis of ways, means, and ends to address the core challenge. The synthesis yields policies, initiatives, and projects.

Programming a strategy. Figure 6-1 describes three phrases, the first being the *fuzzy front end of strategy* and the second being the *structured back end of strategy*. The third phase, *programming a strategy*, encompasses the ways and means of resourcing strategic initiatives.

Strategic initiatives are tools for closing identified performance gaps, typically with a program management structure. The decisions made within these programs apply resources in order to align the ongoing operations with the strategy. (Programs are defined as collections of projects where synergy is developed by coordinating the project efforts through a program leader.) Projects are then chartered, planned, and executed.

Probes

Probes are found on the strategic thinking map but seldom on the operational thinking map because operational thinkers are typically focused on fail-safe performance; that is, making sure that any initiative will succeed. By contrast, probes are safe-to-fail tools intended to gain insight or better understand the characteristics of an emergent phenomenon.

An example of a probe is the technique of "gemba visits" used to identify unarticulated customer needs or opportunities for operational process improvements. Other examples include a package of data-collection instruments sent into outer space or an investigation launched by a prosecutor to search widely for evidence of wrongdoing by a government official. Chess players use their pawns as probes to understand their opponents' responses to a new position.

The following two questions help to orient the strategist's view in order to prepare for a range of plausible outcomes:

- What might we do if the probe reveals benefits that we want to enhance?

- What might we do if the probe reveals threats that we want to dampen?

Give Preference to Set-based Design, Not Point-based Design

The practice of set-based design is useful to the strategist. It contrasts with point-based design, which reflects conventional linear thinking. Set-based design approaches are best suited for high-VUCA environments where one must search for weak signals and probe below the apparent.

An analogy helpfully illustrates the practices of set-based design. Imagine a 19th-century gold prospector overlooking a rugged valley with the intention of finding a vein of subsurface gold. In this analogy, our strategist-prospector is presently in the fuzzy front end of strategy.

An essential practice of set-based design is the early and continuing search for constraints. Our strategist-prospector's constraints include the following: excavation tools are limited to basic hand tools carried by her mule, the rugged mountain peaks and a deep lake are inaccessible, dangerous wildlife might be present, and she has only a few weeks supply of food. These constraints define sets of feasible terrain for further exploration.

Realistically, our strategist-prospector's best opportunities for finding gold are in two kinds of terrain. One set of opportunities is found in caves that penetrate the hillsides. When she finds a cave, she inspects for evidence of gold and begins excavating. This first option has an increased probability of threats from wildlife that might call the hillsides and caves home.

The second kind of terrain involves the small river that cuts through the valley, eroding and exposing ore. This small river offers a high-probability space for using the just-described technique of probes. All our strategist-prospector needs to do is to collect samples at intervals and pan the sample by swishing water to remove lighter particulates. She can determine the amount of gold found in each sample. Then, assuming that higher concentrations have washed out of concentrated veins of gold, she can start digging near the stream bed near the greatest opportunity.

Another set-based practice is *decision pruning*, which involves identifying and eliminating the weakest solutions. In this prospector example, the search-the-caves option is arguably weaker, because of the wildlife threats and the effort involved. The sample-the-stream-bottom option seems to offer more opportunities to our strategist-prospector.

The set-based approach allows her to preserve her flexibility. She can incorporate new insights and refine her choices to exploit them. She can avoid making a premature, costly, all-in bet. In retaining flexibility, she increases her agility.

For contrast to the set-based design approach, our strategist-prospector could use point-based design. She would pick a spot, commit to it, and excavate her gold mine. She has ignored (or neglected) the unpleasant uncertainty that gold might be absent at that spot. Her operational thinking mindset has been activated and her focus is on the best-possible excavation. Point-based design is similar to organizational goal setting in that people select what they initially perceive as the best course of action and concentrate on the dogged implementation of that choice.

The point-based design approach is similar to solutioneering, which I described in Chapter 4 as "the tendency to focus mental energy on promoting a solution rather than fully understanding the strategic context." A person practicing solutioneering perceives a problem, imagines a fix to the problem, and goes to work on the fix.

The strategic thinking microskill of conceptual mapping can be used to explain set-based versus point-based design. In a set-based design approach, a map shows you the terrain and you can use that terrain to evaluate the presence of opportunities and threats. Set-based design helps you imagine the larger terrain for strategy as regions of opportunity where you prioritize your efforts within the region. Your goal is to gain information and limit early-but-difficult-to-reverse investments.

By contrast, many operational managers hear the word *map* and instantly envision a roadmap that tells her, turn by turn, choice by choice, her route to the future. It feels satisfying to make decisions quickly, but this habit often limits your flexibility.

As you will see in the next chapter, futures literacy includes the concepts of discovery-oriented anticipation, opportunity search, and shapes of the future.

The Microskill of Asking High-Quality Questions

You should recall from earlier chapters that there are 20 microskills of strategic thinking. If you're keeping count, this the 15th microskill that I've introduced. Its applicability goes beyond strategy and includes leadership, business acumen, and innovation. It has synergy with other microskills, notably curiosity and skepticism.

A strategy can be incremental, or it can boldly pursue new, significant, emerging opportunities. Which of those two paths is taken is largely determined by the questions asked as part of crafting strategy. Steven French writes, "Better strategy can be generated if answers are found to quality questions, rather than quality solutions found for poorly posed questions." Poorly posed questions usually have easy answers that focus on the solution space rather than the challenge space.

> *A better strategy can be generated if answers are found to quality questions, rather than quality solutions found for poorly posed questions.*

An example of a poorly posed question is, "What do I want to do?" Another is, "What is the best practice?" These questions are mundane, uninspired, uncreative, and conventional. A critical goal for a competent strategic thinker is to ask more questions and better questions. Recognizing the role of ambiguity, a strategic thinker will ask, "What questions are we trying to answer?" Or, alternatively, ask "Are we even asking the right questions?" Enlarging your point of view often stimulates these kinds of questions.

Good questions can help point the way toward bold strategy. Consider the practices of Google X, a division of Alphabet. Google X is trying to solve big problems, which they term moonshots. Journalist Derek Thompson, who spent time with its staff, reports, "Moonshots don't begin with brainstorming clever answers. They start with the hard work of finding the right questions."

The question-betterment technique. You improve your strategic thinking when you challenge yourself to ask important (and not mundane) questions. It's a journey of continuing betterment. An initial question can always be improved. I use the good-better-best technique of question construction, guided by the following Level 0-1-2-3 framework.

- **Level 0 – Ask no questions.** Instead, substitute your assumptions about the situation and aspirations. There are many reasons that people don't ask questions: the answer to the question may involve additional work; they may feel disempowered to ask questions of people ranking higher in the hierarchy; or the answer may be ambiguous.

- **Level 1 – Ask a mediocre (poorly posed) question.** A mediocre question is one that's mundane and asked ritualistically. A poorly posed question often results in goals and goal setting. (See Example 1 below, which asks the question, "What is the vision?") Regardless, any question and any answer are probably better than no question.

- **Levels 2 & 3 – Ask better and still-better questions.** You can improve any question. A good question prompts thoughtfulness. It widens and deepens the understanding of interests and issues.

The following two examples show how you can apply this question-betterment technique to strategy:

- **Example 1 – "What is the vision?"** I criticized visioning in Chapter 2 as being practiced in a way that disintegrates the *ends* of strategy from the *ways* and *means* of strategy.

  Another problem with the what-is-the-vision question is that people often ask it ritualistically. It seems to beg for a single, right answer provided by someone in authority. It can be elitist. It has an unrecognized and problematic assumption that the visionary has extraordinary powers of prediction not available to others.

  The what-is-the-vision question is a mediocre question for strategy. It's better to search for questions that stimulate open-mindedness, diagnosis, and insight.

"What might the organization become?" is a better question because it opens us to a broader set of concepts and assumptions about the future. We're now willing to consider futures that are different from what we wish for and different from what is probable. The word *might* implies uncertainty, and the word *become* implies that our current capabilities will evolve into different forms. If you're sufficiently imaginative, you might develop some preposterous (and potentially useful) ideas. This is an example of a Level 2 question.

"What are the shapes of the future for the organization?" is a still-better question, an example of a Level 3 question. The notion of shapes-of-the-future implies that we should imagine the future in a broader way, one that allows for ambiguity. The concept of shapes-not-points encourages us to consider the edges (where opportunity is often found), the centers (an organizing idea for a new dominating idea for strategy), and the overlaps (places where innovations can diffuse from one domain to another). Questions like these open our minds so that we can test the foundational assumptions of our plans, scenarios, and models.

- **Example 2 – "What are our organization's strengths?"**
  An organization's strengths and advantages are sources of competitive power and a basis for strategy. Probing for competitive strengths can reveal an advantage. Like the earlier question about vision, people often ritualistically identify strengths (it's the "S" in the common SWOT technique).

A strategy should push the envelope of knowledge.

This is a Level 1 question that frequently yields superficial answers such as, "Our organization has good people." The problem with a generic answer is that rivals also have good people.

"Are our strategic resources organized appropriately?" is a better question because 1) it brings attention to the design of strategy, 2) it implies that the organization makes choices to configure its resources, and 3) the desired state is one that fits the present and future environments.

A still-better question would be, "Where might we be able to find new strategic resources that will give us capability and power that we do not presently possess?"

Improve your question asking. The ability to ask short, excellent questions is a skill. Notice how a talented television interviewer helps a subject reveal important information. Since strategy often involves conflicting ideas, status, and hurt feelings, it's better to use a conversational tone rather than an interrogative or argumentative tone. It's better to ask one high-quality question at a time and patiently wait for a thoughtful answer. If the person answers quickly, the answer is likely glib.

This is another opportunity to practice the beginner's mind: Listen for interesting things and expect to be surprised.

This microskill can be supplemented with the microskills of curiosity, pragmatism, open mental stance, and storytelling. You could ask:

- "I'm curious. How does this work?"
- "Does it work the same for your competitors?"
- "What's the backstory to your situation?"

Ask for advice. Another way to practice asking high-quality questions is to recognize that other people have useful knowledge and expertise. In complicated and complex systems (see Appendix A for more on those systems), seek the advice of others who have a higher-quality experience than you.

Interestingly, research suggests that asking for advice boosts others' perceptions of the advice-seeker's competency. Of course, this boost is associated with difficult tasks and not with simple ones. After reviewing Appendix D, most people agree that the various landmarks on the strategic thinking map, and their relationships with each other, are challenging and not straightforward.

Balancing Sensitivity and Specificity

A critical strategic thinking task is to find an appropriate balance of sensitivity and specificity. Sensitivity refers to the ability to detect a weak signal. In medicine, a highly-sensitive test is more likely to detect disease than one with low sensitivity. For diseases (such as some cancers), the ability to detect an early marker of the disease can be critical for an effective treatment plan. However, the risk with sensitivity is that of false positives: suggesting the presence of cancer when there is none present. Some people have temperaments that predispose them to be anxious, and they will distract the organization with warnings about the weak signals that they have noticed.

Specificity is the opposite of sensitivity. A familiar example in terrorism warnings is that of a "specific threat." The once-weak signal now has additional detail on the probable time, place, and methods of the threat. The signal is now much more relevant to those affected by the threat and actionable by first responders.

There's no one right level of sensitivity or of specificity. Both false positives (finding meaning in meaningless data) and false negatives (rejecting useful signals) are undesirable. They are unavoidable, too. As a rule, you want to dial up sensitivity for weak signals in the fuzzy front end and replace it with specificity as you determine and declare a specific core challenge for the organization.

The Knowledge Soup Problem

In Figure 6-1, I note the appearance of the "knowledge soup problem." The term *knowledge soup* invokes the metaphor of a bowl of soup. John Sowa defines knowledge soup as loosely organized, dynamically changing knowledge. The problem is related to ambiguity: parts of the soup make sense to some people and not to others; some people see the same "thing" and label it differently from others, some people see things that others don't, and so on.

The strategist's core task in the fuzzy front end of strategy is the sensing of weak signals. The information isn't perfect, its potential implications for the future of the organization aren't clear, and it's not

110

immediately actionable. Knowledge soup is a natural consequence of an open-minded, curious mental stance.

A person can feel mentally overwhelmed by the data in the knowledge soup. Feeling uncomfortable, she can find many reasons to turn her attention to the more structured world of operations. The microskill of personal resilience is beneficial if this occurs. A strategic thinker retains an open mental stance to sense the big picture. She will be optimistic that she can find a way through the knowledge soup and reach clarity.

The natural next step is the resolution. A strategic thinker will take the broader view and reflect:

- What questions can I ask that will reveal the crux of the matter?

- What frameworks, points of view, ontologies, are relevant?

- Who has the expertise to help me expand my ability to make sense?

When I'm working through the knowledge soup, I scan for interesting things and then postulate two possible outcomes. The speculation could be represented this way:

Interesting observation → interesting outcome

Interesting observation → uninteresting outcome

The Microskill of Abductive Reasoning

Imagine that you have noticed something interesting. It's a weak signal and may or may not have consequences. It's a specific chunk of knowledge floating in the knowledge soup.

Abductive reasoning is the practice of inferring a possible cause or consequence of one's observations. A more familiar phrase is *educated guessing* (where the guess is about the nature and implications of some theory or hypothesis). Abductive reasoning, applied to strategy, is the individual's practice of sensemaking in answering these questions:

- What chunks of knowledge in the soup have possible relevance to the organization's interests?

- Are they issues that might have a broad and long-term impact?

- Do they help me identify the core challenge or a way to make progress on the core challenge?

As an example of abductive reasoning applied to a weak signal, Christopher Columbus saw many interesting items in his early career as a merchant seaman: driftwood from the west, strange bodies in a boat, and stories passed along from people of other cultures. Perhaps these were unconnected curiosities. Or maybe they were evidence of lands to the west.

Abductive reasoning is the practice of developing explanations for observations. Another set of useful questions is these:

- What explanation best fits the data?

- Is the explanation simple enough?

- What new data might invalidate the explanation?

Hypotheses. Abductive reasoning is used to generate hypotheses, which are statements that could be true or false. Evidence is used to support or reject a hypothesis.

Hypothesis testing is a featured technique in much of the work of the well-known strategy consulting firm McKinsey & Company. An important reason is that the data-driven nature of hypothesis testing helps the strategist to sidestep cognitive biases such as over-optimism, loss aversion, and satisficing.

Three levels of abductive reasoning. The simplest and easiest approach for using abductive reasoning is to find and adopt an established theory. For example, suppose a manager notices that her unit sales have declined in each of the last three quarters. She needs to understand the causes so that she can choose effective responses. Microeconomic theory suggests that demand will increase if she cuts the price. Motivational theory indicates that salespeople will respond to a better set of incentives. Both theories offer ideas for plausible explanations and testable hypotheses.

The intermediate level of abductive reasoning would be to find an existing explanation and modify it to the situation. Columbus's adoption of Toscanelli's map, or Billy Beane's use of Bill James's sabermetrics models, provide examples of this intermediate level.

The most complex level of abductive reasoning is important to crafting good strategy. This is because that level of reasoning centers on exploring the implications of novelty. There are no answers to be found in the literature or by asking an expert. Consider the evolution of Starbucks in the late 1980s from a coffee-focused roaster into a unique café business, tailored to the needs of the American market. Traditional subject matter expertise isn't helpful for the emergence of new business models. Instead, the better approach is to use probes and learn about the emerging environment.

A competent strategic thinker is open to novel data and arguments. This frees her to imagine a broader and richer set of assumptions about the system. Perhaps that new information points her in an entirely different direction, even to the generation of big questions and novel strategies. A scientist who chooses uninteresting problems and develops can't-fail hypotheses won't achieve a distinguished career. But an organization that pushes the envelope of knowledge often gains the advantage over others.

Pushing into the Uncomfortable Unknown

Some people are comfortable with being known as smart and are uncomfortable with feeling stupid. They feel that they should know. However, this emphasis on concrete knowledge could be said to be a conventional and orthodox value.

Strategic thinkers focus more on learning rather than knowing. They have a sensitivity to context, a willingness to tolerate the discomfort of ambiguity, and an ambition to explore the unknown.

Martin Schwartz, a scientist, reveals that, as a researcher, he has gotten used to the discomfort and unease associated with not knowing something. He actively seeks out opportunities to feel the discomfort. He notes, "We can't be sure we're asking the right question until we get a result from an experiment or an answer from some other valid source."

The lesson for strategic thinkers is to keep stretching, putting aside the feelings of stupidity and frustration. The fuzzy front end of strategy is a venture into the unknown. The better your questions, the more you increase your probability of learning something interesting and useful.

Strong Opinions, Weakly Held

A useful strategic thinking tool is the practice of strong opinions, weakly held. The adjective strong conveys that the opinion being offered is extreme or unconventional. It also expresses that the impact of the opinion is significant.

Imagine that you've identified a weak-but-potentially-significant factor that could grow in significance (its impact is exponential and nonlinear rather than incremental). As examples, nations could go to war over access to fresh water, or large segments of workers could lose their jobs to automation, such as self-driving vehicles.

Practice the technique of strong opinions, weakly held.

The tool of strong opinions, weakly held, resembles the "believing game," in which credibility is assigned to a belief that's out of the mainstream or unorthodox. It puts you in a mental stance where you can imagine that this belief is plausible and consider more fully the factors (for example, weak signals) that make the belief plausible. I explain more about the believing game in Chapter 12.

In this chapter, we've explored the fuzzy front end of strategy, where the presence of ambiguity is most significant.

Ambiguity often fogs the weak signals needed to craft an effective strategy. We gain an advantage by casting a wide net of scanning because some of those signals have great potential value. Of course, we can never be sure that a signal is useful until later, but that's only one of the dilemmas of VUCA and strategy.

Companies such as Starbucks, Apple, Google, Facebook, and Microsoft gained their early advantages because sharp-minded individuals were attentive to emerging technologies and markets. They stand in contrast to others who neglect the primordial goo of half-baked ideas suspended in a muck of ambiguity.

The next chapter continues an emphasis on finding weak signals and making sense of them. Our focus is on identifying pockets of the future, which are objects and behaviors that are not presently common but will potentially have a great impact in the future. It's worth a reminder that Pillar IV of the definition of strategic thinking is success in the future.

CHAPTER 7

Pockets of the Future

The Future is Here. It's Just Unevenly Distributed.

IN THE YEAR 1996, cell phones were mostly used by business professionals, and fewer than one percent of Americans considered them a necessity. Within a decade, as expected by many industry observers, the cell phone became an everyday part of people's lives.

An interesting tangent to this story concerns the addition of small, cheap, digital cameras to cell phones. This enhancement began around the year 2000. Now, nearly every person carries a digital camera embedded in her cell phone. The digital camera innovation was in plain sight to anyone, including executives at Eastman Kodak, a firm investing billions of dollars to adapt digital photography to its consumer business model. We can plausibly imagine that Kodak's executives might have declared, "A camera on a cell phone is irrelevant to our business. It's just a distracting, odd, fanciful curiosity." It's possible that the Kodak executives might have similarly dismissed any significance from the emergence of MySpace (which shifted its business model to social networking and media sharing in 2003), Facebook (founded in 2004 and by 2006 available to nearly anyone with a valid email address), Instagram (founded in 2010), Pinterest (founded in 2009) and digital imaging initiatives from tech companies such as Google, Apple, and Yahoo.

With the benefit of hindsight, we now know that digital cameras on cell phones are commonplace and that social media companies are among the most valuable of all enterprises. We also know that Kodak declared bankruptcy in 2012, abandoning the consumer business.

William Gibson remarked that "the future is already here, it's just not very evenly distributed." The statement means that in the present moment, an observant person can find some detail that's currently low in prevalence but will become common in the future. A person who noticed, in the early 2000s, the presence of cheap digital cameras on phones, had found a *pocket of the future in the present* (a PoF).

Details found in the present have significant future implications.

A PoF is defined as an observable practice, idea, or thing that is rare and insignificant in the present moment but has the potential to become more prevalent and impactful. PoFs are important weak signals that have the potential to profoundly influence the organization's core challenge.

The Three Horizons

You might recall that I noted three horizons of H1-H2-H3 as landmarks on the strategic thinking map in Chapter 5. The analogy of time and terrain works well to elaborate the three horizons, as shown in Figure 7-1. Imagine that you're on a trail traversing a grassy plain. The path leads toward the foothills of a distant, somewhat-indistinct mountain range.

In this analogy, Horizon 1 (H1) is the foreground. It's the present moment and short-term future. Horizon 2 (H2) is the foothills, representing the intermediate future. Horizon 3 (H3) is the mountains, representing the distant future.

In H1, you can see the details that are close, such as the rocks and trees in the foreground of Figure 7-1. You can make out only the general shapes of the distant terrain. The trees are PoFs that will become more prevalent in the H2 foothills, and the rocks will be more prevalent in the mountains. An important feature of the analogy is that the

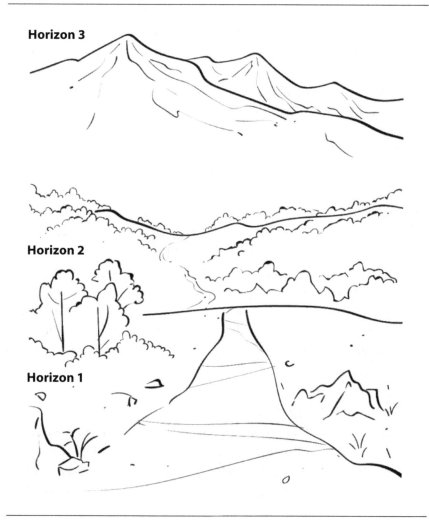

Figure 7-1. The three horizons.

lowlands, the foothills, and the alpine ecosystems are each distinct and qualitatively different. The plants and animals you would find in the lowland ecosystem don't exist in the alpine ecosystem.

Let's apply the three-horizon analogy to time. At present, the dominant system for trans-ocean passenger travel is jet-powered aircraft. Two centuries ago, wind-powered ships were the dominant system. Aircraft are the H3 to the sailing ship's H1. There were intermediary technology-driven shifts during the transition that included using fossil fuels to produce steam, using fossil fuels for powering internal combustion engines, and shifts from propeller aircraft to jet aircraft.

Now, put your imagination to work as you consider this question: If jet aircraft are now H1, what does H3 look like for long-distance travel?

Analogies have limitations. The lowland-to-alpine transition comparison to time is problematic because you can physically ascend and descend a mountain, but you can't physically travel into the past or future. (However, you can use your imagination, which is a major point of discussion for this chapter.) The analogy's power is that each ecosystem is fundamentally different.

The H3 future is qualitatively different from the present.

It is not the passage of time that is significant. An organization's 5-year or 10-year plan typically neglects the potential for unrecognized discontinuities and emergence. Sometimes systems change over relatively long periods, such as the shift in technology from sail to steam to aircraft.

Sometimes change occurs quickly, such as Kodak's experience of disruption in its consumer photography business. Imagine yourself in the 1990s, and your family is celebrating an event. Mom pulls out the camera and takes a bunch of pictures. When the roll of film is complete, she takes it (or mails it) to a photo processor. If she has asked for expedited processing (at an upcharge), she receives the photos a few days to a week later. She then picks out the snapshots she likes, mounts them in an album or frames them, and shares them with others.

Kodak faced disruption because technology was changing the print-the-image part of the consumer experience. Today the customer can snap a digital picture and upload it seconds later for all to see. Printing the image is optional, diminishing the value of photo processing. In the H3 environment, the activity of sharing the picture happens earlier, and the curating and print-the-picture activities happen later (or are eliminated).

H2 is a Zone of Transition and Conflict

H2 is the intermediate horizon between the present and the distant future. PoFs are no longer intellectual curiosities, because many operational thinkers acknowledge the trend. Most agree on the need for reform, although there is no consensus on which policies to pursue.

Let's examine Kodak in H2. Counter to the common story that Kodak was passive, it spent billions of dollars to adapt its business model to its changing realities. For example, in 2001 Kodak purchased a photo-sharing site (Ofoto) and used it as a digital storage platform that consumers could use to print images. It appears that Kodak's decision makers retained an H1 assumption about the importance of printing images. However, the consumer learned that a digital image offered more benefits and had begun to abandon the traditional printing-images model.

Kodak's managers correctly anticipated the importance of digital capture of images. However, they missed the consumer's preference for digital-image consumption. Scott Anthony provides a nice summary:

> The right lessons from Kodak are subtle. Companies often see the disruptive forces affecting their industry. They frequently divert sufficient resources to participate in emerging markets. Their failure is usually an inability to truly embrace the new business models the disruptive change opens up. Kodak created a digital camera, invested in the technology, and even understood that photos would be shared online. Where they failed was in realizing that online photo sharing was the new business, not just a way to expand the printing business.

In H2, it's difficult to distinguish the importance of nuances. Kodak's decisions show that its managers placed importance on rendering images on paper, which was its traditional chemical and print business. They underappreciated the importance of newly emerging social media.

This suggests an important question for strategic thinkers: *Are our present values relevant for the future?*

Should H1 values colonize H3? This is another way to ask about the relevance of values in the future.

Colonization is an interesting analogy that has useful strategic thinking implications. Consider the 400-year period (1500–1900) when Europeans used military, political, and economic power to subjugate the peoples of other continents. The colonial elites enriched themselves by exploiting the resource wealth of the colonialized. Of course, colonialism is a faded model, and the current thinking is that indigenous peoples experienced suffering that didn't justify the wealth gained by the colonial powers.

Elites with a colonial mindset impose their system onto others. The colonialists argue that their power is a signal of their merit and that they are using their power for the benefit of the colonialized. In this analogy, I'm suggesting that powerful elites apply their H1 values onto H2 and H3.

There are three cognitive biases that underlie colonial thinking. The first is myside bias, which is that individuals tend to favor the values and beliefs of their group and diminish those of outsiders. Colonial thinking places importance on H1 values. The second is status quo bias. A colonial mindset assumes, as a taken-for-granted, the lasting power of current institutions. The third is loss-avoidance bias. People don't want to lose their power.

What's conserved from the past gives important information about cultural values and assets. Start with your own life. Financial planners regularly include inheritance and charitable donations in their work with clients' retirement portfolios. What is most important to pass on to your grandchildren or great-grandchildren?

Using a similar line of reasoning, how would you feel if your grandparents imposed their expectations on you? Imagine that they wanted you to live in a certain town for your entire life, vote for their preferred political party, observe the same courtship rituals, listen to the same music, and attend the same church. I suspect that you would resent many of their expectations.

The influences that shaped our grandparents' culture are often irrelevant to emerging H2 and H3 systems. Kodak not only faced disruption born of technology, it was affected by shifts in the culture, such as evolving gender roles for men and women.

Now consider this question: Would your grandchildren welcome the imposition of your expectations? If you don't care, or if you assume that they desire what you believe to be important, then you're practicing colonial thinking about the future.

Reflecting on your legacy helps you to become more sensitive to your values about what is important and should remain important. These values inform the assumptions that guide your anticipation of the future.

Organizations show their concern for values by collecting and displaying artifacts and photographs from early days. As an example, the lobby of the corporate headquarters of Domino's Pizza in Ann Arbor, Michigan, contains a Volkswagen sitting on a pedestal. It was the company's first delivery vehicle, invoking the dominant idea from its 1960s-era strategy: a business model where pizza delivery was an anchor of its strategic narrative. However, this antique automobile is more than just a curiosity; it's a symbol of the company's customer focus and willingness to adapt to new realities.

What's the legacy you want to leave for future generations?

Your strategic thinking is enhanced when you consider this question: What has been conserved from the past and what does it symbolize?

As a final strategic thinking exercise associated with symbols and legacy, visit a museum. Museums are curators of the artifacts that define a civilization. You'll often find longitudinal displays that show how cultural values change over time.

Given that the H3 future involves a new and different system, questions such as these help to inform your strategic thinking:

- What criteria do we use in deciding what to keep and what to discard from the present?
- What will people in H3 most value about H1?

Multiple H3 visions. In H2, an increasing number of organizational stakeholders recognize the patterns in the trends. They can see some things in decline and some things increasing. Disagreements arise about whether the patterns are temporary aberrations or permanent shifts.

Those who see the decline as a symptom of a problem, deficiency, or dysfunction will propose various fixes. Operational thinkers often view the symptoms as showing a need for a new process or a reform of an existing process.

Those who track innovation trends will have proposals to take advantage of trends. There will be multiple H3 visions and numerous advocates for their particular vision.

Metrics

People pay attention to what is measured. If you measure past performance in the existing business model, people will pay attention to past performance in the existing business model. If you measure PoFs, people will pay attention to PoFs.

Most organizational metrics are lagging indicators that tell more about where the organization has been than where it might be going. They're associated with the 5P landmarks of operational thinking and help managers to optimize the organization's performance, since they're commonly measures of productivity or forecasts. Organizations need to use leading indicators to balance the biases introduced by lagging indicators.

As an everyday example of lagging and leading indicators, the odometer on your car tells you the distance you've traveled. While that's useful information, you don't drive your car by focusing on the odometer. Instead, a good driver looks down the road for weak signals such as stopped traffic or children playing a game near the roadside.

Many organizations use the stock market as a leading indicator. A rising market is a signal of optimism about the economy and a falling market is a signal of pessimism. However, this is an imprecise measure, as suggested by this quip: "The stock market has predicted seven out of the last three recessions."

Reframing Time-as-a-Resource to Time-as-a-Place-Where-Opportunity-is-Found

Figure 7-2 summarizes the three horizons and their implications for strategic thinking. I want to call your attention to the fourth column. In H1, time is a resource to be managed and in H3, time is a place where opportunity is found.

	Temporal scale	Qualitative nature of the system	Application	Characteristics of Pockets of the Future (PoFs)
Horizon 1 (H1)	Present moment and foreseeable future	Existing system, qualitatively different from H3	Managerial focus – Time is a scare resource

Operational thinking map that assumes that strategic fit is nearly optimized | PoFs are low in frequency

The prevailing operational culture considers PoFs irrelevant |
| **Horizon 2 (H2)** | Intermediate future | Transitional: elements of old and new are present and competing for attention | Entrepreneurial focus – Time is a place where conflicts are experienced and resolved | PoFs seen as emergent trends of new practices, tools, and elements |
| **Horizon 3 (H3)** | Distant future | A transformed system, qualitatively different from H1 | Aspirational focus – Time is a place of potential

Assumes a new configuration of system elements | H3 has become H1 as a new system dominates

Watch for new PoFs |

Figure 7-2. The three horizons have implications for strategy.

On the operational thinking map, H1 is the sole emphasis (it's the fifth P of the present). The focus on time establishes an organizational cadence of predictability for the operational thinker that further reinforces her aspiration of productivity and production.

When you accommodate H2 and H3 in your imagination, you regard time as a source of opportunity rather than a resource to be managed.

On the strategic thinking map, the landmark of the future is more specifically consideration of H2 and H3.

Five Questions to Guide Your Strategic Thinking

These five questions provide a useful start in developing a fuller view of your strategy's present and future landscapes. They also contribute to an understanding of the implications of the three horizons.

Q1. What are your present concerns, frustrations, and issues? This question will help you to identify present-day H1 elements that influence your perceptions of the core challenge. This is an opportunity to practice critical thinking to get the clearest view that you can of the current situation.

Q2. What are your future aspirations? The organization's stakeholders have interests, including their expectations, hopes, and dreams. The answers to Q2 are natural expressions of the preferred future of the organization.

Q3. What are the pockets of the future? These are weak signals that may (or may not) increase in prevalence, contributing to a new H3 system.

Q4. What emerging innovations and trends are likely to shape the intermediate-range future? This question helps you to include opinions on trends and their impact on the defined core challenge.

Q5. What's the legacy that you want to leave for future generations? This question points directly toward individual and institutional values. Some values endure, and some values change with each generational cohort. To reiterate an earlier point, what's conserved from the past (and what's preserved for the future) implies important information about the organization's interests and the strategic issues connected to those interests.

Prevalence and Strategic Fit

Figure 7-3 displays the three horizons in a different format. The Y axis on the left side of the graphic shows the prevalence (the frequency of

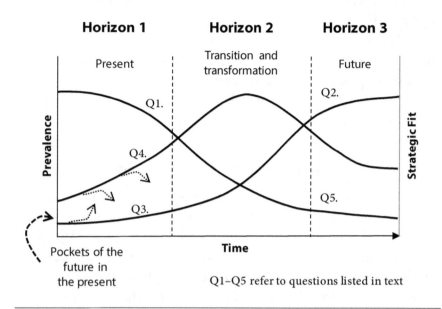

Figure 7-3. The three horizons, prevalence, and strategic fit.

something at any given moment). The curves show how prevalence of things changes over time. In H1, things that are of high prevalence are expected to decrease. Also, in H1, PoFs should be expected to emerge, with some of them increasing to define new H2 and H3 future systems.

The Y-axis on the right side of the graphic shows the fit of the organization to its environment, implying that organizations that have a tight fit in H1 will lose fit as new systems emerge. The Kodak story confirms this dynamic. In the late 20th century, Kodak's consumer business was successful in marketing to women as gatekeepers of memories. It was a profitable business. However, it had many legacies in supply chain and capital investment assumptions. Kodak was unable to reconfigure itself in time to be relevant in the different H3 environment.

The smaller offshoot arrows in Horizon 1 indicate that the prevalence trendline can suddenly increase or decrease. Stated differently, a PoF may quickly grow in prevalence. It shifts the situation to H2 or

H3 and thus the organization's strategic fit. Likewise, a PoF may fizzle and remain an anomaly within H1.

Also, in Figure 7-3, you should note the five previously discussed questions of Q1 to Q5. A useful exercise is to include the questions in your sensing and sensemaking practice (that is, when you're focusing on the fuzzy front end of strategy). You write answers to the questions on sticky notes, and then position them on the appropriate lines.

The Microskill of Anticipation

Anticipation is the ability to imagine the later-than-now.

Some people spend so little time considering the future that we could say that they deny the future. Some people rely strictly on the prognostications of mystics or of religious end-of-the-world dogma. Others use scenarios and quantitative forecasts to shape their planning. Others hold to a strong-willed view that they can create their own future. Some people are optimists who trust that they will discover the success that they want. Each of these examples reflects anticipatory assumptions that, to one degree or another, influence its present-moment decisions.

The microskill of anticipation is the skill to develop and examine a broad range of anticipatory assumptions.

There are three different kinds of anticipation. The first two are preparation and planning, both of which operate with the assumption that the future is "closed" in that the X-factor of emergence is ignored. Stated

Strategic thinking provides benefits when people are proactive – they have a functional forward-looking worldview.

differently, in the first two kinds of anticipation, the strategist operates with the assumption that everything worth knowing is known. The third kind of anticipation is discovery and is "open" to emergence. Let's take a closer look.

Preparation (anticipation as backcasting from an imagined future, contingency). This first kind of anticipation involves envisioning a future state. Then you backcast to anticipate how you would use your resources to advance your interests. Another name for this kind of anticipation is *contingency planning*.

For example, a plausible scenario is that your home has caught fire. Your anticipator assumptions help you develop responses to questions like these: What's the family escape route? Where would you meet if separated? What items are kept in a fire-proof safe? What kind of insurance is purchased?

Another example: Imagine that a cyber hack has victimized your organization. How would you mitigate the impacts and recover to resume operations? How would you inform and work with your bank, your customers, your employees, and your suppliers?

A third example of this kind of anticipation is the faith-based reliance on prophesy, such as predictions of the end of the world.

Planning (anticipation as creating an imagined future, optimization). This kind of anticipation is familiar to anyone who has practiced planning. Consider a vacation trip to a foreign country. You have a budget constraint. You use anticipation to develop your itinerary and develop a packing list of resources to carry with you. You imagine the tradeoffs of carry-with-you versus obtain-locally resources.

For another example, imagine a farmer who intends to harvest a crop of corn. Once she commits to planting, it's unlikely that she'll change to a different crop. Given her desired outcome of a corn crop, her secondary goal is to optimize the yield. Accordingly, she'll balance the seed and fertilizer inputs to production while considering conditions for soil, precipitation, and pests.

People often practice planning with an unrealistic belief that everything worth knowing is already known.

Like anticipation-as-preparation, the assumptions of anticipation-as-planning embrace a settled and single vision of the future: the only plausible outcome is a field of corn. The limitations of this analogy are that enterprises have greater VUCA. New opportunities often present themselves. Sometimes goals should change. Yet people often maintain a commitment to irrelevant goals and then blame the bad results on poor strategy implementation.

Did you notice that this example included several landmarks on the operational thinking map? The goal was productivity of corn yield and implied prediction of results.

Discovery (anticipation as a search for novelty). Novelty is an essential theme of strategy. Billy Beane found an innovation in fantasy baseball and adapted it to overcome the conventional strategies of rivals. Spence Silver created a novel substance, microspheres, and found an application for them in 3M's Post-it Notes. Christopher Columbus wanted to prove the unorthodox concept of sailing west from Europe to Japan.

When you practice this kind of anticipation, you are sensitive to novelty and the PoFs that imply the X-factor of emergence. I find it useful to imagine a "futures scout," a person with an open-minded stance who searches for PoFs. She senses these weak signals and makes sense out of them in the context of the future. Her goal is to find and consider the broadest possible range of anticipatory assumptions.

This futures scout can also step into a leadership role, where she helps others to interpret those signals. She helps others to increase their capacity to tolerate ambiguity, practice sensemaking, and challenge assumptions about what's relevant.

You should consider H3 in your definition of the core challenge for your organization's strategy. As an exercise, contemplate these three approaches and consider the anticipatory assumptions that you are using:

- Imagine a radically different H3 future such as a dystopian future where governments everywhere control economies and personal choice. What will be the new dominating idea? How might that affect the definition of your core challenge?

- Imagine a new dominating idea, such as fighting wars over water, alliances of African nations with China, artificial intelligence technologies that make now-venerated professions such as medicine or law obsolete, or the decline of bricks-and-mortar universities. How will those ideas manifest in a new, radically different H3 future? How might those PoFs affect the organization's choice of the core challenge for the strategy?

- Flip the good-bad valence of outcomes. Devalorize what is good to make it bad, and vice versa. This helps you to better understand the influence of context on your perceptions of reality. For example, most people say that it's good to hold a winning lottery ticket. However, there are stories of past winners who found that their good fortune led to misery. Consider the range of options that would have opened up if Kodak had regarded print-and-film as an undesirable business. It might have been more assertive in seeking out alternative business models.

Discovery-oriented anticipation is most compatible with imagining the H3 future as remarkably different and qualitatively new. Exercise your knowledge of history to find major shifts like those mentioned earlier: sail to steam, steam to jet power, and physical photo sharing to online sharing. The H1-H2-H3 framework explains well past transformations.

It's been said that history doesn't repeat itself, but it does rhyme. Historical thinking can provide useful analogies for questioning anticipatory assumptions and considering alternative narratives.

Leveraging other microskills. Anticipation is the sixteenth microskill presented in this book. I encourage you to review the list of microskills in Appendix B and identify how each applies to the tasks of strategic thinking.

Here are two examples that connect the microskills to the future:

- **Skepticism** – When offered a prediction, investigate the sources of data and the model used in that prediction. What are the anticipatory assumptions in use by the person making the prediction?

- **Personal resilience** – The future might bring you adversity. Resilience includes believing in your own agency, your determination to make good choices, and your volition to achieve the future that you want. What strengths help you deal with any present adversity? What are you doing to improve your resilience to cope in a changed future? Can your organization do more to improve its capacity for resilience?

Shapes and Scenarios

The three horizons can help your organization develop better input for constructing scenarios.

Shapes of the future. In Chapter 6, I suggested a high-quality question: "What are the shapes of the future?" I also discussed set-based design, where we identify constraints and try to find solutions within the boundaries. The shapes-not-points idea benefits our strategic thinking by offering our imagination more options and flexibility.

Now, let's consider this more-specific question: "What are the shapes of the future, given your children's or grandchildren's choice of college (or not) and vocation?"

Each child's choice has the potential to powerfully influence the shape of her future: her income, status, and family size. You'll see the power of the question as you imagine it specific to an individual. Otherwise, it remains an abstraction that lacks relevance.

Our goal is to get a richer understanding of H1, H2, and H3 systems and the relationships between causes and effects. We're less concerned with correct forecasts and linear marches of trendlines.

Scenarios. Many managers and strategists construct scenarios.

Returning to the above example of college choice, two possible outcomes of college choice might be wealth and number of children.

It's a common practice of scenario construction to use a 2×2 matrix, as illustrated in Figure 7-4. It shows parameters of wealth and number of children. Each of the quadrants is a target for further

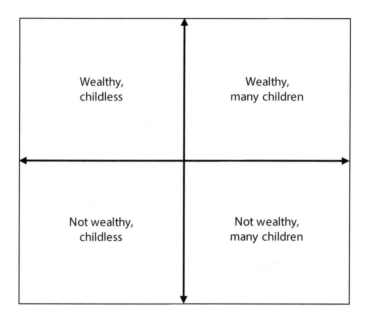

Figure 7-4. Example scenario.

exploration and analysis. Depending upon your point of view, each of the four scenarios could be a utopian or a dystopian scenario. I will leave for you the exercise of elaborating the specific implications of your own situation.

The final step is to backcast and imagine your anticipatory assumptions behind that scenario. It's possible that there are decisions and actions you can take in the present that can stimulate your preferred future or help you to be more prepared for any of the scenarios.

Futures-Sensitive Strategy

Given the future, strategy needs to address potential for change, the organization's present interests, the beliefs of stakeholders, and the definition of the core challenge.

The key principle of futures-sensitive strategy is to build awareness of anticipatory assumptions. Increase the number, quality, and range of those assumptions and you'll find that you develop more sensitivity to the consequences of present-moment decisions. You'll have a more proactive attitude.

◆ ◆ ◆

In the next chapter we examine a success story of a transformation to a new environment. As you read, keep in mind how IBM's success contrasts with Kodak's failure.

We examine the strategic-thinking narrative of Louis V. Gerstner Jr. and his experience with IBM and its external environment. The IBM case provides a good contrast of the culture of operational thinking with the culture of strategic thinking. The chapter will help you to identify more landmarks of strategy, and it provides another example of writing strategy, which will clarify tactics as an organization's decentralized adaptation to a more strategic decision.

Looking ahead to Chapter 9, I continue the Lou Gerstner strategic-thinking narrative and explain the X-factor of insights. You'll see more evidence of the reconfiguration of resources to fit a new and emerging environment.

Looking even further ahead to the final chapter on extra-ordinary leadership, I want to tease you just a bit and mention that I've already placed several small pockets of hints to help you distinguish ordinary and extra-ordinary leadership.

CHAPTER 8

Strategic Decisions

The Logic of Fit and Focus

Everyone that has ever done anything significant first found themselves in the place where the status quo no longer was enough.

— TemitOpe Ibrahim

THIS CHAPTER INTRODUCES the strategic-thinking narrative of Lou Gerstner, the chief executive officer of IBM and a leader of one of the most remarkable business turnarounds in history. The many quotes in this chapter are drawn from Gerstner's book, *Who Says Elephants Can't Dance?*, which is his account of his experience in crafting strategy.* This narrative shares many of the same principles as those of Billy Beane and Christopher Columbus, but it differs in that it takes place in a complex, large, and global technology business.

---

* *Moneyball* (the book) was an interpretation by a third party, Michael Lewis. *Moneyball* (the movie) was an interpretation of Lewis's book. The Christopher Columbus narrative was drawn from the interpretation of historians. The Gerstner example enriches our understanding of Pillar II and Pillar III because he described his reasoning for his actions.

Lou Gerstner and the Business Turnaround at IBM

Louis V. Gerstner Jr. was the only outsider hired as CEO in IBM's history, serving from 1993 to 2003. Gerstner had previously held top roles at American Express and RJR Nabisco. He had been a customer of IBM and had experienced disappointments arising from IBM's preoccupation with its own needs, policies, and technology. Before those roles, he was a partner at the consulting firm of McKinsey & Company. He reflects, "The most important thing I learned at McKinsey was the detailed process of understanding the underpinnings of a company. McKinsey was obsessive about a deep analysis of a company's marketplace, its competitive position, and its strategic direction."

In the early 1960s, IBM recognized the significance of the integrated circuit and launched an integrated set of product offerings that delivered powerful, reliable, lower-cost computing. Wrote Gerstner, "For customers, System/360 would be a godsend. For IBM's competitors, it would be a knockout blow." System/360 was engineered with a closed architecture, which meant that only IBM's products could function with other IBM products. IBM had a tremendous amount of control over all the major system operations. Customers, once committed to IBM, had to follow IBM's lead and adapt their business processes to the system architecture.

In the 1980s and early 1990s, emerging new technologies, platforms, and business models were undermining IBM's advantages. UNIX, the open operating system, obviated many of the benefits of IBM's closed approach. The new technologies and business models were disruptive forces that undermined IBM's business model. Gerstner relates, "After UNIX cracked the foundation, the [personal computer] makers came along swinging wrecking balls." New entrants such as Microsoft and Oracle captured big chunks of industry value. IBM's business model had lost its tight, effective strategic fit with the environment. Like all incumbents, IBM was vulnerable to the forces of disruptive change.

The new competitors and technologies were pockets of the future, and they led to an industry structure where customers would pick

	Past situation (prior to Gerstner)	Situation when Gerstner arrived at IBM	Future situation (expected)
Description of the external situation	1960s Growing demand for data processing, growing global companies	Major waves of change in industry New group of competitors capturing value Global customers unhappy with IBM	Expectation that there will be continuing waves of change Search for new dominating ideas for industry leadership
Description of the internal situation **(The internal configuration of its strategic resources)**	IBM leverages breakthroughs in microprocessors and creates an endowment with System/360	IBM has vast resources, which are aligned toward legacy ideas	Will need insights to guide reorganization, realignment, and addition of resources Culture will need to be reshaped
How well the internal situation fits the external situation	Very good fit IBM becomes so dominant as a competitor that from 1969 to 1982 it faced an anti-trust suit	Poor fit Many people believe the only way to achieve fit is by breaking up the company into smaller business units	BM can lead again by reconfiguring its resources to fit a changed competitive environment

Figure 8-1. Strategic fit for IBM as a dynamic concept.

and choose technologies from different suppliers to build their information systems.

Strategic Fit is Dynamic

Figure 8-1 shows the situation facing IBM before, at, and after Gerstner's arrival in 1993. IBM's business model was a good fit for the situation in the 1960s, and it followed the natural inclination of operational thinkers to use specialization and process to solidify its advantages. The good fit of the 1960s became a misfit in the 1990s.

IBM's experience reflects a general pattern. Organizations specialize and gain efficiencies of scale. Unfortunately, a loss of flexibility is a natural consequence of specialization. Too, over a span of time, the external environment changes and the fit of resources erodes. Incumbents can hold power for decades but need to invest in reform and renewal.

You can use Figure 8-1 as a diagnostic tool for your situation. Start by examining the past situation (external and internal) for your organization.

- If your organization was once much smaller, what was the factor that allowed it to scale?

- What is the present external and internal situation and what is the fit between them?

- Why has the fit tightened or loosened?

- What are the future scenarios and evidence that points toward a misfit?

Revisiting discontinuity and disruption. A familiar story in market-based economies is that a firm gains advantage, becomes an incumbent, and then is disrupted. IBM first gained success with its accumulated proprietary expertise in the computing industry. Over time, it gained advantages over rivals and became an incumbent leader. Eventually, discontinuities emerged, such as personal computing and competitors Microsoft and Apple. IBM noticed the discontinuity (emergent opportunity) and responded with a new strategy.

Unless they're in a crisis (or one seems imminent), people focus more on the day-to-day than on discontinuities.

Any organization might be an incumbent or might be a disruptor. These questions can help you use the incumbent-disruptor designation to clarify your situation:

- If we are the incumbent, where are we most vulnerable?

- Are we prone to laxity, inertia, and weak responses?

- Are we basking in our past successes rather than looking to the future?

- Might rivals or substitutes be more skilled at recognizing the needs of our customers and stakeholders?

- If we believe we might be a disruptor, what specific strengths and strategies might enable us to disrupt a rival?

Strategy starts in the fuzzy front end. Chapter 6, The Fuzzy Front End of Strategy, describes a useful framework for understanding the origins of any strategy. In the fuzzy front end, individuals sense weak signals and make sense of those signals. Gerstner spent his first three months learning about IBM's business situation. He visited IBM sites throughout the world, its customers, and even its competitors. He asked many questions.

The fit of internal capabilities to the external environment is an essential element of strategy.

He saw that the core challenge involved strategic fit. IBM's formidable resources weren't configured to serve large global customers.

Rivalry (and Its Neglect)

This next quote describes an incident that took place six weeks into Gerstner's tenure as CEO. Gerstner was the audience for corporate strategy presentations by 26 senior IBM executives and summarized the meeting this way:

> There was little true strategic underpinnings for the strategies discussed. Not once was the question of customer segmentation raised. Rarely did we compare our offerings to that of our competitors. There was no integration across the various topics that allowed the group to pull together a total IBM view.

This kind of discussion remains common to this day in organizations everywhere. Executives neglect competitor's intentions (and other kinds of ambiguity) and focus on short-term performance goals. Perhaps this is acceptable if the organization is in a stable situation, but IBM's experience shows that complacency and laxity often mask fundamental changes in the external environment. It illustrates a weakness in the literacies of strategy and judgment.

Gerstner's Most Important Decision

IBM's financial difficulties were evidence that it had not responded quickly enough to shifts in the competitive environment. John Akers (Gerstner's predecessor as CEO) had put into motion a plan to break IBM into smaller independent companies to compete in segments, each offering a specialized piece of the enterprise solution. In Akers's view, IBM's closed-architecture approach (the tight integration of hardware and software) was less relevant in an industry where computing had moved to the desktop and where thousands of upstart companies could specialize in chips, or monitors, or software. "He was disaggregating IBM to embrace what he thought the new industry model was going to be," reports Gerstner. Following the break up, each smaller business would specialize in a product niche.

The decade-earlier breakup of AT&T was an exemplar suggesting that the future of big companies was to become more like small companies. For many journalists, leaders, and practitioners, the AT&T experience anchored a belief that the future belonged to smaller, focused, nimble, innovative companies.

Was the AT&T breakup analogy relevant to IBM's situation? Although both were large, dominant companies, they were unlike in many ways that strained the analogy. IBM held unique advantages: deep expertise with technology, global reach, and established relationships with global business customers. Rather than defining the problem in this two-fold way, "IBM is too big, and IBM is too integrated with its products," Gerstner believed that IBM had not properly fitted its competencies and resources to the needs of its most important customers. Customers told him (and he knew from his own prior experience) that the future of computing was that large-scope information technology investments would have a transformational impact. In other words, the future was not with personal computers, because the PC would never be able to take on intensive processes such as airline scheduling. Buying technology piece by piece would frustrate customers.

Gerstner reversed the plan to break the company into smaller businesses, explaining, "I can't tell you exactly when I decided to keep IBM together, nor do I remember a formal announcement. I had always talked about our size and breadth as a distinct competitive advantage. However, I do know that it wasn't a particularly difficult decision for me."

Writing the IBM strategy

In the following paragraphs, I provide a written statement of IBM's strategy. It follows the template introduced in Figure 2-1. Like the Moneyball example, it shows crafting of strategy as a series of statements showing "we believe, we choose, we adapt." Both examples reinforce the definition of strategy as a specialized tool for addressing the situation and establishing a program for action.

This provides you additional analysis of Gerstner's decision to keep IBM together and will serve as context for distinguishing strategic decisions from tactical decisions.

1. **The collective interests.** An organization practices strategy to advance its interests. IBM had interests that included its shareholders, employees, customers, suppliers, and host countries. Perhaps most important to Gerstner's strategic-thinking narrative was his focus on the interests of IBM's large, global customers. IBM's collective interests could be stated like this:

   > IBM's interests include serving our many global stakeholders. Those stakeholders include shareholders, employees, customers, suppliers, and host countries. Each of those stakeholders has high expectations of IBM to deliver value and to choose well in how it conducts its business.

2. **The collective beliefs about context, situation, and issues.**
   This next part of writing strategy presents the person's underlying justified knowledge based on the organizational context. IBM's collective beliefs could be stated like this:

   > Given our interests and circumstances, we believe:
   > - Our capabilities and strategic resources are a misfit with the situation
   > - Standalone computing will give way to networks, and many competitors will begin to offer networking solutions
   > - Large global customers will find value in a large firm that provides genuine problem solving on behalf of customers, the ability to apply complex technologies needed to address business challenges, and integration
   > - The industry is attractive to new entrants

   Gerstner was an outsider, not part of the entrenched IBM culture. It is unlikely that his beliefs were widely shared. He had to use the formal organizational power of his position as CEO, as well as personal influence, to convince people of his beliefs.

3. **The collective beliefs about the core challenge.** Lou Gerstner faced many issues and stakeholders. IBM's core challenge could be stated as follows:

   > The core challenge is that large customers are angry with IBM (for many reasons) and are shifting their spending to competitors. As a result, IBM's financial outlook is precarious.

   Behind this concise statement is an extensive backstory, which includes that IBM held on too long to an old business model and that it had many problems because of changes in the external environment, including new competitors in the industry. IBM's culture was inwardly focused, which made it difficult to overcome complacency.

   Bluntly, IBM was floundering. This is a word that brings to my mind the image of a fish flopping about in a struggle to find water, or a boat stuck on a sandbar. Organizational floundering is common as a response to disruptive change, and it requires a frank assessment of its presence and strong messages on needed actions.

4. **Choosing the ways to configure the means.** The diagnosis of the core challenge leads to the next step, which could be stated like this:

> Given our interests and our diagnosis of the situation, we choose to reverse the breakup of IBM.

Recall from Chapter 2 that one way to define strategy is as the integration of ends, ways, and means. Here we apply that definition to this example. The word *reverse* means that IBM chose to cancel activities and projects associated with launching new stand-alone companies. This was a statement of ways. The breakup plan involved billions of dollars of resources; these resources (the means of strategy) would no longer be allocated to new activities but would now be retained by IBM. The ends of this strategy were to preserve a unique combination of capabilities and resources. People had told Gerstner that IBM was a national treasure, and its customers saw in the company the potential to deliver value in a unique way.

5. **State the adaptation of the organization.** This last part of the writing-strategy template reinforces the principle that good strategy is coherent. As I will explain shortly, a good strategy involves centralized decisions that guide others in their decentralized execution. IBM's adaptation could be stated as follows:

> Given the choice to keep IBM together, we will adapt by terminating contracts with investment bankers, who are arranging initial public offerings of the pieces of the enterprise, and by stopping internal activities for creating separate processes and systems for each of the units (examples being new advertising and human resource benefits activities).

These statements help others to understand their roles in tailoring their actions (the ways and means) to the local situation.

Clarifying Strategic versus Tactical Decisions

As I mentioned in the first chapter, people often use the adjective *strategic* rhetorically to signify importance. An example is that many people use *strategic* to contrast with *tactical* – the strategic level is analogous to the brain and the tactical level is analogous to the hands. This results in a meaningless distinction between "choosers" and "doers," because people in low levels of an organization's hierarchy can and do make decisions.

Sometimes those lower-level decisions are catastrophic, as in the case of James Liang, a Volkswagen engineer who found a way to fake reports on vehicle emissions testing – Volkswagen paid over $20 billion in fines. Clearly, it's not only the CEO of an organization who makes consequential decisions.

Tactical decisions must adjust to other, more-strategic decisions.

I generally advise avoiding the use of the word *strategic* as a substitute for the word *important*. However, I make an exception for the phrase *strategic decision* if it's used deliberately and coupled with the distinct phrase *tactical decision*.

The application is in this rule: a strategic decision constrains a tactical decision.

An example of a strategic decision was Gerstner's decision to keep IBM together. He revealed it to be "the most important decision I ever made – not just at IBM, but in my entire business career."

The first essential characteristic of a strategic decision is *stand-aloneness*, which means that the decision is independent of other decisions. Gerstner's decision to keep IBM together was stand-alone because Gerstner decided it on its own merits.

Gerstner's decision arose out of his specific nuanced understanding of the situation and was influenced by his unique perspective. A stand-alone decision could also be called a subjective decision, in that it's guided by a person's perspective, personal values, and experiences. Throughout his book, Gerstner recollected his first-hand frustrations as an IBM customer.

The decision to reduce the price of mainframe computing systems was a tactical decision. It was not a stand-alone decision, because the pricing decision involved a considerable sacrifice of profits at a time when IBM was under extreme financial pressures. The pricing decision's logic depended on IBM's commitment to large, global customers. IBM had no good reason to reduce prices if it was going to abandon those customers.

Figure 8-2 is a two-part graphic that illustrates the adapting of tactical decisions to strategic decisions (top half) and then shows the IBM example (bottom half). The tactical decision to change mainframe pricing was a necessary choice *because* IBM was remaining together and because IBM was going to continue to give attention to large global customers.

Similarly, the tactical decision to eliminate international business units was an adaptation with the same rationale: IBM was not breaking up into smaller companies.

The other essential characteristic of a strategic decision is *centralization*, which means that it originates from the center of the organization. Centralization is important to strategy because effective strategy is the coordinated and coherent use of resources. Strategic decisions are centralized decisions because they involve substantial commitments of scarce resources. Gerstner's decision was a centralized decision because Gerstner used his formal power as CEO. He then informed the rest of the organization, which adjusted its local operations to that decision.

The alternative to centralization is decentralization, where each person makes decisions based solely on local issues.

Policy is a tool. Sometimes, coordination must be imposed upon the organization. Sometimes coordination is achieved by influencing the decisions of others.

Many people associate the concepts of bureaucracy and procedure with the word *policy*, and accordingly the word has a negative connotation. Although many people find the word *policy* uncomfortable, I

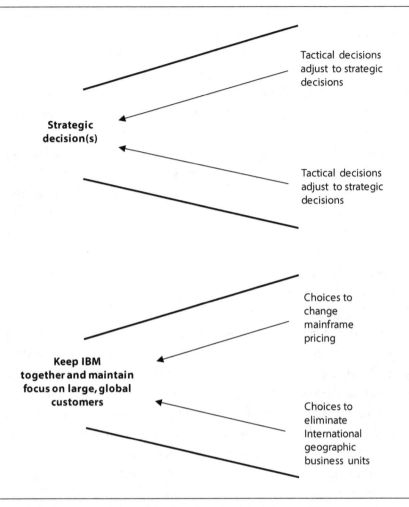

Figure 8-2. A framework for strategic and tactical decisions, with an example from IBM.

believe that it's an accurate and useful word. Policy describes a pattern of decisions that originate from a centralized point and influence the decentralized decisions of those who are not in the line of sight of the decision maker.

Focus and leverage. The focused application of power is fundamental to any good strategy. All organizations have limited resources. Most

146

of those resources are committed in some way and can only be reconfigured with great effort. Gerstner explained that his challenge was a "bone-jarringly difficult task of forcing the organization to limit its ambition and focus on markets that made strategic and economic sense."

In the first chapter, I explained that good strategy involves deciding what the organization can't or won't do. A few examples: Gerstner and his team decided that IBM was not going to operate as regional fiefdoms, it was not going to pursue certain lines of business (for example, IBM divested itself of its Federal Systems Company for $1.5 billion), and it was not going to pay its full customary dividend to shareholders.

IBM's focus on securing its cash flow gave it time to stabilize and shift resources to more productive purposes. It could now leverage its existing relationships with large global customers – a distinctive strength. This became a decisive factor in the IBM turnaround.

As a contrast to making the tough choices about what to do and what not to do, many organizations conduct strategy as a brainstorming of ideas that get summed up into a wish list of organizational goals that are disconnected from the resources available to accomplish the goals.

Empowerment. A tactical decision is made to adapt a strategic decision to the local context. Empowerment, rather than being a generic buzzword, can be used to improve the quality and speed of tactical decisions.

Empowerment is a function of the person's authority, resources, information, and accountability and can be described by this formula:

Empowerment = f (authority, resources, information, accountability)

Empowerment = 0 (if authority, resources, information, or accountability = 0)

By unpacking each concept, you can assess the organization's readiness to make tactical decisions. Does the person have the authority?

Has she been allocated the resources for her part of the strategy, or will she have to generate the resources? Is the rationale and overall strategic intent clear to her?

Accountability is defined as a person's willingness to have her performance measured. Naturally, good or bad performance is associated with consequences for the individual. If a person is accountable, then her choices are visible to others, which helps to decentralize strategic decisions.

A network of dominating ideas. I focused on the decision to keep IBM together as an example of a strategic decision. However, it wasn't the only strategic decision in this story. Each choice is part of a network of decisions. One decision was to reinforce the principle that IBM's business was a market-driven and customer-focused enterprise. Additionally, Gerstner de-emphasized behaviors that suggested that IBM was an internally-focused, process-driven enterprise. Other strategic decisions included that IBM would reinvest in the mainframe, protect the fundamental R&D budget, and remain in the core semiconductor technology business.

Strategy as a Bet

Strategy is a bet. That assertion is typically one of the biggest surprises to operational thinkers and their aspirations of predictability. The proof of the assertion is found in the strategic-thinking narratives in this book.

Gerstner explained IBM's strategy as a series of wagers. He writes, "The saga would pivot on two big bets: one on the industry's direction, and one on IBM's own strategy." Gerstner explained his thinking on the first bet: "I believed very strongly that customers would grow increasingly impatient with an industry structure that required them to integrate piece parts from many different suppliers."

Strategy involves making bets. No strategy can be guaranteed to succeed.

The second bet was an extension of the first. Gerstner's hypothesis was this: "Over the next decade, customers would increasingly value companies that could provide solutions." As we see in the next chapter, Gerstner's strategic thinking migrated toward an insight about a new business model centered on services.

With the benefit of hindsight, we now know that Gerstner's strategic thinking generated an effective strategy. IBM changed its basic structure from a confederation of product-centric subsidiaries to a more integrated services-centric, customer-focused enterprise. IBM remains a formidable global company. It accomplished perhaps the most significant turnaround of any large organization, anywhere, at any time.

Gerstner spent many pages in his book discussing the specifics of IBM strategy, including the changing strategic landscape for IBM. He could see, in retrospect, the importance of emerging things such as the internet. He and his colleagues must have struggled with interpreting weak signals and emergence, as implied by this quote: "All of this wasn't so neat, tidy, and clear to us at the time."

The specific lesson is that every strategist needs to acknowledge that most individuals will feel discomfort from the uncertainty, tentativeness, and indeterminacy in her strategy craftwork. Too, she needs to be skeptical of any story that says that the outcome is inevitable. No one can predict the future and no strategy can be guaranteed to succeed. You don't know the future, but neither do your rivals.

The End of One Strategy and the Start of a New Strategy

As he concluded his first eight months at IBM, Gerstner took a long walk on the beach, reviewing IBM's success in stabilizing its organization.[†]

In his reflections, Gerstner began to consider a new question: How might IBM regain industry leadership? A new core challenge beckoned. Gerstner's mind cleared, and he came to another strategic

---

[†] One simple and effective technique for your own strategic thinking is to take a walk, preferably in nature.

decision: "We were going to take our best shot at making the long climb back to industry leadership." This was an identification of a new core challenge that signified the genesis of a new strategy.

As Gerstner walked the beach, he knew that IBM possessed a collection of powerful strategic resources. IBM's size and resources were advantages. However, size is also a design constraint because it's tough to grow an already large-scale organization.

If this is your situation, you need to follow Gerstner's example. You should persevere with your strategic thinking and remain confident that you and your team can craft an effective strategy.

◆ ◆ ◆

I continue the Gerstner strategic-thinking narrative in the next chapter, explaining how IBM transformed from a product-centric organization to a services-centric organization.

It's an important chapter because it explains the X-factor of insight. I explain how analysis can spark insights by bringing the mind's attention to new story anchors or by strengthening or weakening an anchor. This can spark development of a new strategic logic. I introduce the microskill of reframing as a tool for generating insights.

CHAPTER 9

The Spark of Insight

Insights Are the Secret Sauce of Strategy

It's better to fail in originality than succeed in imitation.

— Herman Melville

E VERYONE HAS EXPERIENCED AN INSIGHT. It's a sometimes-unexpected, newly realized, clearer understanding of your situation and the action you should take. An insight can have a significant impact on your strategy, which is why I designate it as an X-factor.

This chapter gives you additional strategic thinking tools with a focus on sparking insights and using them in strategy. We'll examine one Lou Gerstner insight and that insight's role in providing a compelling new strategic logic that became fundamental to IBM's turnaround.

Recall that IBM was in trouble when Gerstner, an outsider, assumed the CEO role. Gerstner's early activities were sensing and sensemaking. He met with executives in the organization to understand their perspectives. Gerstner counts a meeting with Dennie Welsh, held early in his CEO tenure, as one

An insight connects to and improves the strategic logic.

of his luckiest moments at IBM. Welsh ran IBM's USA services business, which at that time was a small branch of the sales organization.

Welsh described an expanded role for a services organization that could take over (on the customer's behalf) all elements of information technology. "My mind was afire," recalls Gerstner.

Gerstner was excited by the logic of integration-through-services because he "imagined new possibilities" for growth. Gerstner found the services idea "meshed exactly" with his desire to retain IBM's strengths as an integrated entity. This insight is the reason why we now know IBM as a global-services consulting firm, replacing the old, dominating idea of IBM as a manufacturer of computing equipment.

The Rudiments of Insights

An insight is a person's realization of a new and better explanation of the situation. Gary Klein explains it as replacing a mediocre story with a better story.

A working knowledge of insights is essential for competent strategic thinking. From largest to smallest, the building-block elements of insights are story frames, story anchors, cues, and emotional responses to those cues. The mind realizes insights through three pathways: finding connections, exploring contradictions, and using creative desperation.

You might find this analogy useful: A chemist uses her understanding of chemistry to synthesize new compounds. A strategic thinker uses her knowledge of the elements of insights and pathways to understand and create insights.

Story anchors and frames. Just as a nail anchors a picture frame to a wall, a story anchor is something that anchors our attention to some idea, person, or action.

As an example, three story anchors describe the basic contours of Christopher Columbus's strategy: The Earth is spherical, the winds can be leveraged, and there is an opportunity to open a new trade route to Asia by looking to the west.

Gerstner mentally combined the expanded-role-for-services story anchor with his existing anchors: the importance of global customers, empathy for the customer and the customer's problems, the evolving path of the information technology industry, and the commitment to integration. His insight was the result of this mental synthesis.

Cues and responses are the elements of an anchor. An anchor is composed of yet-smaller elements: cues and responses. A cue is a weak signal that might appear as an inconsistency, an anomaly, or an irregularity. The cue for this example was *an expanded role for services* in the IBM business model. The response was Gerstner's mind-afire excitement about the possibilities. Gerstner *sensed* a cue, and he *made sense* of it.

Another example of an anchor was Gerstner's recall of an unsuccessful attempt to outsource a data system during his tenure as the CEO of RJR Nabisco. Gerstner's response to this cue (his memory of the event) was the emotion of frustration.

The emotional component of storytelling is powerful. People become excited, frustrated, disgusted, intrigued, anxious, and fearful. The more powerful the emotion, the more powerful the anchor.

> An anchor is a cue and a person's visceral response to the cue. Connection-type insights occur when we add an anchor and explore the implications.

I have a warning for those who hear the word *insight* as a contemporary buzzword (along with the popular words *data science* and *analytics*). In those usages, the term *insight* is blandly defined as "useful information." This is unfortunate, since it gives the impression that number-crunching methodology is at the heart of success.

Instead, you want to pay attention to the emotional components of stories. In Chapter 5, I argued that strategy is better defined as an art rather than a process. Gerstner's mind was afire with excitement about the possibilities invoked by his insight. That insight, not number crunching, changed IBM's strategic logic.

The connection pathway. This is the first of three insight pathways described by Gary Klein. The connection pathway involves a new anchor to an existing mental frame, leading to an exploration of the implications and opportunities suggested by that new anchor.

Lou Gerstner's reaction suggested that services was a new anchor. The connection sparked his new strategic logic of making services a focal point for IBM, which would serve as a technology integrator on the client's behalf.

Other examples of connection-pathway insights are those of Christopher Columbus adding the anchor of Easterlies blowing from Africa and Billy Beane's understanding of Bill James's writings on sabermetrics. Essentially, a connection insight helps us see broader implications about the workings of the world and the possibilities of the future.

The contradiction pathway. Have you ever seen something strange or incongruous? Was that observation inconsistent with your expectations? The contradiction pathway for insights involves identifying a weak anchor and strengthening it.

As an example, Lou Gerstner noticed that many managers had a tremendous concern for internal status. He felt that this was inconsistent with a business principle of placing customers and market needs foremost in the organization's priorities. Gerstner restrengthened the emphasis on the fundamentals and de-emphasized the preoccupation with status and privileges. (We discuss the return-to-fundamentals heritage story archetype later in this chapter.)

The creative desperation pathway. If you face some obstacle or intractable problem, pay attention to this insight-development pathway. It involves discarding weak anchors to escape from a dangerous situation. You're searching for flawed assumptions, and that often means that you're deviating from conventional wisdom.

A familiar bit of organizational jargon is the burning platform, which refers to making an immediate and radical change because of a dire problem, using the metaphor of workers jumping off an offshore oil rig to save themselves. The situation is desperate, and the act of abandoning the safe and familiar is both an act of creativity and an act of survival. Both IBM and the Oakland A's were in dire situations that prompted searches for novel strategies.

Culture as a Frame

Culture was one of Lou Gerstner's most significant challenges. Even as he met with Dennie Welsh, Gerstner realized that "the culture of IBM would fight it." The effort to introduce new ideas in a conservative culture is one of creating new pairings of cues and responses. Here are a few examples of how Gerstner changed the story anchors:

- He strengthened the anchor about IBM's size and breadth as a global business rather than it being a group of geographic regions pursuing their individual interests.
- He strengthened the anchor of enterprise computing.
- He weakened the anchor of desktop computing as the inevitable evolution of the industry.

> *Culture is defined by anchors and changed by reframing.*

- He weakened the anchor about the importance of small, agile, niche competitors in the future of the industry.

Using the language of insights (cues, responses, anchors, frames), a culture is a group of anchors that form a coherent frame (or a coherent story, if you like). Coherence, when referring to culture, describes the degree to which the anchors reinforce each other. A thickly coherent culture has a sturdy frame that resists insights. An extreme example of a thickly coherent culture is a cult. Less-extreme examples might include military and police forces or institutions like universities. A thinly coherent culture allows and tolerates differences.

In thickly coherent cultures, people don't usually remember the source of their most-deeply-held beliefs. Those beliefs are taken for granted, and people become defensive when their beliefs are tested. Their logic is this:

- Our beliefs are *the* truth.
- The truth is obvious.
- Our beliefs are based on real data (cues).
- The data (cues) we select are reliable facts.

This frame is also considered a strategic narrative.

One important influencing task of leadership is helping others to examine the anchors and frames of the prevailing culture. Sometimes those anchors and frames are appropriate (for the declared strategy) and sometimes not. Leaders help others adopt better anchors, realize insights on their own, and improve the organization's narrative.

Don't fix culture, exploit its strengths. Many organizations try to "fix" culture. A better practice is to use existing cultural anchors to strengthen the response to the core challenge. Gerstner wrote of "tremendous strengths in the company's culture – strengths that we would not want to lose." Gerstner's new strategy was enhanced by IBM's positive cultural anchors, such as the intelligence and talent of its employees, the mutual respect that individuals held for others' points of view, and pride in the IBM legacy.

Don't fix culture. Leverage its existing strengths to support the strategy's direction.

As a communicator, Gerstner focused on the issues relevant to the core challenges facing IBM. Gerstner realized the insight of services-as-a-integrating-logic by using the connection pathway. However, he communicated it to the organization by strengthening a weak anchor, which was the contradiction insight pathway. He flipped the anchor of service, "so that it was viewed, not as a threat, but as a great new ally of our traditional product units." Eventually, services became a strong anchor for IBM's identity.

The Ladder of Inference as an Insight Analysis Tool

The ladder of inference is illustrated in Figure 9-1 and describes and distinguishes specific kinds of inference activities in an individual's reasoning. It provides a framework for unpacking the explicit logic inferences that undergird a belief. When you learn the logic behind others' beliefs you are less likely to have a misunderstanding.

I use the ladder of inference to make the mechanisms of insights more explicit, thereby increasing the number and quality of insights.

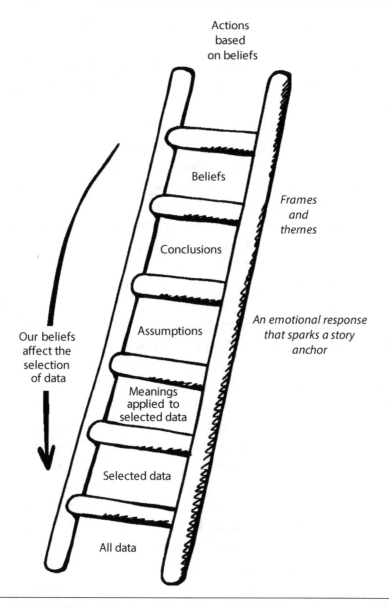

Figure 9-1. The ladder of inference, with elements of insights.

Start with the bottom rung. Your specific task is to find and isolate the cues. These cues might be interesting things such as coincidences or other patterns, or they could be outliers that are anomalies and curiosities. The cues might be small, familiar details that you or others take for granted. Helpful microskills are those of sharpness, empathy, and open-minded stance.

The more cues considered, the greater the chance of adding or changing an anchor, resulting in the increased probability of realizing an insight.

The next step up the ladder is considering possible meanings for each cue. It might be as simple as "this cue is important" or "this cue is irrelevant." Perhaps the cue signifies a low-prevalence pocket of the future. When other people identify an insight, you can probe for that cue-meaning relationship and thus better understand their mental model.

The next step up involves assumptions. Recall that an anchor is a cue plus an emotional response. Here is where the emotional response to the cue intrudes into our awareness, creating an anchor. Perhaps, like Gerstner's "mind afire" reaction to services, you will feel excitement. Alternatively, you might feel passion, pain, fear, or anxiety. Feelings are valid strategic thinking signals and the power of the "What-am-I-feeling?" question will be discussed in the next chapter.

The top rungs of the ladder are those of drawing conclusions, generating beliefs, and acting upon beliefs. Here our minds jointly consider the anchors' relationship to each other. Our minds are framing and reframing (which is the very definition of an insight) and postulating how those insights affect the strategic logic. I encourage you to review the previous description of Lou Gerstner's insight about service to see if you can identify each of his inferences.

To get more and better insights, you need to consider more cues and evaluate the relative strength of the story anchors to the overall frame. It's worth reiterating the three insight pathways. The connection pathway involves adding a new anchor and exploring the implications. The contradiction pathway involves strengthening a weak anchor. The creative desperation pathway involves discarding a weak anchor.

Note the presence of the reflexive loop, illustrated on the left side of the ladder. The dictionary definition of the word *reflexive* says that it involves actions that are performed as a reflex, without conscious thought. People tend to habitually narrow frame so that they only consider cues that are consistent with their existing beliefs and limit their exposure to sources that might offer disconfirming evidence. The steamrolling idea mentioned in Chapter 4 is an example of the reflexive loop.

The obvious advice is to recognize the reflexive loop and its potential to create unrealistically strong anchors for people's stories. You have two options, each of which may spark an insight. You can discard the weak anchor, or you can find alternative weak anchors and strengthen them.

Recognizing the Garden-Path Story

Imagine a garden filled with beautiful plants and sculpture, and a path twisting and winding through it. You follow the path and unexpectedly encounter something entirely out of place. This is the meaning of *the garden path*. Everything seems natural. However, the path ends with something unexpected or unintended.

A garden-path sentence is a sentence that's grammatically correct, yet leaves you feeling confused. An example of a garden path sentence is, "The old man the boat." The trick is that the word man is used as a verb, so the sentence is explained this way, "The old people serve on the boat."

A garden-path story is similar in that at each part of the story things seem normal. Consider these four anchors of IBM's 1970s–1980s-era frame: we have world-class products, we have industry leadership, we have talent hired from elite universities, we have a global delivery capability. The garden path leads you toward a conclusion that IBM must have a great strategy and a great future. However, the garden path abruptly turns to tell a story about a company that's hemorrhaging money, losing customers, and terminating employees.

So, there's a question for you to consider: "Might your organization (or its rivals) be telling itself a garden-path story?"

I believe the answer to this question, for many organizations, is yes. The managers are merely following a routine of tried-and-true assumptions that may no longer be valid for the situation.

The mediocre-story hypothesis. Gary Klein explains that an insight results in a better story than the prior story because the previous story is mediocre. Mediocrity is a descriptor for something that is less than excellent. Something that's mediocre is middling, unexceptional, uninspired, undistinguished, and ordinary.

I use the mediocre-story hypothesis as a tool for orienting my coaching by establishing a hypothesis that the organization's current story (its strategy, its frame) is mediocre. This question prompts a search: "What's the evidence for the mediocre-story hypothesis?"

We've seen several examples of mediocre stories in this book. The mental frame that located Japan as east of Europe was habitual and narrow. Oakland's rivals pursued conventional wisdom and were vulnerable to a clever strategy. The Moneyball strategy was brilliant in contrast to the rivals' orthodoxy. IBM operated under a mediocre strategy and story for years, if not decades. The breakup strategy relied on a weak analogy that IBM was like AT&T. IBM's largest customers didn't welcome the business model of IBM as a vendor of components. The better story was that customers valued more an integrated IBM.

It's understandable that people want to hear compliments about themselves and their organizations. It's also understandable that they sugar-coat their conversations to highlight the good and pretend to be excellent. One of the difficulties of leadership and of strategic thinking is seeing reality clearly. Moreover, that reality is that many organizations are telling mediocre stories about themselves. Like IBM in the two decades before Lou Gerstner's arrival, many successful organizations are on a path to mediocrity. They're coasting on the value created by past strategies, an example being IBM's reliance on System/360.

You can test the mediocre-story hypothesis with evidence such as the following:

- A strong operational culture focused on quantitative measures and the 5Ps

- The neglect of VUCA in the external environment

- Hubris

- Solutioneering

- Bureaucracy and people's misconception that hierarchy defines the most relevant information for decision making

- Cultural preoccupation with status and gossip

- Cultural emphasis on niceness (telling others what they want to hear)

- Goal setting that's disconnected from the issues facing the organization

- Assumptions that one group of people (the thinkers) set goals for others (the doers), who then implement work to achieve those goals

- Financial statements

Seeing reality clearly. Essential characteristics of leadership include the abilities to sense reality for oneself, help others to see reality more clearly, and confront the implications of change.

The Microskill of Reframing

Like the microskill of devalorization, reframing uses imagination. It's a speculation that you can perform privately or with a group of trusted associates.

The microskill of reframing is a technique of synthesis that involves adding, deleting, strengthening, and weakening anchors. By examining cues and responses, the strategist can explore the sensemaking implications of changed anchors. A new frame isn't always an improvement, but it does increase the possibility of discovering a better explanation for the situation and the strategy.

The microskill of reframing involves deliberately altering the relationships of anchors.

The following four concepts can help you imagine new frames: narration, abstraction, partitioning, and projection (NAPP).

Narrative framing. The technique of narrative framing begins with analysis, using the earlier-described components of frames, anchors, and cues to gain an understanding of the present story. Next, the strategic thinker can synthesize a new, alternative story.

Within any story are numerous themes, so the storyteller (the influencer) establishes a theme as a further tool of sensemaking. Themes help to answer the question, What is this story about? Moneyball is commonly seen as a theme of analytics, but I have shown that the strategic thinking theme is also appropriate. However, as an alternative, I could have positioned the Moneyball, Christopher Columbus, and IBM stories as different themes. Examples include the topics of culture, a leader-is-persistent, economics, a band-of-brothers, and the use of tools and innovations.

Themes also serve as archetypes. The first of two familiar narrative archetypes is that the organization has strayed from its traditional values. This heritage archetype has a theme of rediscovering or returning to a past "purer self." IBM's legacy was on Gerstner's mind. "For IBM the lesson was about rediscovering something we've lost." Gerstner further explains, "Our strategic moves had much to do with returning IBM to its roots as a research-driven builder of large systems and infrastructure." The back-to-basics message is common in other organizations as a rationale for focusing on critical value-adding activities.

> The heroic-quest narrative is most applicable for strategic situations where you are venturing into new areas. Examples are growth, new business models, and entrepreneurial opportunity.

In contrast with the heritage narrative's search for a purer self, the heroic-quest narrative (the second archetype) is a search for a new self. In this case, IBM's new self was transforming into an integrated business with services (rather than products) at its core. You can review Chapter 4's discussion of the microskill of storytelling for a larger discussion of this archetype.

I described some of the elements of a heroic-quest narrative in my earlier discussion of the microskill of storytelling. Gerstner, at times, was in the role of a reluctant hero pulled into a quest to save IBM as a national treasure. He didn't journey alone, but instead had a team of fellow travelers.

Abstraction. People interpret abstract ideas in their regular lives. For example, many people enjoy abstract art. Abstraction, also called upframing, is the practice of removing non-essential details to find essential characteristics. The IBM services strategy was an upframing of the definition of services from an old anchor that defined it as a maintenance activity of fixing and trouble-shooting already-sold products. By defining services more broadly as client-focused consultative problem solving, Gerstner built a logic for keeping IBM whole and for regaining industry leadership.

As another example of abstraction in everyday life, people speak abstract words such as *love, honor, cherish,* and *obey* in marriage vows, and then go about interpreting the meanings in personal ways. Individuals persist through the ambiguity because the outcome is important to them. Likewise, strategy includes abstract concepts such as power, advantage, issues, commitment, and execution. Your challenge is to interpret, in your specific context, those abstract concepts.

Earlier in this chapter I described the ladder of inference. A similar tool is the ladder of abstraction, which places detailed, granular concepts at the bottom and more generalized and abstract items at the top. Imagine stepping up and down this ladder of abstraction. When you take a step up the ladder, you place things in a category. The category "organization" includes entities such as businesses, churches, schools, and armies. When you step down the ladder of abstraction, you're adding specific detail that grounds the concept in its unique features. At the very bottom level, the concept is unique to a situation.

Partitioning. Partitioning involves separating elements of a concept into distinct components. Partitioning allows you to narrow or broaden your view or filter out data. When you crop a photograph, you're partitioning the image.

This question helps you to apply partition: "What is this a part of?" A deeper probing should reveal the relationships between the elements, the functioning of the elements, and the value added.

Partitioning is a useful supplement to the task of identifying a core challenge, especially for larger organizations with complicated business models. An organization may have multiple business models, each with a distinct core challenge. Some of those business models are filled with growth opportunities, and others should focus on rationalizing their cost structure. A useful strategic thinking exercise is to determine if the organization has multiple markets, multiple ways to reach those markets, and multiple value propositions. If the markets are distinct, identify a core challenge for each.

Projection. The reframing technique of projection uses imagination to visualize situations from different points of view. Broad framing facilitates a fuller diagnosis of the strategic situation.

Use the techniques of narrative framing, projection, abstraction, and partitioning to help you reframe.

Here's another exercise for your imagination: Assume that an outside organization is eyeing your organization with the goal of inviting it into an alliance, such as a merger. What parts would they find valuable? What, if they took over, would they change?

Walking the fenceline. This technique begins with an analogy: the property line of a residence resembles the periphery of an organization. (The analogy assumes a detached residence with a fenceline separating it from the neighbors.) The first step is to walk the fenceline (property), stopping periodically to look out at your neighbors, and then turn toward your house to take your neighbors' points of view. A sharp-eyed examination might provide the surprising realization that you've been blind to defects that are readily detectable from an outsider's perspective.

The next step is to use your imagination to examine various stakeholders' points of view. For example, how does a customer see your organization? Or a new hire? Or a government regulator? Or a supplier?

As a variation on the walking-the-fenceline technique, imagine a realtor looking at your house, from all angles, to assess the curb appeal and offering price for the house and property. What would the realtor notice? Peeling paint or stained roofing are possible anchors of value and would lower the estimated offering price.

The walking-the-fenceline exercise will increase your empathy for the perspectives of others and help you to identify the issues that may have a broad or long-term impact. You can spot opportunities for innovation, which are often found at the fringe of the organization, where things are murky and ambiguous.

> *Every person has had an insight at one time or another, perhaps while taking a shower, when exercising, or in the middle of the night.*

Time travelers. Imagine a time traveler (from the past or future) who has just appeared in the present. This involves the reframing technique of projection (because this is one person's point of view) and narrative framing (because the time slice has changed).

The visitor from the past sees the present as a special world, full of changes in technology and culture. The visitor from the future sees the missed opportunities. This time traveler scenario can help further elaborate the time horizons (H1, H2, H3 as discussed in Chapter 7) through questions such as these:

- What would the time traveler recognize as familiar?
- What would the time traveler recognize as new?

IBM's incumbent business model (H1) was losing its fit with the environment. Services were lower in prevalence than products. Services would increase in prevalence in the future horizons. H2 is a zone of transition for nearly every element of organization, metrics, and culture.

Searching for Opportunity in the Upframed Future

This next three-step technique combines the reframing techniques of abstraction and narrative framing. It's based on Richard Normann's advice to look for opportunity in the upframed future.

- **Step 1 – Identify the essential nature of your organization.** In this step you describe the current reality, not as you wish it to be but as it actually is. You want to understand the story that others tell about you, not the story you tell to yourself. The earlier-described walking-the-fenceline technique can help you to get a better understanding of your business model. A useful question is this: How does our offering help a customer or stakeholder get a job done?

- **Step 2 – Frame your organization's mission to see broader descriptions of a category.** As an example, IBM became an e-business. For other examples, Xerox became "the document company," Ford Motor Company became a "mobility business," and Allegiant Airlines redefined itself as a "travel company."

  In Chapter 7, I discussed the plight of Kodak. It had successfully upframed from an images-on-paper to its "Kodak moment," which was a well-embedded meme of popular culture, referring to something that was picturesque or sentimental and deserving of an image to record the memory. Kodak had the good luck to have the "moments" part of the strategic logic in place. Kodak was unlucky in that the anchor of "curating moments" versus "sharing moments" was a subtle discontinuity that eventually had great impact. Companies such as Facebook, Instagram, and Pinterest emerged with a lucky advantage, which was that their social media platforms leveraged the anchor of sharing moments.

- **Step 3 – Imagine the upframed organization in the future.** How might that upframed mission be affected by discontinuities and pockets of the future? What are your speculations about the possible shapes of the future? How might your organization's strategic resources be better organized?

166

System Resilience and Bounce Forward

A disrupted organization is not a destroyed organization; it's an organization that will recover in some way. Some would say that IBM "bounced back," but I prefer to say that it "bounced forward" to a business model that was more adaptive to the evolving future of the industry.

System resilience characterizes how a system recovers from disruption and chaos. Consider the surprisingly rapid emergence of small plants and animals after a forest fire. Another example is the changes in cities after earthquakes or fires. System resilience has implications for strategy because the emergence of a new set of conditions is an opportunity to take the initiative.

How do we characterize our fundamental identity as an organization? What are our strategic resources? What stories do we tell ourselves? What stories do we tell others? What is our capacity for learning and change?

IBM had an inherent capacity for resilience, perhaps stronger than that found in other floundering organizations. First, and maybe most important to its turnaround, was that IBM had extremely strong relationships with large customers around the world. If a global customer wanted to deploy a world-wide technology, IBM was one of the few suppliers who could deliver a large-scale effort to multiple sites. Although IBM had made missteps, the global customers continued to trust in IBM's capabilities. Second, IBM employed some of the world's best-educated and accomplished talent. These people quickly learned new things and put them to work. A third resource for resilience was related to IBM's experience and intellectual property.

The idea of system resilience offers an important landmark for strategic thinking. Given the potential for disruptive change, how might your organization increase its capacities for resilience?

Insights Differ from Intuition

Insight is a concept different from intuition. A straightforward way to remember the distinction is this statement: You drive a car intuitively; you don't drive a car insightfully.

Intuition is associated with the mind's efficient mental processing, which is why experienced drivers seldom get mentally exhausted from a routine commute. Intuition is a kind of memory and habit, built up through experience with thousands of repetitions and exposures. The presence of intuition explains why accomplished athletes and musicians appear to perform effortlessly.

By contrast, an insight is the result of *effective* mental processing. Insights point you toward better explanations of the situation. It's insight, not intuition, that's the secret sauce of strategy.

Orient Toward Insights

In Chapter 5, I declared that the future is an essential navigational beacon of strategic thinking. The navigational beacon of insights is just as important.

The IBM turnaround is an excellent example of what one insight can do. Gerstner declared that the services strategy was a "powerful logic" that would undergird "IBM's unique competitive advantage." From that quote you can extract this compelling question: Does your organization's strategy have a logic that is unique and provides an advantage?

Insights, more specifically cues and anchors, are critical navigational beacons on the strategic thinking map. A strategic thinker is continually searching for cues in the data and paying attention to each cue. She applies sensemaking to that cue to test for the spark of an emotional response. It might be as simple as, "This request for X from a stakeholder is new, and it's interesting. I wonder if there's any further significance to it?"

Does your organization's strategy have a powerful logic?

When presented with a strategy, a good question is: What's the insight behind this strategy?

Nurturing a New Insight

It's best to treat the initial development of insight as an idea that needs to be nurtured to gain its full value. Particularly when considering the

X-factor of emergence, the strategist assumes that context is evolving, and so are customer requirements, markets, constituencies, technologies, and industries. It's not about who's first to market with a new idea, it's about who's first to get their strategy right. It can take years to fully integrate an insight into an organization's strategy.

The goal is to gain learning at a low cost. One useful tool is the minimum viable product. This is a product that delivers the smallest set of essential functions needed by a customer to get a job done. Similar to the benefits from prototyping, the developer gains relevant, useful, customer information quickly and at low cost.

Although this chapter highlighted the X-factor of insight, the other three X-factors of drive, chance, and emergence were present in the Gerstner strategic-thinking narrative. The presence of each of the X-factors influenced the outcome. Had Gerstner not been passionate about serving the customer and winning in the market, the story would have been different. Had he not been willing to take a chance and place big bets, the story would have been different. Had the internet not emerged, the story would have been different.

Lou Gerstner, like other strategic thinkers, didn't craft strategy by following a prescriptive planning methodology. Instead, he applied his unique perspective, which reflected his unique professional and personal journey. His perspective colored his diagnosis of the situation and his strategic logic.

I'll take up the essential topic of perspective in the next chapter. I explain, using six guiding questions, an approach for developing a strategic-thinking narrative for your own strategic situation.

PART II

Personal and Interpersonal Mastery

THE FINAL FOUR CHAPTERS build upon the Part I discussions of the principles of strategic thinking. You achieve mastery when you manage the forces within yourself and lead with influence.

Chapter 10 (Perspective) explains that the strategist's perspective originates in the authentic, unique self. It's her personality and her point of view. The chapter provides a series of questions that can help you craft strategy for your own situation, organized around context, confidence, choice, character, commonsense, and commitment.

Chapter 11 (Shoulder Angels) suggests that there are two angels whispering in your ear. The angel of dullness often wins, and I provide an example of a bad decision made by an intelligent and educated executive. Everyone has cognitive blind spots that affect her judgment and her ability to act competently. The chapter explains the critical microskill of metacognition, which is the ability to recognize and regulate your thoughts, feelings, and behaviors. This chapter's essential advice is to listen to the shoulder angel of sharpness.

Chapter 12 (Dialogue and Deliberation) explains that thoughtful conversation leads to good strategy. A crucial task of strategy is transforming the "I" of individual beliefs and choices to the collectively agreed upon "we." The chapter introduces you to useful tools such as dyads, the believing game, the achieve-preserve-avoid technique, inquiry and advocacy, the ladder of inference, and the five types of decisions.

Chapter 13 (Being an *Extra*-ordinary Leader) describes a style of personal leadership that exceeds the norms. The chapter introduces the last of the 20 microskills of strategic thinking. Courage is acting despite anxieties and is the opposite of conformity. A strategic thinker uses courage when she speaks truth to power and lives into the future. Leadership is a choice to commit to the service of others where often a commitment to the future is a bold leap.

CHAPTER 10

Perspective

Develop Your Own, Unique Common Sense

I like to use the word perspective *because it makes it possible for anyone to have one. When you say vision, it feels like only a few selected visionaries of the world can have one.*

— Jensen Huang

PERSPECTIVE IS THE COMBINATION of an individual's personality blended with her point of view. Her perspective is the foundation of all aspects of her strategic thinking: the way she senses her unique situation, makes sense of data, synthesizes, and programs her strategies.

An innate part of personality is temperament. Parents know that their children are different from each other in fundamental ways and have been so since birth. Temperament is a source of personal strengths and weaknesses and shapes how a person processes information and makes sense of signals. Psychologists have many well-known tools for characterizing temperaments, such as the Myers-Briggs or FIRO-B assessments. These tools can help a person understand her preferences for concrete versus abstract data, openness to possibilities, and other proclivities

Perspective is personality plus point of view.

that affect her personal approach to sensemaking. Some people are temperamentally suited to the microskills of strategic thinking, and others must apply extra effort.

A person's point of view is the second part of perspective. Point of view includes a person's sensing of data and her sensemaking, which inform her opinions, feelings, and reasoning.

Perspective, then, has some stable components that change little over a person's life, some philosophical components that evolve and settle, and some moment-to-moment changes in interpreting the details of a situation.

How to Develop Your Strategic Perspective
Six Questions

Figure 10-1 provides a three-step framework for developing perspective, with two orientation questions for each step. (To help you remember this framework, note that there are six words, each word beginning with the letter *C*.) The questions in Step 1 are easier to answer, and those of Step 3 require more deliberation.

Context. The orientation question for context is, What is happening?

The development of good situational awareness may be one of the most critical goals for individuals and for organizations. The real world is complex and messy. Neglecting VUCA is easy. Likewise, it's easy to oversimplify.

The path toward developing strategic thinking perspective is to avoid oversimplifying. A person grows in perspective as she develops the knowledge and tools to grapple with complicated and complex systems. She embraces the messiness of the world by developing an awareness of weak signals and the potential that they have for the future.

Strategic thinking is enhanced by an enlarged point of view. All the microskills encourage a broader perspective, especially mapmaking questions such as these two:

- Am I using the right map to describe my reality?

- Where am I on that map?

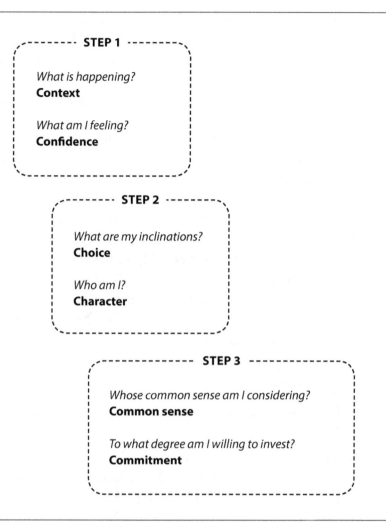

Figure 10-1. Helpful questions and concepts for developing perspective.

Invoking the microskill of storytelling is also helpful. Here are three good questions to ask:

- What's going on that's unique to this time and place?
- What are the discontinuities?"
- How does the context of the situation affect the events that are taking place and how people perceive those events?

Confidence. The orientation question for confidence is, What am I feeling?

Confidence is a kind of feeling. Your feelings and those expressed by others are signals. Emotions and opinions are a natural part of human existence and can be a window into the inner mental life of a person.

Consider the feeling of excitement associated with gaining an insight. An insight energizes a person and creates an impetus for action. On the other hand, it's also natural for a person to feel anger, frustration, irritation, fatigue, and indifference when grinding through an analysis of ambiguous data and that same insight proves elusive.

Of particular interest to the crafting of strategy is a person's feelings of over- and under-confidence. Billy Beane's rivals knew of sabermetrics but had little confidence in the technique. Christopher Columbus was overconfident in his belief in the diameter of the Earth and the distance to Japan. Questions such as these help you to develop your perspective and point of view:

- Could I be overconfident and committing to action that's not supported by facts and logic?
- Could I be underconfident and avoiding taking necessary action?"

Confidence is a powerful force for leadership. A natural consequence of low self-confidence is indecisiveness or inaction. The result of inaction is the status quo. On the other hand, overconfidence is also a common cognitive bias.

We should also examine statistical confidence. More and more organizations are increasing their use of quantitative approaches. Data and models increasingly guide decision making. We need to improve our literacy in the use of terms such as *confidence intervals, sample sizes, dispersion,* and the like.

Choice. The orientation question for choice is, What are my inclinations?

People tend to use a habitual way of problem solving. Some individuals approach every situation with solutioneering, offering up the first solution that comes to their mind. Other individuals may rely on designated experts for analyzing the situation and then making a recommendation. The Cynefin framework, discussed in Appendix A, recognizes that different kinds of problems need different approaches. One should avoid defaulting to problem solving out of habit.

This orientation question is straightforward, and it reminds you that you can choose to act or chose not to act. It reminds you that there's a difference between urgency and importance. Answers to questions such as the following enhance your perspective:

- How might I test my inclinations?

- Am I inclined to seek or avoid risk-taking?

- Whose counsel might I seek?

- Where might it be appropriate to probe and establish hypotheses?

- How might a competitor or substitute react to this decision?

- What might be the consequences of this decision?

Character. The orientation question for character is this general question, Who am I?

The generic answer to the who-am-I question reflects your role, in the literary sense, as an individual character who plays a consequential role in an unfolding narrative.

As you consider your past, what have been the critical lessons about strategy that you've picked up in each position or project?

Recall the earlier description of the ordinary world of operations and the special world of strategy. Operations are familiar and comfortable. It requires effort and courage to leave that ordinary world and go on the journey.

We've now reviewed the first four Cs of the six-Cs model of perspective. This next strategic-thinking narrative provides an opportunity to identify their use in crafting a strategy.

The Story of STF

There's a story behind my development of the Figure 10-1 framework. It involves STF, a small, community-based, not-for-profit organization. STF had been founded a decade earlier with funding from local development agencies and a handful of local corporate sponsors. Its stated mission was to facilitate networking of an ecosystem of technology professionals and companies for the benefit of a region. One of STF's ongoing challenges was that the technology industry in the region was a minor part of the local economy. Further, the Great Recession of the early 21st century took a toll on the organization as its sponsors significantly reduced their funding commitment. As a response, STF reduced the quantity and quality of its programs. STF held on, but barely.

STF's newly elected president believed that STF faced a stark choice: either it should develop a new strategy appropriate for the current reality, or it should dissolve its charter and cease operations. His first preference was for a turnaround, so he recruited several new board members to support this decision.

One of the new members was William Cords (not his real name). Whenever William introduced himself, he referenced his service in the U.S. Marine Corps. There could be no doubt that William strongly tied his self-identity to being a Marine.

People are not just board members, or employees, or elected officials, or volunteers. They're unique individuals who say and do things that reflect their nature and their nurture. Indeed, we could say that the primary task of any person is to find her unique spot in the world. For William, that identity was as a Marine.

As a Marine, William's prior experience was that strategy and planning were identical activities, both oriented toward optimizing resources and execution. This approach was straightforward: the commander stated the intent, and the planners arranged the resources to assure that the intent was met. The necessary mindset was quantitative, involving backcasting from a goal to identify the successive steps necessary to reach that goal.

William was now in a role more resembling a military commander than a military planner. He was facing the ambiguity of advancing the interests of yet-to-be-defined stakeholders and yet-to-be-articulated interests. His habits of mind, useful for other contexts, were inadequate for this situation. As an example, I have explained insight as a "secret-sauce" X-factor that's essential to strategy. I still vividly recall William's sarcastic complaint when I encouraged the board to seek insights: "What are we waiting for? An epiphany?"

To William's credit, he tried to leave his comfort zone, and he recognized that the role of a board member of a community organization requires a broader consideration of issues than is involved in planning a technical activity in support of a military operation.

Not long afterward, William resigned from the STF strategy-crafting project and eventually from the STF board. Facing the realization that there was a weak mission, feeling the frustration, and having little enthusiasm for finding an appropriate purpose, the president and several other board members also resigned. The organization ceased operations two years later.

I mentioned that the six-Cs model had origins in the STF experience. My insight came from connecting two anchors: William's actions and the topic of difficult conversations. A worst-case outcome for a difficult conversation is the blame frame, a breakdown of the relationships between people. As I mentioned, William resigned, and STF lost the benefit of his energies and knowledge.

A difficult conversation resembles a conversation on strategy because individuals have different perceptions of the same events. They need to reach agreement on the nature of the reality and the need to cooperate for future mutual gains. A useful tool is to unpack the situation into three subconversations:

- What has happened?
- What am I feeling?
- Who am I?

For me, William's answers to the second and third questions were obvious: William was feeling frustrated, and William was a Marine. William's story of "what happened" must have been different from mine.

I developed the remaining parts of the perspective model as I further elaborated my initial insight.

There are several other learnings from the STF story.

First, I have some general comments about strategy in not-for-profit organizations. There are hundreds of thousands of them doing good work for their communities and constituencies. Local businesses encourage their employees to serve on the boards. Board membership is a significant development opportunity for the employees as they get to extend their visibility and gain exposure to board-level decision making. However, these employees-turned-board-members often only know the operational-thinking map and are more comfortable with conventional, linear, event-oriented goal setting.

Many board members are disinclined to spend time in the fuzzy front end of strategy. They're reluctant to lean into the work of strategy because of their discomfort. Further, the not-for-profit's professional staff and executives tend to be deep into the details of running the organization. The staff looks to the board for strategy and the board looks to the staff for strategy; the consequence is that no one is thinking strategically and the organization drifts toward irrelevance. Mediocrity is a too-common result.

A second learning concerns what academics call the "agency problem," where the word *agency* describes the relationship of individuals to their organization. One of the board members, Margaret, was the owner of a small business. She never showed much interest in STF's strategy and mission. Instead, she appeared to value her board membership because it provided opportunities to network with potential new clients. Margaret wasn't selfish, but it seemed clear that her loyalties were to her own business. Margaret was understandably interested in developing her business clientele, but she also agreed to be an agent of STF. The dilemma is this: Given the potential for conflict, what is the priority of interests?

In developing a strategic-thinking narrative, we must recognize that principals (employers and companies) and the agents who represent their interests (employees) can conflict. Individuals often pursue the goals of their home department over the broader goals of the enterprise. Each may have different attitudes toward and tolerance for risk. The principal and agent may be inclined to take different actions, a continual and ongoing tension that affects strategy. It's why the definition of *strategy* provided in Chapter 1 includes the concept that strategy is a tool used to advance the organization's interests. These two questions help to enhance your perspective:

- Who are our stakeholders, and what are their interests and loyalties?

- To whom or what do I feel loyal?

A final learning is that people often hear the word *strategy* and assume that the output of an institutionalized strategic planning process will give them the relief that they seek. It is difficult to leave the familiar world of conventions and operational thinking to journey to the map of strategic thinking.

Putting the Character into the Story:
Your Challenge

Recall the microskill of storytelling and the quest narrative archetype, in which the hero is in the ordinary world and hears a call to journey to the special world.

Now, place yourself in the role of the protagonist of an evolving strategic-thinking narrative. What role will you play in this specific strategic-thinking narrative? Maybe you're the hero who must make a difficult choice to cross the threshold from the ordinary world of operations to the special world of strategy. Perhaps you're the mentor who will give a nudge that helps the hero.

It's rare that there's complete agreement on the strategy among a group of managers. Maybe you're one of the allies of the protagonist, but you don't agree with her beliefs about the strategic situation. The movie *Moneyball* starkly showed that many of Billy Beane's staff strongly disagreed with Beane's definition of the core challenge and the direction to take. Lou Gerstner described several situations where his direct reports undermined his efforts to integrate IBM.

The six orientation questions provide a useful framework for your narrative. Following are two examples you can use as models for the first four C questions. The first one is what William might write based on his experience as an STF board member. (I identify each of the Cs inside the parentheses.)

> I have been told that STF needs leadership help from the business community and that a new strategy is required. I've listened to other board members speak about STF's history and its marginal impact on the community. *(This describes the context of "What's going on?")* In the Marines, we established our goals and built the strategy by planning the needed steps to reach our goals. As a Marine, I know that it's essential to act rather than waste time. *(This is a statement reflecting William's character.)* My frustration is strong. Why can't this organization set a direction and a plan? *(This describes confidence, "What am I feeling?")* I'm inclined to listen at this point, out of caution, because this doesn't match my expectations. *(This describes choice, "What are my inclinations?")*

This second example draws from the Chapter 8 scene where I described Lou Gerstner walking on the beach, contemplating the situation. Here is a restatement of his thoughts, implying the same concepts of context, confidence, character, and choice.

> We have achieved a turnaround, and IBM will survive. The industry continues to be dynamic. We can expect emergent new opportunities. I'm feeling satisfied and yet unfulfilled because I didn't come here to merely rescue the company. I want to accomplish more. I've spent my career in business making companies better, and the question, Can IBM lead again? is a test of my leadership. I'm ready to answer yes and engage the company to take advantage of our strengths.

A Second Meaning of Character

The word *character* has two meanings that are significant for understanding perspective. The first meaning designates a role for an individual in a narrative. The second meaning describes a person's essential nature. We trust those people whom we judge to have good character and distrust those of bad character.

The following paragraphs describe four ideas that can help you develop your character and improve your strategic thinking. Recognize that character is developed through tests: why it's crucial to separate ego from decision outcomes, ethical reasoning, and respecting others' perspectives.

Tests of character. Rick Warren writes, "Character is both developed and revealed by tests, and all of life is a test." In being tested, you learn and grow, giving you the confidence to challenge the status quo.

In heroic-quest narratives, the hero's external battles provide drama and help resolve the essential tensions of the story. In the STF example in this chapter, the external battles were with competing priorities and the struggle to gain attention for the STF brand in the local community.

What have I gotten myself into? is a common question of self-reflection.

A person can have internal conflicts, too. Perhaps each of the STF board members was struggling with her own place in STF (in particular) and the world (in general): Who am I? Do the labels placed on me hinder or help my ability to think strategically?

People find that, as they come to understand the complexity and risks of a strategic situation, they have doubts about themselves and what they're doing. What have I gotten myself into? is a common question of self-reflection and is an example of an inner obstacle. Asking that question reveals that you're outside your comfort zone. And that's where you should be.

The X-factor of drive is essential to strategic thinking. Drive, ambition, and courage originate from within the person. Some people have grit and they rise to the challenge of strategic thinking. Others do not, and they retreat.

The consequences of our decisions are independent of our self-worth. Some people punish themselves excessively for bad decisions, even for accidents. Consequently, they become more conservative and risk-averse, which keeps them in the status quo.

An alternative perspective is to develop and hold the "trader's mentality," which is the psychology of people who are successful in trading financial tools. Examples are day traders of stocks or financial futures. Successful traders separate their ego from their trading decisions. Their self-worth is unaffected by making a bet that didn't work out. Likewise, they don't believe themselves to be geniuses if bets pay off. Much of the psychology of successful traders originates in broad framing: the market is a complex system that can't be fully understood, but with enough bets, the probabilities can work in the traders' favor.

You may have made a wrong decision, but that doesn't make you a bad person.

This attitude toward risk distinguishes and strengthens perspective. A trader's mindset for strategy is to be reflective, to keep in check emotions that might lead to impulsiveness, to stay open to new data, to be skeptical about trends (the trend is your friend until it isn't), and to accept the four DICE X-factors of strategic thinking. A trader knows that she's not in control of the markets, but she also knows that the markets will offer an opportunity to the sharp-minded person.

Ethical reasoning. Many organizations and professions publish codes of ethics that spell out expected behaviors for members. These codified ethical standards are ideals that describe rights, obligations, benefits to society, fairness, or specific virtues. You would find the landmark of codified ethics close to the landmark of perfection on the map of operational thinking.

Ethical reasoning is more than compliance with an ethical code.

However, these standards can't apply to every situation. An alternative to published codes is to rely on ethical reasoning. This resembles strategic thinking in that understanding the context for the choice is essential to the practice. Ethical reasoning begins with a person's awareness of her moral leanings and the moral leanings of others. Those leanings include assessment of good and bad, virtue and vice, justice, and freedom. Here are a few "bigger" questions:

- What is right and wrong?
- Should I follow the letter of the law even if I'm violating its spirit?
- What are my obligations beyond my employment (e.g., family, society, the planet)?

A respect for others' perspectives. Many other people have invested thought into their views and perspectives of strategy. Seek them out. Practice the microskill of open-minded stance to understand their perspective. Even if you don't agree with their mental models of strategy, you'll find that your effort to understand their reasoning strengthens and refines your perspective.

The Fifth and Sixth Cs:
Common Sense and Commitment

Let's consider the two questions in Step 3 of Figure 10-1. A person's perspective includes her own common sense about the situation and her willingness to commit their resources to strategy (or to operations).

Common sense. The orientation question for common sense is, Whose common sense am I considering?

It helps to distinguish the common from the sense. What makes something common sense is that there is a group of people (the common part) who agree on what is practical, useful, or real (the sense part).

I mentioned earlier that I had an insight about connecting a person's feelings with difficult conversations. Another insight strengthened the framework. It came from hearing Jen-sen Huang's story of founding Nvidia, a graphics chip manufacturer. He explained that, as a member of the video-game generation, it seemed obvious that there would be a continuing demand by video gamers for better-performing computer chips. Huang saw the opportunity for a business model focused on creating and supplying those chips. To him it was common sense, albeit a common sense that was unique to his team. It wasn't a matter of having a vision, it was a matter of holding a unique perspective.

One person's strong signal is another person's weak signal, and one person's nonsense is another person's common sense. Everyone has their unique perspective, and that's a source of value.

People are often shocked to hear that subjectivity is a desirable quality of strategy. If they're on the operational map, they value objectivity. They've learned that subjectivity is nothing more than opinion and is worthy of disdain. Subjectivity means that context influences truth and facts. For example, imagine one person saying this to another, "I'll telephone you tomorrow at six o'clock." Does that mean 6 a.m. or 6 p.m.? What if the person is in a different time zone? You can't understand the "truth" of the fact labeled "six o'clock" in the absence of the context of social and cultural conventions such as time zones or a.m. and p.m.

> One person's common sense is another person's nonsense.

For the crafting of strategy, subjectivity is a good thing, especially if the subjectivity is associated with a proprietary insight that's unavailable to your rivals. A broad common sense may be bland and mediocre. If most of the mainstream agree on the interpretation of the situation, then common sense could also be labeled commonplace, conventional, and orthodox.

This subjectivity provides opportunities for entrepreneurs: If common sense is that which is familiar to the mainstream, it's reasonable that this mainstream familiarity is ordinary and orthodox. There's a delicate irony here: the more common the acceptance of a set of ideas, the more likely that the culture complacently accepts them, exposing the organization to the effects of discontinuities and disruptions.

In Christopher Columbus's time, it was a common-sense assumption that Japan was located to the east of Europe. Columbus had a different common sense: Japan was located to the west of Europe. As with other aspects of strategic thinking, a nuanced view of details is helpful.

Commitment. The orientation question for commitment (the sixth C) is, What resources do I commit to what actions?

In Chapter 3, I used a chess analogy as a way of distinguishing Pillar II (the cognitive element of strategic thinking) and Pillar III (the actual configuration of resources). The Pillar II construct in strategy is to take a systems perspective to consider the consequences of decisions. Using the criteria described in Chapter 8, a person makes a strategic decision because her own subsequent choices will adapt to this move, and her opponent may also react to her actions. She assesses the situation, imagines the array of next positions, and makes a resource commitment decision.

Next, let's consider this more-revealing question: To what degree am I willing to invest?

The "to what degree" segment of the question suggests nuance. If you have serious doubts, you might decide to make a smaller investment than if you were wholly convinced. Our earlier discussions of probes and experiments are helpful in establishing the ways and means of implementing a strategy.

The Strategist's Perspective

Throughout this book, I have valorized the concepts of being unorthodox, unconventional, nonconformist, and unordinary. A person's strategic perspective is grounded in her personality, life experiences, and present point of view. No two people will have the same perspective because each person has a unique path in life during which she accumulates resources: experiences, knowledge, attitudes, ambitions, common sense, and outlooks. That path establishes her perspective and influences her strategic thinking.

Your own life's journey is a source of your strategic perspective.

My advice is to regard your unique self and perspective as a strength. It adds diversity to the organization and, through that diversity, resilience. An individual's perspective on strategic thinking, combined with her perspective on leadership, provides an important source of power for helping the organization advance its interests.

Writing Strategy for Your Situation

The starting point for an assessment of strategy is straightforward. You begin with a character (you or someone else) taking note of the situation and her feelings. Stakeholders have many beliefs about their interests and the nature of the situation. They hold some firmly and some weakly.

A tip for explaining your beliefs about the situation, when writing strategy, is to express doubts about the stability of the status quo. For the IBM example (described in Chapter 8), it might be powerful to state, "We're skeptical that the dominant configuration of the future is desktop, stand-alone computing," and then establish one or more hypotheses about the future.

I encourage you to continue with the remainder of the questions in our discussion of the six-Cs technique. You can augment this technique with the five-part approach to writing strategy described in this book. (You've probably noted that the techniques overlap in that they include the elements of context and character.)

I'm sure that you've noticed that there are many questions posed in this book. The best answers are going to require substantial reflection. It's easy to understand why managers won't invest energy in probing and reflection and instead default to the much-easier practice of goal setting.

In the next chapter, I describe the microskill of metacognition, which is the ability to regulate yourself based on your self-awareness of your knowledge, skills, blind spots, and feelings. Metacognition is a characteristic of high-performing people.

Looking toward the final two chapters, we address the practical problem of converting an individual's "I believe" to a collective "We believe." How might we build a common base of beliefs and consensus on decisions when the situation calls for new strategies?

CHAPTER 11

Shoulder Angels

Pay Attention to Sharpness and Not Dullness

*Unfortunately, the world is not black and white.
Senior managers spend most of their life in the
gray regardless of their responsibility and that can
be a dangerous and hard place to be.*

— Stephen Richards

THERE ARE A SURPRISING NUMBER of top executives who have
been convicted of white-collar crimes.

Consider the case of Samuel D. Waksal, holder of a Ph.D. and
founder and CEO of ImClone Systems, a pharmaceutical company.
Waksal knew that the U.S. Food and Drug Administration had rejected a critical ImClone product, an announcement that typically
causes a decline in the price of a pharmaceutical stock. Waksal tipped
off his daughter and others, who sold their ImClone stock before the
announcement.* This action was a violation of securities law.

Why did this smart and talented executive decide to put his career, family, wealth, and social standing in jeopardy?

---

* One of the tipped people was media personality Martha Stewart, who was
imprisoned for using insider knowledge for her own financial benefit.

Many people opine that Waksal was fundamentally of bad character: immoral and greedy. There was little in Waksal's background to suggest that prison was his life's destiny. A better explanation is found in Waksal's admission that he didn't carefully consider his situation and the consequences of his decisions. I believe he was dulled in his thinking rather than sharp-minded. Waksal relied on his intuition and made a bad decision when he could have made a good choice.

Waksal is one of many examples of successful executives who became white collar criminals. Eugene Soltes of Harvard met with many of them over an extended period. Soltes found, in many cases, that their criminal activity arose from "intuitions and gut instincts," and they "expended surprisingly little effort deliberating consequences of their actions. They seemed to have reached their decisions to commit crimes with little thought or reflection."

Smart and talented people can act incompetently.

Let's examine a second story involving poor decision making. The 1960 Bay of Pigs fiasco is a well-studied strategic decision that occurred in the early part of John F. Kennedy's presidency. JFK was troubled by the belligerence of the Castro regime in Cuba. He approved a plan, brought forward by his advisors, to launch a military operation that was intended to lead to the overthrow of the regime. The operation went poorly.

Noting the collective stupidity of the decision, Kennedy reflected afterward, "I guess you get walled off from reality when you want something to succeed too much."[†]

Kennedy's decision (in contrast to Waksal's impulsive choice) was made with deliberation. A planning team had developed the logistics and tradeoffs for the endeavor. They discussed and worked through the implications before bringing it to Kennedy. Kennedy's advisors

---

[†] To Kennedy's credit, he and his advisors took a critical look at their perceptions and decision-making style, which proved to be beneficial for the subsequent Cuban Missile Crisis.

participated in the decision, and yet they made one of the biggest blunders in U.S. foreign policy history.

For yet another example, return to Chapter 8 and Lou Gerstner's recollection of an IBM strategy meeting. In that meeting, despite the reality that the organization was in a dangerous situation, the 26 senior executives failed to address the core challenges and were unable to hold a big-picture point of view. Gerstner stated that IBM was an organization filled with some of the most talented and intelligent people he had ever met. However, this group of top executives showed no inclination to recognize the big picture or address core challenges facing the organization.

The theme of these examples is that smart and talented executives can fail at the common-sense tasks of looking at the long term, considering the big picture, and embracing multiple points of view. Degrees from prestigious universities are not a vaccination. Knowledge of benefit-to-cost calculations is not a vaccination. It raises a question essential to the concept of strategic thinking competency:

> If smart executives are vulnerable to mistakes of impulsiveness, in-deliberation, and narrow framing, might they also be susceptible to taking mental shortcuts when they craft strategy?

The answer to the question must be yes, a sobering thought for any organizational stakeholder. It's easy to become dulled, and this is an obstacle for competency in strategic thinking. Any organization is subject to the potentially disastrous consequences of a decision.

What might be the solution to dullness?

Andy Grove, former chairman of Intel Corporation, provides one answer. In his book *Only the Paranoid Survive*, he comments on why incumbent organizations become undermined by disruptive organizations. He explains, "Success breeds complacency. Complacency breeds failure. Only the paranoid survive." Grove used the word *paranoid* rhetorically, intending to remind people to pay attention to the presence of external discontinuities and avoid attitudes of entitlement and laxity.

It's worth mentioning, because it reinforces Chapter 10's discussion on perspective, that Grove, a Jew, had survived many tests in his early life in Nazi-controlled Hungary. He arrived in the United States in 1957 with no money and barely able to speak English. He became one of the top businesspersons of the 20th century, and *Time* magazine named him person of the year. In Grove we see an excellent example of the drive of a strategic thinker (X-factor #1).

Another technique for avoiding dull decisions is to encourage more conversation between stakeholders. Often all it takes to stop a dumb decision is another point of view or a reminder of basic principles.

Perhaps you're alone with your thoughts. Can you have a better internal conversation? Let's examine two voices.

Shoulder Angels

A shoulder angel is a familiar literary trope, a bad angel and a good angel each sitting on a shoulder. For this analogy, the angels are named dullness and sharpness, respectively.

The good angel is the person's conscience encouraging her to take a moral path. This contrasts with the malevolent figure on the other shoulder, which encourages her to indulge her selfish desires or reminds her that she's tired, busy, and can take satisfaction in her achievements. Figure 11-1 presents examples of each angel's whisperings.

The Microskill of Metacognition

Metacognition is "the *intentional* and ongoing *interaction* between awareness and self-regulation." You practice the microskill of metacognition when you pay attention to the angel of sharpness and act upon her suggestions.

You practice metacognition by looking inward and adjusting your behavior.

The microskill of metacognition has many similarities to the microskill of reflection. Metacognition is directed toward self-awareness of your current knowledge, thoughts, actions, and feelings.

"You have a
busy schedule."

"You have a lot of
responsibility."

"Time and other
resources are scarce."

"You like to keep
things simple."

"You've been successful
in the past by trusting
your gut."

"No one will notice that
you're cutting a corner."

*"Time is not always a
resource that needs to be
managed. The future is a
source of opportunity."*

*"Consider your legacy to
future generations."*

*"Opportunity is all around us,
waiting to be discovered."*

*"Nuance and small details
often determine who wins
and who loses."*

"Don't be complacent."

*"Shortcuts often lead to rework
or worse. It is better to be
rigorous about those things
that matter."*

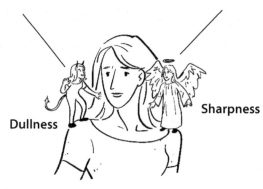

Dullness

Sharpness

Figure 11-1. Two shoulder angels.

Self-regulation is an essential feature of metacognition. You may notice yourself thinking, "I'm not using my mind in the way that I desire." People who effectively use metacognition are aware of their thoughts and change their behavior in response to that awareness.

These three steps enhance the mechanics of metacognition:

- Step 1 is normative and identifies your ideals. This question is useful: What should I be valuing, knowing, learning, thinking, doing, or feeling?

- Step 2 is assessing your real, current situation. Your question is this: What am I actually valuing, knowing, learning, thinking, doing, or feeling?

- Step 3 is acting to close the gap between the ideal and the reality.

The microskill of metacognition is a counterbalance to intuition and gut instinct. Let's imagine that Waksal's metacognition was more active, and it identified compliance with the law and long-term consequences as the standard for his conduct. He might have recognized the gap between values and actions. He might have recognized that he was neglecting useful information, suffering from overconfidence, and considering an impulsive decision. With more metacognition, he might have made a different decision.

Four Trigger Questions for Metacognition

In contrast to the angel of dullness, the shoulder angel of metacognition is whispering questions to trigger your self-awareness and self-regulation. Here are four good ones.

TRIGGER QUESTION #1
Am I in learning mode?

This trigger question helps your metacognition invoke and reinforce other useful microskills, such as curiosity, sharpness, open stance, abductive reasoning, reflection, reframing, high-quality questions, and empathy. While people like to learn, they often don't want to leave their comfort zone to acquire new learning. Often, they steamroll through the material, looking for entertainment or for information that confirms what they already believe to be true.

The learning associated with strategy and strategic thinking is challenging material for many. I suggest that you review the topics of meaningful learning (introduced in the preface) and the beginner's mind (Chapter 1).

TRIGGER QUESTION #2
Am I using the operational thinking map or the strategic thinking map?

The second trigger question is related to situational awareness and orientation. In organizations, people tend to rely exclusively on the operational thinking map, unaware of alternatives.

These additional questions can reinforce and deepen this trigger:

- Am I aware of the current focus of my attention?

- Am I oriented to the landmarks of the operational thinking map or of the strategic thinking map?

- How dominant are those landmarks in my thinking habits and physical habits?

- Are my choices and actions being guided by insight, or are they relying on impulse, intuition, and instinct?

- Am I searching for interesting things and not mundane things?

- What stakeholders are affected by strategic decisions, and how are they affected?

TRIGGER QUESTION #3
What am I feeling?

This trigger question should be familiar from Chapter 10. Your feelings about a situation can be a window into your current point of view.

Perhaps you're feeling great because an insight energizes you. You become more focused as you activate that insight with action. On the other hand, if an insight eludes you, you might feel a desire to persevere with the hard work of sensing and sensemaking.

Perhaps distracting mind energies are hindering your strategic thinking. I use the acronym DAYRT to remember five troublesome states of mind.

- **Doubt** – I know that some strategists have occasionally mumbled to themselves, "What the hell am I doing here?" Feeling doubt is natural and to be expected. A strategic thinker can gain a fuller understanding of her inclinations through examining her misgivings: "What doubts am I feeling?" Those doubts are essential because they might be an indicator that you're grappling with ambiguous signals.

- **Aversion** – People get angry. Some organizations stress harmony, and when a person expresses anger, that's enough to disrupt any conversation of strategy. Consequently, there's less candor and more conflict-smoothing behavior. In the STF case described in Chapter 10, aversion contributed to people's reluctance to engage in helping the organization regain its strategic footing.

- **Yearning** – This is the energy of wanting something that you don't have. The Bay of Pigs failure is an example of a group of people whose focus on their desires caused them to neglect relevant information.

- **Restlessness** –A restless mind often sparks the emotions of worry and anxiety and manifests itself in fidgeting and attention deficit.

- **Torpor** – Some people find themselves in a state of low energy. For any number of reasons, they disengage from their work and responsibilities. They're passive in responding to their environment.

When I notice any of these, I first remind myself that each feeling is transient and that my mind might flow from one state to another, moment to moment. I also remind myself that an important goal of strategic thinking is seeing reality as clearly as possible. I remain confident that there are counterforces to those troublesome mind states, notably the microskill of reflection. I find benefit from taking a walk, exercising, getting some sleep, or talking out the issues with a trusted friend, advisor, co-worker, etc.

TRIGGER QUESTION #4
In what ways are cognitive biases affecting my judgment?

The Samuel Waksal example highlights the mental elements of decisions, supporting a general argument that people fail to perceive the situation and act reasonably and therefore are incompetent. Waksal selected certain cues and neglected other cues. He paid attention to the cue of losing money and ignored the cue that it's against the law to share certain information about publicly traded companies.

This provides us an opportunity to review the role of story anchors and the microskill of reframing. Recall that an anchor is composed of a cue and an emotional response. Waksal's frame had a strong cue – that the stock price would drop – and the associated emotional response of aversion to the loss.

There was another relevant story anchor, which was legal compliance. Waksal could have decided to sell his ImClone stock at any time *except* when he was taking advantage of his insider knowledge of an announcement. Waksal appeared to ignore the legal compliance cue, making it a weak anchor. We can see, in retrospect, that a strengthening of the legal compliance anchor would have led to the insight, *fight your impulse to take a criminal action.*

A natural tendency of all people, managers included, is to neglect the ambiguity of weak signals. Managers favor the status quo, even in the face of mounting evidence of strategic misfit. Managers often fail to act in the best long-term interests of the organization.

Understanding the source of dullness allows us to prevent its occurrence. I imagine the shoulder angel of metacognition whispering to me: "Judgment is being applied here; watch for the encroachment of the availability heuristic and the substitution effect, because they often lead to dullness."

The one-two punch behind dullness. Consider this question and the answer to it:

- Generic question: What is important to my organization and me?
- Generic answer: The first thing that comes to mind.

Two terms from cognitive psychology give us a more precise understanding of the mental process and help us to understand the source of mental errors.

A heuristic is a mental shortcut (or rule of thumb) that allows the mind to process large amounts of information efficiently. The *availability heuristic* is a shortcut by which the mind adopts the first acceptable answer that presents itself. Recall Figure 1-1, the old-lady/young-lady graphic. Most people see one of the two faces and move on. Since the answer is satisfactory, the mind rarely expends additional mental energy to continue searching for new information. The risk is this: the first answer is often not the best answer.

Perhaps you've heard the story about the person who is searching for her car keys under a streetlight. Although she lost her keys elsewhere, she search there because "that's where the light is brightest." The same fallacy affects our search for strategic information; we often search where we can best see what's available, rather than where we're most likely to discover useful information.

The availability heuristic is the first punch that dulls your thinking. The second punch is the *substitution effect*, which is this: when faced with a question or problem that doesn't have an immediately available answer, the mind tends to substitute an easier question for the original question.

Now let's look at this one-two availability-substitution punch as an explanation of many strategy discussions in organizations.

Imagine that you've asked a busy top executive this question: "What's your strategy?" The availability heuristic is likely to kick in: she answers with the first thing that comes to her mind, for example, revenues. Unless there's some sort of mental alert to cause her to pause and broad frame, she mentally substitutes a question about strategy with a statement about goals: "My strategy is to increase revenues." The activity is subconscous and quick. The easier the mental process, the more likely she will feel confident with her answer and neglect strategic issues.

The success of the angel of dullness is based on your satisfaction with what comes to mind readily.

The availability heuristic and the substitution effect are a characteristic of everyone's mental life. The availability heuristic explains why so many otherwise smart and talented people neglect ambiguity. The substitution effect explains why most organizations settle for a list of goals and aspirations in place of good strategy.

Fallacies, Illusions, Neglects

The angel of metacognition reminds me to "Watch for FIN," which is an acronym for fallacies, illusions, and neglects.

The following paragraphs provide a sampling of common fallacies, illusions, and neglects that affect strategy.

Neglects. I began Chapter 1 with the assertion that people neglect ambiguity. People overlook things that are mentally uncomfortable, including ambiguity, competition, and complexity.

The illusion of physical appearance. A familiar example of an illusion is found in the advice to "dress for success." A person's appearance has little relationship with her talent, intelligence, or character. Despite that fact, we continue to emphasize the wearing of nice and appropriate clothing because it gives others the impression that we have desirable qualities. In the Moneyball example, professional baseball scouts used the physical appearance of a player as a basis for their recommendations.

The illusion of overconfidence. People are very skilled at fabricating explanations and predictions. Another common example of illusion is people's overconfidence in their knowledge and abilities and in their belief that they *knew* that something was going to happen.

The illusion of nostalgia. Often people remember the past as a much simpler, more pleasant, and more virtuous time. In politics and elsewhere you'll find people who treasure nostalgia and want to return to an earlier era that never really existed. IBM's Louis Gerstner remarked, "The company's golden age – much of it reality, but at least part of it an illusion – had such a powerful hold on the imaginations and the hearts of some IBMers that every change was perceived as a change for the worse."

The illusion that experience is a signal of expertise. Experience as a stand-in for expertise becomes problematic when we encounter novel and emergent situations. One famous example concerns Captain John Smith and his role in the tragedy of the supposedly unsinkable *Titanic*. Smith had considerable general experience at sea, but he admitted that he had no experience in crisis situations. Smith's broad experience wasn't sufficient for him to take reasonable actions to avoid icebergs nor to save as many passengers as possible once the unthinkable occurred.

A person's experience with implementing solutions tells you little about her ability to diagnose novel situations or solve unfamiliar problems. Some people are smart because of what they've learned. Others are smart because of how they learn. Expertise, in this fast-changing world, should begin with searching the unknown, understanding the context, generating alternative solutions, and then finding the most appropriate solution.

The planning fallacy. People often make and commit to plans and forecasts that are essentially best-case outcomes that neglect two things: 1) uncertain external events and 2) the possibility that they will change their mind sometime in the future! This is faulty reasoning (a fallacy) because a reasonable person would consider uncertainty and would consider that people commonly change their minds about their requirements and intentions.

A common set of mental errors undergirds poor strategy.

One way of avoiding the planning fallacy is to gather statistics from other similar projects before committing. This is the "base rate," and an example is the high failure rate of restaurants. It's reasonable to inquire about their average performance. Despite the high base rate of failure, every year there are thousands of people who invest their life savings into opening a restaurant.

The sunk-cost fallacy. The sunk cost fallacy involves investment decisions and reduces to this rule: costs that have already been expensed should now be considered in future investments. The rational investor only considers expected future returns.

Bad Information and Cognitive Bias

Humor often reveals a truth. An example is the following riddle, which identifies two important sources of bad strategy.

> Q: What do you get when you combine bad information with cognitive bias?

> A: Our business strategy.

Let's use the riddle to identify the role of bad information and cognitive bias better.

Bad information takes many forms. It has many causes. It could be inaccurate data provided by faulty instrumentation or reports. It might be the deceptiveness of a rival, or an effort to spin bad news into favorable news. It might be a result of ignorance, such as people confusing budgets or goals for strategy.

The phrase *cognitive bias* is not defined as a corruption of logic by emotions. Instead, *bias* is used in the statistical sense, meaning a tendency: an average professional basketball player is taller than the average of all people. A cognitive bias is a way of expressing everyday mental habits and tendencies in sensing information, processing it, and making decisions. Cognitive biases often affect strategy because they're blind spots that obstruct perception and reasoning.

> When you see the phrase cognitive bias, *replace it with the phrase* mental tendencies.

Bernhard Gunther, of the German electric utility RWE, found that several cognitive biases negatively affected several large and disappointing investments. He explained that RWE had made poor bets (capital investments) on "the assumptions of ever-rising commodity prices, ever-rising power prices" in its business case. The company wasn't prepared for the discontinuities related to the demand for and economics of renewable energy or for the Fukushima disaster in Japan.

Gunther reports that several cognitive biases undergirded RWE's poor business decisions. He found evidence that the investment rational assumed that past trends would continue. This is called status quo bias. RWE also identified the presence of confirmation bias, the preference for overweighting evidence that favors one belief and discounting or neglecting evidence that disfavors the belief. The sunflower bias is the tendency to look toward the boss and not offer dissenting opinions or evidence. They found it extended into the deepest levels of the hierarchy.

RWE knew it could do better, so it provided training to encourage individuals to develop self-awareness and corrections for their own and others' cognitive biases. The program included training in patterns of decisions and in judgment literacy. The company encouraged more use of prototypes, probes, and experiments and increased the use of independent outsider reviewers.

Stay Sharp!

In this chapter I've presented evidence that smart and talented people have inherent flaws in their cognition. Smart people are human, so they forget things, overlook things that are obvious to others, and utter regrettable statements. They pay attention to the concrete and superficial rather than the sublime. Any person is *always vulnerable* to errors in cognition. However, just because a person might make a mental mistake, it doesn't mean she'll commit those errors. She can override those tendencies if she's alert for fallacies, illusions, neglects, and biases.

Strategic thinkers do not rely on intuition and impulse.

As I wrote earlier, I imagine two shoulder angels chirping in your ear. The good angel is encouraging you to be more attentive to weak signals. The dull angel retorts, "Those good and noble intentions are hard, take time, are impractical, and may be irrelevant." Further, the dull angel will sneak in some distracting illusions: "Everything is fine" and "You're successful and should follow your intuition."

A competent person is a reasonable person. A useful question for metacognition is to imagine yourself as an observer of the situation and ask, "How would a reasonable person act?" Sam Waksal might have made different choices if he had asked himself this question.

Cognitive limitations (biases, fallacies, illusions, neglects) are fundamental components of our mental life that affect every person's judgment. A conversation with a thinking partner can increase awareness of these cognitive limitations. Any individual can, on occasion, sidestep her cognitive limitations with the microskill of metacognition.

The next chapter describes several tools of dialogue and deliberation for improving the effectiveness of conversations about strategy. We discuss how strategic thinking partners can help each other manage their cognitive biases and improve their abilities of sensing and sensemaking.

CHAPTER 12

Dialogue and Deliberation

Better Conversations Generate Better Strategy

"Conversations are the smallest units of change."
– I have no idea who said this but I wish I had.

— Mark Storm

THERE IS STRONG EVIDENCE that conversation is often a turning point for strategy. Billy Beane's conversation with Sandy Alderman pointed toward an unorthodox logic that evolved into the underpinnings of the Moneyball strategy. Lou Gerstner's meeting with Dennie Welsh led to a "mind afire" realization that IBM's future was a service-centric business model. It's possible that a conversation between Christopher Columbus and his brother sparked the insight that a voyager could exploit the prevailing winds to sail west and the westerly winds to return.

The big idea of this chapter is that better-quality discourse can lead to better strategy. These three brief definitions provide an essential grounding:

- **Dialogue** – The word *dialogue* (dia-logos: through the word) describes a high-quality conversation that provides a deeper understanding of mutual interests and specific issues that are important to the organization and its many stakeholders. Dialogue, in its purest form, is an open, ongoing, and ever-expanding exchange of ideas. This generates deep learning than can be valuable for mastering complex, emergent environments.

- **Deliberation** – Deliberation builds upon dialogue with an emphasis on reaching a decision, such as when a jury deliberates to decide on guilt or innocence. Deliberation is the careful, unrushed consideration of the evidence, arguments, conclusions, and solutions being offered.

- **Dyad** – A dyad is a two-person group. The examples in this chapter focus on temporary dyads, which meet for approximately 15 minutes. Each person comes to the conversation with her own perspective, which encompasses her assumptions, beliefs, and choices. Each has the opportunity to share her ideas with someone who is solely focused on listening.

The goal of dialogue and deliberation is to deepen and enrich the sharing of knowledge. They are tools that enable strategists to detect and resolve ambiguity, enhance people's understanding of strategic issues, advocate for unorthodox ideas, test the validity of unconventional approaches, and gain agreement for tough decisions.

The benefits of dyads are that they promote the sharing of first-person perspectives about the strategic situation. Introverts often have high-quality ideas but are reluctant to share them with a larger group. A one-to-one discussion is easier. Also, complicated and nuanced ideas are difficult to articulate, and a good listener can help the speaker clarify her ideas. Dyads also avoid some of the social biases such as groupthink and sunflower management.

The Analogies of Speed Dating and Jury Duty

When I facilitate groups, I explain the dyad conversations as a combination of speed dating and jury duty. The speed-dating analogy relates to the rhythm of moving from the first two-person discussion to the next dyad. Time is limited to approximately 15 minutes per iteration, so each must communicate her interests, beliefs, and recommendations. And each must listen carefully to her partner and learn as much as she can. Then, they separate, and each joins a dyad with a new partner.

The jury-duty analogy is that individuals deliberate to reach agreement. In doing so, they debate the facts and implications with a determination to gain agreement. Because stakes are high, juries accept the commitment knowing that the activity may take them away from their normal pursuits for many hours. The jury's verdict is analogous to managers agreeing on a strategy.

Continuing with the jury-duty analogy, the top decision maker (say, the general manager or president) resembles the courtroom judge in that she sets the rules and confirms or rejects the jury's verdict. The judge has the role of confirming facts, challenging assertions, and issuing orders and findings. The judge can also overturn a jury's verdict. In strategy and courtroom trials, one top individual has the final approval.

Also, courtrooms have individuals who are responsible for recording information. A similar function is needed for strategy conversations to assure that important information is captured and retained for future deliberations.

The jury analogy falters because strategy is often associated with novelty rather than precedent or nuanced points of case law. It also falters because court proceedings are zero-sum – either the plaintiff wins or the defendant wins. By contrast, strategy can be generative, with multiple winners who obtain their benefit from the strategy's synergistic effects. Regardless, just as juries need to reach verdicts, the organization needs to find agreement on the essential elements of its strategy.

Include More Stakeholders in the Fuzzy Front End

Throughout the book, I have argued for sharp-minded people paying attention to discontinuities. The activities of searching and sensemaking for weak signals and pockets of the future take place in the fuzzy front end of strategy.

The more effort applied to sensing and sensemaking, the greater the opportunity to gain an insight. Thus, as much as is practicable, these activities involve a large group of stakeholders, including next-generation leaders, high potentials, and any person interested in strategy. This is crowd-sourcing for strategic intelligence and is not unlike asking citizens to be watchful for signs of terrorism: see something, say something.

> *The inclusion of many stakeholders in sensing and sensemaking provides more intelligence about sources of opportunity.*

Another benefit is that stakeholders feel more invested in the organization's future. They better understand the reasons for developing their personal leadership and resilience.

Although there is a real risk of information overload, technology is rapidly emerging that can help manage the plethora of weak signals.

Ideas and Tips for Better Conversations about Strategy

In the paragraphs that follow, I describe several ideas and tips to help individuals prepare and conduct conversations about strategy.

The achieve-preserve-avoid technique. These three questions help people to clarify their goals and keep the conversation focused:

- What do I want to achieve?
- What do I want to preserve?
- What do I want to avoid?

Here are some examples of things you might want to achieve: identifying a pocket of the future and its implications, learning from others, leaving a legacy of resilience for future members of your organization, and contributing to a good strategy.

Preserving good working relationships with your colleagues is a nice response to the second question.

An example of something you might want to avoid would be release of sensitive and confidential information and possible exposure to the legal system. Some topics of strategy have criminal implications, such as required financial disclosures (recall Samuel Waksal's situation in Chapter 11). Others have civil aspects, such as trade secrets, moves of personnel, and contractual agreements. It's always good to understand what information is permissible for sharing and what is not.

You should be sensitive to people's power, prestige, and status. I have learned that people have an unspoken concern: Could any revealed information be exploited in some way to embarrass another?

Inquiry and advocacy. Inquiry and advocacy are basic modes of conversation. They are complementary and expand the capacity for dialogue.

Advocacy is presenting your mental model to others. When you advocate, you provide the supporting evidence and reasoning for your conclusions. An example statement of advocacy is this: "I believe that our core challenge is that we are floundering. The external environment has changed. We're neglecting our reality, using the excuse of being too busy. We need to start reconfiguring our resources." If your logic is sound, you can convince others to adopt your conclusion.

As a general observation, most managers are better with advocacy than inquiry.

You use inquiry to learn about another person's mental model of the situation and her proposed course of action. As you might guess, the practice of inquiry leans heavily on microskills such as curiosity, reflection, empathy, and open mental stance. Of great usefulness is the microskill of high-quality questions, and this essential question should be applied often: "What do you believe is this organization's core challenge?"

Sometimes a stream of questions begins to feel like an interrogation. Questions are not the only tool of inquiry. You can make requests, such as, "Help me understand your reasoning behind your conclusion." A variation is this statement, "I'm curious and want to learn your data and reasoning."

Listening with an open mind is essential to good inquiry. You want to show that you're willing to change your mind and are open to the unexpected.

Use the map of strategic thinking. Another suggestion is to use inquiry and advocacy to examine the landmarks on the map of strategic thinking. You will find Appendix D useful in identifying important navigational beacons.

Culture is always important to strategy. Since operational thinking tends to dominate the culture, you can use the strategic thinking map to keep the conversation focused on interests and on broad, long-term issues.

Paraphrasing. One of the most valuable of conversation practices is paraphrasing your understanding. As a rule, you should never leave a conversation without paraphrasing.

Let's say that you and your dyad partner are talking about the organization's core challenge in general, and customer relationships in particular. She has listed several specific instances and deficiencies.

Here is an example of paraphrasing:

> I just heard you describe a pattern involving five customer complaints where we failed to deliver on our promises. You suspect that an unfavorable trend is forming and, if ignored, will diminish our brand. You believe our statement of the strategy's core challenge must include that emerging pattern of poor performance. Do I understand the essence of your concern?

Effective conversation and ladder of inference. I introduced the ladder of inference in Chapter 9, explaining it as a tool for analyzing and fostering insights. The bottom rung represents the details and facts. The middle rungs are the mental inferences of interpreting the data. Sometimes, an inference results in an insight. The ladder's top rung represents the visible actions that manifest a conclusion or belief.

You can use inquiry and advocacy to step up and down the ladder. To practice inquiry, you ask the other person to share her data and logic. For advocacy, you might say, "I'd like to start with my data and use the ladder of inference to step you up to my belief." An alternative approach is to step down from conclusions into data.

Here is an example of how you might present your data and logic to your dyad partner:

> I was visiting a supplier's R&D laboratory, and I saw some interesting technology in use. I've never seen anything similar. As I reflected, it seemed to me that the technology could fundamentally reshape many products. It could offer a significant competitive advantage to those organizations that can apply the technology. I've concluded that this is worth some budget for further investigation and that we should also review our product roadmaps for the implications of this new technology.

Ideally, your partner in the dyad would expand the conversation with inquiry. She would be in learning and not fault-finding mode and make a request, "Tell me more about the details and implications."

I encourage you to practice using inquiry and advocacy, supplemented by the ladder of inference, to make clearer your arguments and to understand others' mental models. You will also find that this attention to detail will help you discover insights.

The believing game. The believing game is a useful practice for improving dialogue. The primary objective of the believing game is to expand the number of beliefs and thoughtfully consider their implications. The beliefs can be about the situation, core challenge, anticipatory assumptions, dominant ideas, and choices facing the organization.

A secondary objective of the believing game is to examine, with objectivity and open-mindedness, those beliefs that are unconventional, unfamiliar, unorthodox, and disruptive.

> *Replace the ease of doubt with the willingness to believe.*

This word game encourages a playful attitude. Knowing that it's a game helps to manage the anxiety of making commitments. Also, games are social bonding experiences that facilitate the development of mutual respect and trust.

The first person begins with an assertion of a claim (a belief about something) and an opinion of the claim's valence (why that claim is good or bad). This template is useful:

> I claim that _____ is true, and I believe that the impact is _____ (good or bad) for our organization.

Here is an example application of this template. Imagine a manager at Kodak saying:

> I claim that print-and-film is no longer viable as a consumer business model, and that the impact is bad for our business.

Your partner reacts to the claim. If she agrees with the statement, you have moved from an "I believe" to a "We believe" statement. If there is disagreement with any part, the partner offers one or more counterclaims.

This practice continues as you exchange dyad partners. With each iteration, you find more openness to the unorthodox, unconventional, and frivolous. You find the disappearance of overconfidence and neglect of ambiguity. Also, individuals become more creative in developing flexible solutions and strategic options.

For a variation of the believing game, each person provides a list of statements of claims and valences. Her dyad partner reviews her list, selects the most disagreeable statement, and makes a counterclaim (unbelievable becomes believable) or expresses a new valence (good becomes bad). The conversation can deepen the mutual understanding. Consider:

- Assuming that this claim is true, how is it good/desirable (or bad/undesirable) for me (or for us)?

- Assuming that the counterclaim is valid, how might it be good/desirable (or bad/undesirable) for me (or for us)?

The believing game suppresses your natural inclination to doubt unfamiliar ideas. It encourages you to identify conditions and circumstances that make plausible a preposterous assertion. In using it, you will find that your decisions are more futures sensitive because you have expanded and validated your anticipatory assumptions.

The game supplements the microskill of reframing, which is vital for sparking insights. All you need to do is exercise your imagination. What are the implications of a new cue? What changes when you challenge the validity of an old story anchor?

The Structured Back End of Strategy Is Critical

Perhaps the toughest work in crafting strategy is done in the structured back end. Here the group needs to converge on its beliefs, make choices (strategic decisions), and design an approach for deploying those choices (the tactical decisions that adapt to the strategic decisions).

Dialogue and deliberation are useful for transforming an independent "I" to a collective "We." (I'm now referring to the Figure 2-1 framework for writing a statement of strategy.) Stated differently, the "I believe" (referring to interests, beliefs about the situation, and beliefs about the core challenge) enlarges to become a statement of "We believe." The "I choose" decisions (referring to the core challenge and strategic decisions) aggregate to a more-powerful commitment of "We choose." The "I adapt" (referring to tactical decisions and programming) becomes more coherent as it becomes an agreement that "We adapt." Building agreement is one of the major tasks in the structured back end of strategy.

That task is not an easy one. People in organizations have legitimate differences of opinion, different goals, and different personal styles. Further, smart people stubbornly justify their beliefs. They can act with passive aggression and announce that they agree with a strategy when they, in fact, don't agree or aren't yet ready to commit themselves to make changes.

Designing a Conversation Using Dyads

I favor an informal approach to organizing dyads. Pick an individual who is different from you. Maybe you don't know her very well. Maybe you know that the two of you frequently disagree. The dyad partners don't need to be in the same management level in the hierarchy: a top executive can spend time with a junior manager.

Figure 12-1. In a dyad, each person shares her perspective and discovers areas of agreement and disagreement.

The dyad's first task is to find a physical space for a 15-minute conversation. They can sit or stand as is their preference. During that conversation, they share individual opinions on the target question. A general template to spark discussion is this: "What is your opinion on X?" The "Xs" are landmarks on the map of strategic thinking (see Appendix D), but they could include other topics.

In Figure 12-1, the "X" for the dyad is perspective. Each person explains her perspective. Both search within the conversation for nuance and find areas of agreement and disagreement.

Short, iterative conversations. When the initial 15-minute conversation concludes, the individual finds (or is assigned) a new discussion partner. Importantly, the topic of "X" is the same. Individuals should expect, in the new dyad, to hear new evidence and logic. This process of forming and reforming dyads can stop when people feel that the discussions are no longer contributing to the shared learning.

Eventually, the larger group reconvenes for sharing and discussion. They should find some common ground about the situation. They might have a common sense of the meaning of weak signals and pockets of the future. They can expand the scope of the discussion, if they wish. The intention is to gain a deepened, enlarged, mutual understanding.

Consider a facilitator. This dyads approach delivers benefits because it leverages the authenticity of one-to-one conversation. However, its pacing requires application of good meeting management principles. Because of this, you should consider an external facilitator to help keep the group focused and efficient.

As you may recall from Chapter 2 and elsewhere, this book does not advocate for aspirational statements of vision. Beware of facilitators who have been indoctrinated in mediocre strategy concepts such as writing mission and vision statements and brainstorming goals.

Also, be skeptical of promises to make the meeting fun or high energy. Quality strategy requires deep thinking about serious matters and often confronts the team with difficult and painful decisions. People's feelings may get hurt and emotions may run high. Strategy is inherently ambiguous and a source of discomfort. As I discuss in the next chapter, leadership is the willingness to experience discomfort in the service of others.

Glossary. A glossary is an excellent tool and is especially useful for helping to resolve ambiguity. Appendix E lists the terms that I provide to clients (in the form of a handout) to help them craft strategy.

In early chapters I made the point that the adjective *strategic* is often a synonym for the word *important*. The word *strategic* ought to connect to strategy and not be a tool of rhetoric. The one exception that I make is to clarify strategic decisions from tactical decisions.

I also remind you that you want to craft a strategy that's good, powerful, clever, effective, and brilliant and not one that's bad, weak, stupid, ineffective, and dull. Although each of these descriptors is subjective, sharing your criteria for them can enhance your dialogue.

Using conversation to connect strategic and tactical decisions. There are two tensions that must be balanced in order to make decisions. The first is between individuals and groups. Sometimes it's better for individuals to make decisions and sometimes it's better to involve others. The second tension is between centralization and decentralization. Sometimes it's better to coordinate decisions from the center.

Effective decisions lead to good implementation of strategy.

Sometimes it's better to allow people who are close to the issues make the decisions.

The goal of any decision maker or decision-making group should be to make choices that are appropriate for the specifics of the situation. I have found value in (and have taught many people) Barry Johnson's five types of decisions. I first describe them and then explain their application to strategic and tactical decisions:

- **Type 1 decision** – The boss (individual) decides and tells others. Autocrats who have formal organizational power can be effective with Type 1 decisions, but those decisions may reflect her inaccurate, narrow-framed diagnosis of the situation or her personal preferences. A Type 1 decision has the advantage of being fast and efficient. However, managers who don't like the decision often act passive-aggressively and undermine the decision.

  A decision maker often finds herself reflecting, before making the decision:
  - Who is with me?
  - Should I go it alone?
  - Have I considered all the relevant perspectives?

- **Type 2 decision** – After discussion with others, the boss (individual) decides and announces the decision. This type of decision allows for the input of stakeholders, enabling a fuller consideration of relevant information. When people feel that they have contributed to a strategy, they're more likely to align themselves with it.

- **Type 3 decision** – In a joint discussion, all members of the team make a consensus decision, based on this definition: "Consensus is the unanimous agreement of a group to support the implementation of a decision regardless of whether individual members of the group agree with the decision." The major benefit of consensus is that it creates a firm, collective commitment to support a single course of action.

  The word *consensus* is often misunderstood to mean "majority rules" or "there's no objection." There are two necessary conditions for consensus. First, group membership is explicit, and decision participation is restricted to members. Second, the group needs to agree to a reliable visible signal to indicate agreement (I like thumbs up to signal agreement to support the implementation of the decision).

  A consensus decision will have the fullest support from a group of people because participation in decisions increases the sense of ownership during implementation. However, a downside is that individuals who are opposed to the more extreme elements of the strategy will search for compromises. Because of politicking, a powerful strategy can be suboptimized and lose much of its focus.

- **Type 4 decision** – After discussion (with input from the boss), team members decide and inform the boss. When an organization defers a strategic decision to an outside expert, they are making a Type 4 decision.

- **Type 5 decision** – Team members make their own choices and inform the boss. Some highly decentralized organizations allow each manager to make decisions in her own zone of interests. There is coordination only insofar as each team member agrees to cooperate with others.

Strategy often involves making tough choices about what to do and what not to do, and it benefits from the use of centralized, formal, organizational power. Recall from Chapter 8 that strategic decisions are standalone and centralized. It's probably better for one well-informed person to establish the direction. I recommend Type 2 as your default for making strategic decisions, where a designated authority makes a final decision, with the input of others.

Type 2 is appropriate because strategy is inherently ambiguous, and there are many power bases, many issues, and many opinions. Dialogue and deliberation are needed to make sense of these factors.

There are circumstances where Type 1 is more appropriate for a strategic decision. Perhaps there's a crisis, where any direction provides a way out of the chaos. Perhaps it's a big bet or a matter of principle. Lou Gerstner's decision to keep IBM together is an example of a Type 1 decision, whereas his decision to elevate the services strategy was a Type 2 decision because he considered others' points of view.

People find the Type 3 decision attractive because it signifies broad support for the decision. Type 3 decisions are appropriate for both strategic and tactical decisions. Earlier I mentioned the drawbacks and emphasized that it takes time to develop consensus.

A tactical decision is one that is decentralized and adapts to the relatively more strategic decision. This means that front line people design and implement the tactical decision using their context-specific knowledge of the local environment. Often, the front-line manager must subordinate her local interests to advance the overall interests and success of the entire enterprise.

Types 4 and 5 are most appropriate for tactical decisions involved with programming the strategic decisions into projects. A Type 4 decision implies that the front-line manager seeks information and advice before making a tactical decision. She might ask for help in interpreting a policy. Or she might confirm her interpretation of the strategic decision before she makes a painful decision about discontinuing an operation.

A Type 5 decision is made when there is no need to clarify the strategy.

A conversation about strategy can't, and shouldn't, go on and on and on. Nor should a decision always default to the boss. I recommend that the organization decide which of the five types they want to use *before* they start discussions.

Organizational Development

Communication skills continue to be a top need and priority for organizations. This is especially true when considering the collaboration needed to craft strategy and convey it so that tactical decisions can be made. Expect to find synergy as you integrate strategic thinking competency and skills into talent and leadership development programs. Also, because there are many weak signals in the environment, the organization needs to integrate scanning and sensemaking technologies into its operations.

In the next chapter I explain leadership as a specialized tool, just as strategic thinking is a specialized tool. Both practices require courage, authenticity (a leader and a strategist strive to be their own person), and integrity (acting in accordance with the truth as they understand it). Both grow out of one's perspective, which results from one's uniqueness, unconventionality, and personal values. Leadership enhances your strategic thinking competency.

CHAPTER 13

Being an *Extra*-ordinary Leader

Helping Others Live into the Future

*We are called upon to do something new, to confront
a no man's land, to push into a forest where there
are no well-worn paths and from which no one
has returned to guide us. . . . To live into the future
means to leap into the unknown, and this requires
a degree of courage for which there is no immediate
precedent and which few people realize.*

— Rollo May

LEADERSHIP AND STRATEGY each consume considerable space on the executive bookshelf. A strategic thinker who chooses not to practice leadership is functioning as an analyst. A leader who doesn't think strategically is merely a cheerleader for operational efficiency.

If strategic thinking is a personal competency, so is leadership. My discussion in this chapter describes the "small L" capability of personal leadership rather than "capital L" leadership from the top echelon of the organization.

> *A leader who does not think strategically is merely a cheerleader for operational efficiency.*

Here is my elevator-speech definition:

> Leadership is a choice to grapple with the multi-faceted nature of reality and the courage to help other people do the same.

I find it helpful to define a *leadership zone* that is distinct from non-leadership. A person chooses to enter and exit the leadership zone guided by her assessment of the specifics of the situation. I believe that the most compelling reason for entering the leadership zone is altruism: the desire to be of service to others. (Other reasons for entering the leadership zone include noticing an absence of leadership by others, the desire for power, a loyalty to truth, or a loyalty to an institution.)

Sacrifice and the Willingness to Tolerate Discomfort

The leadership zone is accessible to anyone, yet many people choose to not enter it because the zone includes discomfort.

The practice of leadership is much like the practice of strategic thinking. Both strategic thinking and leadership involve activities that require effort: reflecting deeply on self and situation, recognizing nuance, recognizing the legitimacy of people's emotions, and challenging the status quo, to name just a few. Both involve speaking and behaving in unconventional ways.

Personal leadership bears many similarities to the heroic-quest narrative in that both involve an individual who chooses to leave an ordinary and comfortable world to enter a special world, where she is tested with difficult choices. The hero is a person who serves and sacrifices on behalf of a greater good.

People find it easier to remain in comfort. Accordingly, they deny the data, procrastinate, default to the process paradigm, or resort to using the formal authority of their position. The practice of non-leadership is often easier than personally engaging and influencing others.

Influencing

When in the leadership zone, the leader uses influencing behaviors such as persuasion, not to manipulate or coerce but rather to encourage others to make decisions that are in their best long-term interests. Words are immensely powerful, and skillful use of rhetoric enables people to better define and pursue their interests.

Leaders help others make choices for themselves. I find the BALD framework useful for recognizing motivational forces:

- **Bond** – People want to have personal, authentic, trusting relationships with others. These bonds between people are instrumental for defining a brand (or identity) for the organization. Similarly, the organizational brand helps to define and strengthen the bonds between people.

  One leadership task is in helping people expand their scope of conversations with others, both internally and externally.

  Similarly, the leader helps deepen relationships. This results in increased trust, which becomes an asset for the sharing of information, sensemaking, collaboration, resilience, and innovation.

- **Acquire** – People aspire to wealth, status, prestige, power, and experiences. Organizations allow people to acquire greater benefits than the individual can acquire by herself. Good strategy is a tool for focusing and leveraging people's desires toward advancing the organization's interests.

- **Learn** – People want to grow in their knowledge and capabilities. I like to say that an organization *learns its way* into strategy. The activity starts in the fuzzy front end of strategy and proceeds through the structured back end and into programming. Each step of the way adds to the base of individual and collective knowledge.

- **Defend** – People are loss avoiders and will often go to disproportionate ends to avoid losses, even if the potential for gains is great.

  In defending against loss, I advise people to balance messages about pain and gain. Generally, it's better to keep the conversations directed toward the audience's benefits. However, sometimes those messages don't have enough punch to change behavior. That's when it's useful to introduce the potential for pain: "If we don't take this action, we increase our vulnerability to disruption and the loss of our advantaged position."

Often people are reflexively defensive, sourced deep in the psyche by scars from trauma from childhood events, crime, bullying, and substance abuse. Top managers are not immune from this. It's probably best to assume that someone in the group is feeling pain and shame. Her defensive routines include ambiguity avoidance and perfectionism. She is closed to new ways of thinking.

Strategy work can be very frustrating, and the microskill of empathy is helpful in fostering good working relationships.

Multi-faceted Reality

As you know from experience, people hold different sets of facts, interpret facts differently, and hold different beliefs.

Reality has many facets. The real world is messy, and it is an idealistic notion that only one definition of truth can prevail. Yet for the purposes of crafting good strategy, we must try.

The microskills of strategic thinking mostly encourage you to seek and appreciate constructs and ontologies: be pragmatic, be sharp, be open-minded, and understand the stories that others are telling themselves. Be prepared to have your truth challenged and be prepared to challenge others, especially the orthodoxies.

Five Tips for Speaking Truth to Power

Leadership involves exposing people to new facets of reality and sometimes the facts are presented bluntly. Unsurprisingly, hearing the words "you're wrong" provokes a defensive reaction.

Speaking truth to power can be dangerous, and many people have experienced the truth of the cliché *shooting the messenger*. Those in power can and do retaliate with anger when they're surprised or embarrassed or contradicted.

- **Tip #1 – Express your respect.** The obvious advice for presenting inconvenient truths is to express your respect for the person, their perspective, and their accomplishments. A leader respects civility and reveres candor. Be courteous and cordial. *And* tell the truth.

  A leader need not set aside civility, courtesy, or politeness when discussing strategy. Most people (at least when rested and calm) want to know the facts of the situation. They want communications that are candid, clear, and plain.

- **Tip #2 – Ask permission to share.** Because people like to feel in control, ask permission to share your perspective. "I've formed an opinion. Would you be interested in hearing it?"

- **Tip #3 – Unpack adjectives.** Recall from Chapter 2 that I suggested that adjectives can help you uncover useful nuance. Rather than saying, "You are stating goals and not strategy," ask, "Do you think your strategy is good (or effective, powerful, clever, nuanced)?" Approach the answer with curiosity, intending to learn more rather than score points by declaring the other person's weakness.

  > *Civility is respect for the person and the institution. Candor is an honest appraisal of the situation.*

- **Tip #4 – Ask about assumptions.** People's plans and mental models are based upon assumptions. Those assumptions are frequently biased observations and speculations. When it is your turn to talk, you may be able to advocate for better assumptions.

- **Tip #5 – Being kind is essential, being nice is optional.** This last tip is probably more of an insight and principle than a tip, yet it may help you approach powerful people more effectively. The insight is this:

  > Leadership is a practice of kindness, but it's not always a practice of niceness.

Kindness is helping others by showing that you care about their well-being. Niceness is the practice of courtesy and politeness. A nice person tells others what the others want to hear. A person can be nice, but simultaneously unkind when she withholds uncomfortable truths or fails to share critical information.

The Microskill of Courage

Courage is the last of the twenty microskills described in this book.

Courage is distinct from bravery. A firefighter who rushes into a burning building is brave because she's been trained to step into danger. People are taught to be brave, and that often involves compliance and cohesion to a group norm. Bravery is the setting aside of fear.

Centuries ago, people used the word *bravery* to signify goodness. Being called a brave person was a compliment not unlike complimenting a person for wearing fine clothing. Also, in past centuries, the word *courage* meant "what is in a person's thoughts." Bravery is part of a person's physical life, and courage is part of a person's mental life. The opposite of bravery is cowardice, the opposite of courage is conformity.

Courage is acting despite anxieties. There are three tasks for increasing one's capacity for courage, and thus leadership. The first task is to recognize the presence of anxieties and understand their source, probabilities, and impact. Humans evolved in a dangerous world, and the careful ones survived to pass on their danger-alertness genes. Our modern world is characterized by more stimuli, and many people have a disorder called anxiety that is related to their hyper-alertness to threats.

In Chapter 11 I declared that anxiety is a signal of a restless, overactive mind. Calming techniques such as meditation, exercise, and walking in nature are well established and recommended habits for the strategic thinker.

The second task is a choice to act or to be passive. If you choose to act, you do so with knowledge that courage is the acceptance of anxiety. If you choose not to act, is that due to torpor or some other kind of distracting mind energy?

The discussion of perspective in Chapter 10 provides some tips for examining the choices in front of you. As you develop a confidence in your perspective, you become more willing to make unorthodox and non-conformist choices.

> *The opposite of bravery is cowardice.*
> *The opposite of courage is conformity.*

The third task is your commitment of physical and emotional resources. I encourage your review of Chapter 6's discussion of set-based design and abductive reasoning. You can make strategic decisions and commitments, yet still retain agility.

Separation anxiety. Many important decisions are done to avoid conflict because decision makers are affected by a fear of loss of peer connection. Many people withhold the truth because they value their group membership and feel anxiety at the possibility of ostracism or falling out of favor.

Jerry B. Harvey suggests four useful questions to ask yourself:

- What action would I like to take?

- What keeps me from taking such action?

- What support do I need from others in order to take sensible and moral action?

- What action do I plan to take?

Leadership is an authentic display of perspective and integrity. The sunflower bias occurs when people look to the organization's top management for direction, rather than staking out their own perspective.

A well-developed perspective originates from clarifying one's deeper personal values. Consider this question: When faced with a challenge, are my words and actions motivated by complying with others' expectations of me? Or are they originating from someplace deeper: what I believe to be fundamentally true and right?

Integrity is the alignment of a person's thoughts with her words and actions. It flows out of her well-reasoned perspective and ethical reasoning. Consider, as examples, individuals such as Mohandas Gandhi or Martin Luther King Jr. who concluded that some laws are unjust and ought to be disobeyed. Each reflected deeply on the interests of others and with justice as a high principle. Their desire to serve others and desire for justice compelled them to act with courage.

Willing to stand apart from norms. Leaders are willing to pay attention to that which is unconventional, unorthodox, and unfamiliar. Consequently, others might regard the leader's words and actions as unorthodox, nonconformist, odd, abnormal, unproductive, and possibly traitorous.

How would you feel if someone used those words about you?

Extra-ordinary Leadership

Especially for strategic thinking, organizations need extra-ordinary leadership. I add the hyphen to emphasize that this practice of leadership is *extra to ordinary* and not a gratuitous superlative. More specifically, it exceeds what one would expect from leaders in an operational environment. This statement nicely elaborates a key idea:

> Ordinary leadership involves "perfecting the known," whereas the chief task of extra-ordinary leadership is "imperfectly seizing the unknown."

To imperfectly seize the unknown, the extra-ordinary leader must explore beyond the edges of the known, familiar, and conventional. The idea of imperfectly seizing the unknown reflects the X-factors of chance and emergence and implies the value of probing, experimenting, and tolerating failures.

Improvisational jazz music offers a useful analogy. Often, when a jazz musician hears a "wrong" note (it's musically in the wrong context), it becomes an opportunity to shift the performance into a different modality. The musician learns to grapple and grok with the unexpected and transform the music into a new, different, and often much better composition. Strategic thinking is similar in that both involve the artistry of coping with the unexpected.

Ordinary leadership is leadership on the operational thinking map. Ordinary leaders serve others by harmonizing work activities and inspiring people to give effort to their assigned work. Ordinary leaders rely on common tools such as goal setting, optimization, simple principles, incremental improvement, classification into categories, visioning, and planning. Ordinary leaders assume that everything that needs to be known is already known, or at least can be discovered by consulting a knowledgeable reference.

Extra-ordinary leadership is "imperfectly seizing the unknown."

An ordinary leader is typically satisfied with incremental improvements. She might find proposals for bold leaps of improvement to be risky, impractical, or irrelevant.

DICE to the extreme. An extra-ordinary leader pushes beyond the ordinary. The four X-factors of strategic thinking (drive, insight, chance, emergence) are natural areas for emphasis, taking leaders well beyond the ordinary.

The first X-factor, drive, means ambition both for yourself and for others. A leader's drive to distinguish herself and gain rewards is one component. Too, her ambition might be to help others achieve success.

Insight, the secret sauce of strategy, is the second X-factor. In the quest to "imperfectly seize the unknown," the leader needs to push for insights, knowing that they might be tentative and merely a starting point for creating new strategic logics. Extra-ordinary leadership for strategy should include more-than-usual effort in searching for weak signals and practicing reframing.

The third X-factor is chance. Extra-ordinary leaders recognize and embrace risk, knowing that an event can be a threat or an opportunity. Once a strategic decision is made, an extra-ordinary leader works to improve the probability of success and reduce the probability of failure. This risk management can include developing better models, expanding the number of potential events considered, and improving the estimation of probabilities and impacts.

The X-factor of emergence implies a search for pockets of the future, recognizing that they can become prevalent and stimulate a new system. Just as with the X-factor of chance, using more probes and experiments provides early and quality information. It allows the organization to respond with agility.

Living into the Future

Watch people's body language in your next meeting. It's likely that you'll see many people leaning back in their chairs, showing through their body language that they're disengaged.

An extra-ordinary leader doesn't lean back from strategy, she leans into it, as implied by the title of Facebook COO Sheryl Sandberg's famous book, *Lean In*. When a person *leans in*, she engages with others, confronting both external and self-imposed obstacles.

Let's take that leadership idea further. Consider the Rollo May quote that introduces this chapter. May writes that we *live into* the future. This is not a common phrase in English. A person who *lives into* an idea is committed and is not stymied by obstacles. May suggests the grand gesture of leaping into the unknown.

Don't lean into the future, use your imagination to leap into the future.

I like to imagine the extra-ordinary leader as a trail-blazer rather than a path finder. There isn't a proven path into the future. Rather, the leader has to push into the unknown with courage and an eye for novelty.

Coaching Others

If leadership is fundamentally an act of service, then leaders have responsibilities for teaching, coaching, and mentoring others.

Given that competent strategic thinking is rare and valuable, I encourage you to step into the leadership zone and teach others about the nature, purpose, and scope of strategic thinking. You don't need to sponsor a big training-department initiative, but you could perhaps make it a discussion topic for meetings and grassroots communities of practice.

A useful coaching idea derives from the principle that leaders lead by asking questions. Consider asking *questions in the service of the asked*, which are questions that help protégés discover their own answers. Here's an example: Jeff was an engineer at a high-tech company and was offered a career move to one of two positions. Each position had positive as well as negative aspects, and the pay was equivalent. Jeff felt stuck and called me for advice. I listened and asked this question: "Imagine yourself in each of the new positions: What's the most probable future for you?" The question stimulated an immediate insight for Jeff. He now knew which of the two positions was better for him. A few weeks after he assumed the new job, a corporate reorganization occurred, and Jeff found himself in a very favorable position compared to the alternative.

Helping others realize insights might be one of the most powerful contributions of a leader-as-coach. Jeff was stuck because his story anchors were limited to the present-day scope of each position and its responsibilities. When he added the new anchor of the future, and explored implications, Jeff quickly realized that one position had more potential.

Four microskills can stimulate your ability to ask *questions in the service of the asked*. They are the microskill of empathy, the microskill of high-quality questions, the microskill of abductive reasoning, and the microskill of reframing. Empathy helps to shift your focus toward leadership rather than your comforts. High-quality questions help others to discover their truths. The hypothesis-testing skills of abductive reasoning can stimulate discussions on experiments that reveal and validate beliefs. Questions about narratives, abstractions, partitioning, and projection (NAPP) can reframe understandings and spark insights.

A leader serves others when she helps them develop their microskill of personal resilience. In a *permission culture*, people default to acting only on those things that are explicitly permitted; they take the simpler route of looking upward into the chain of command for answers. Initiative is rare. When personal resilience is desired, a leader might ask:

- How might this experience strengthen my protégé's perspective?
- How might an expert approach this situation?
- Where might insights be found?

Lastly, leading-by-example is one of the strongest of coaching practices. Through actions and conversations, you show your ability to think strategically in your daily work.

Overcoming the "I'm-too-busy" Excuse

Another leader-as-coach idea is to confront, head-on, the common excuse, "I'm too busy to think strategically."

Reframe and redefine what it means to work hard. Many people use an agricultural age definition: hard work is about the hours that you spend at your job. A better framing is needed for the modern era, and Seth Godin has an interesting one:

> Hard work is about risk. It begins when you deal with the things that you'd rather not deal with: fear of failure, fear of standing out, fear of rejection. Hard work is about training yourself to leap over this barrier, tunnel under that barrier, drive through the other barrier. And after you've done that, to do it again the next day.

To work hard is to choose to be courageous.

For extra-ordinary leaders, hard work is doing things that ordinary leaders won't do. They know that their present-day sacrifices are investments.

Increasing purposefulness. Heike Bruch and Sumatra Ghoshal explain that most managers in organizations are distracted (their mental energy is absorbed by the strong signals of day-to-day work) or disengaged (they're exhausted and approach their work halfheartedly) or immobilized by procrastination. They reveal that only about 10 percent of workers work in a purposeful way, defined as having both above-average energy and above-average focus. What might the organization achieve if it could raise the proportion of purposeful people by just a percentage or two?

They propose a two-step approach for increasing purposefulness. The first step is to issue (or recognize) a challenge. The second step is to provide people with the freedom to choose whether to accept or reject it.

Although their approach is a personal development activity, the comparison to organizational strategy is clear: focus on the strategic thinking map and leave the comfort of the operational thinking map, focus on a small set of significant issues that define the core challenge, abandon orthodoxies that no longer make sense for the future context, and make tough policy choices on how to apply the organization's scarce resources.

I challenge you to become a competent strategic thinker and an extra-ordinary leader. The choice is yours.

Discovering the essence. This third idea for people who are too busy draws its inspiration from the artist Vincent Van Gogh, who wrote to his brother, "You really have to understand how I consider art. To reach the essence of it, you have to work long and hard. What I want and what I am aiming for is infernally difficult, and yet I believe I am not aiming too high."

In the spirit of Van Gogh's words, I offer this description of strategic thinking's essence:

> A strategic thinker is willing to work long and hard to develop her unique perspective on the nature, purpose, and scope of her art: strategy. The essence of strategic thinking is a clear-eyed view of the situation, a future orientation, a recognition that resources are finite but creativity isn't, a willingness to focus on significant issues, a striving toward discovering insight, a willingness to be tested, a willingness to learn, a desire to serve, and the courage to be different from the conventional.

Ambiguity and Leadership

I launched Chapter 1 with the assertion that ambiguity is an essential but overlooked factor of strategy. Since leadership is a complement to strategic thinking, it's appropriate to examine ambiguity and the tasks of leadership in this final chapter.

The concept of ambiguity isn't on the radar of the mainstream thinkers in leadership. Perhaps, in ordinary environments, one need only support the organization's processes. After all, a strength of process is that it eliminates ambiguity and creates predictability.

Because ambiguity is a source of discomfort, one could argue that it's a natural leadership act to reduce the pain. However, an extraordinary leader might consider ambiguity as an opportunity to explore weak signals or as a mechanism for building personal resilience.

There are at least six leadership practices for managing ambiguity:

- **Unpack ambiguity.** One leadership option is to unpack the ambiguity to identify the sensible alternative stories. In Christopher Columbus's time, a sensible story, the most common-sense story, located Asia to the east of Europe (an idea that lingers in modern language, as the term *orient* comes from the Old French word for east). The alternative story of Asia located to the west was also a sensible story.

  Ambiguity is relevant to leadership as well as strategy.

- **Absorb ambiguity.** Lou Gerstner absorbed ambiguity with his strategic decision to keep IBM together, which eliminated some of the discomfort of people who were paralyzed by the chaos.

- **Reframe ambiguity.** Gerstner managed ambiguity by reframing. In his first months, with the IBM workforce filled with anxiety about the company's future, he strengthened the story anchors on the importance of executing the basic tasks of serving the customer. He weakened the anchors associated with rumination and worry. Later, he reframed ambiguity to create new dominant growth ideas and strategic logic for services and e-business.

- **Eliminate ambiguity.** You can eliminate ambiguity by defining words and acronyms that others might misconstrue. Strive for plain tellings of stories and avoid presentations filled with pretentious words and complicated graphics.

- **Exploit ambiguity.** Another option for ambiguity is to incorporate it into the strategy. For example, Billy Beane used ambiguity to disguise his intentions and to encourage his competitors to retain their mediocre existing stories. By exploiting ambiguity, he was better able to deal for the talent he wanted.

- **Tolerate ambiguity.** A last leadership option for ambiguity is to tolerate it. Leaders must be patient and encourage others to be patient. Fight the habitual urge for impulsive action. Although it seems uncomfortable, leadership sometimes means sitting quietly, in the mess, sensing and sensemaking for the underlying structure.

Be Extra-ordinary, Be Humble, and Good Luck

It's customary to wish others good luck on their journey. The expression is a hope for the favor of opportunity and the avoidance of bad luck. Chance is inherent to strategy, and it's pertinent to your leadership style.

One significant benefit of acknowledging chance is that you realize that there are things bigger than your ego and willpower. Your leadership capacity is enhanced when you embrace humility rather than entitlement, hubris, narcissism, arrogance, and grandiosity. Research shows that humility is linked with better job performance, academic performance, and leadership excellence. Humble CEOs are valued, but hard to find.

This question is an interesting conversation starter: *Have you been lucky in your life?* You'll find that many people have given that question little thought, but they only need a few moments of reflection to arrive at a list of the many ways that good luck has favored them: the fortune of birth by their parents, the kindness of schoolteachers, the timing of an early interest in some emerging technology or art that didn't become widely prevalent until years later. Or in the inspiration and instruction found in a good book.

Humble executives are valued but hard to find.

Although an individual's efforts and talents are essential, those efforts are but one small part of the story. A helping hand may make a significant difference in someone's success. Lou Gerstner was able to afford college because he got a scholarship. Billy Beane was handed a book on sabermetrics by his boss.

A gratitude mindset is an interesting marker of extra-ordinary leadership. Gratitude promotes resilience, an appreciation of opportunity, and stronger relations with others. When you feel gratitude for your good fortune, you have a greater desire to be generous to others. This gratitude-to-generosity logic fosters extra-ordinary leadership: the leader serves other persons by helping them to be in a ready position to capture emerging opportunity.

It's with gratitude that I offer these last words. Thank you. I am honored and gratified that you chose to invest your valuable time to consider this book's ideas.

◆ ◆ ◆

The appendices provide more information and tools that can help you become a competent strategic thinker. They include more detailed description of VUCA, a statement of a strategic thinking manifesto, a listing of landmarks on the strategic thinking map, a glossary, a brief description of the 20 microskills of strategic thinking, and a short discussion of personal branding as a competent strategic thinker.

Volatility, Uncertainty, Complexity, and Ambiguity (VUCA)

THE PHRASE *fog of war* originated in the 19th century to characterize rapidly changing and sometimes-chaotic environments. More recently, the acronym *VUCA* has become popular in military and non-military organizations.

Interestingly, the VUCA concept itself is fraught with ambiguity because users of the acronym seldom define the specific meanings of each of the four elements. Nor, do they explain how each affects the crafting of strategy. I've found it best to present each VUCA element from the most straightforward to the least: volatility, uncertainty, ambiguity, and finally complex systems.

Volatility. In physical chemistry, gasoline changes from liquid to gas (it boils) at a lower temperature than water. Gasoline is more volatile than water. The fact that gasoline is volatile is a good thing if you want to use your automobile to drive across the country, but a bad thing if you spill gasoline in a confined space.

In financial markets, volatility refers to rapid changes in trends. As an example, consider a high-tech stock that might rise in price 8 percent on Day 1, drop 15 percent on Day 2, and rise 10 percent on Day 3. For contrast, an electrical utility stock might rise 0.25 percent on Day 1, rise 0.1 percent on Day 2, and fall 0.15 percent on Day 3. The high-tech stock would be considered the more volatile and risky stock.

Generally, volatility is desirable if you're seeking emergent opportunities (growth) or you're in a relatively weak strategic position. Volatility allows the strategist to take a strategic position at low cost, assuming the risk that the option may become worthless, but also increasing the upside potential.

Generally, volatility is good if you're seeking opportunities and bad if you're seeking predictability.

On the other hand, volatility is undesirable if you require predictability. Some investors prefer the less volatile utility stock. Incumbent organizations are risk averse, so for them volatility implies unpredictability.

Uncertainty. The dictionary tells us that *uncertainty* is a broad term about unknowns and is the opposite of certainty.

I find it better to use a narrower definition of *uncertainty*, as an unknown that can be revealed with an explicit answer, such as the following:

Q: What is the probability that it will rain today?

A: The weather service reports a 50 percent probability.

Uncertainty is associated with building predictive models and optimizing them. The better the characterization of uncertainty, the more accurate the prediction. Besides weather forecasting, you can find examples in insurance, medicine, finance, the military, and engineering.

Uncertainty is the focal point of classic risk management because it's concerned with specific events, the probability of those events occurring, and the impact of those events if they do occur.

Ambiguity. Ambiguous language is language that can be interpreted differently or holds different meanings depending on the context.

Ambiguity is inherent to strategy in that people can interpret differently the meaning and implications of weak signals. Of the four VUCA elements, ambiguity probably causes the most frustration for strategy.

These questions can help you with sensemaking in ambiguous situations:

- What is the crux of the matter?

- Are we asking the right questions?

- Would someone with a different background define this problem differently?

- What could happen if someone misinterpreted the situation's context?

- What mistakes could be made by me or others?

Complexity and complex systems. The layperson uses the word *complexity* to describe a situation where there are many elements that seem relevant, with unclear cause-and-effect relationships between the elements. *Complexity* is a general term that implies that a person is overwhelmed with information.

It's useful to instead distinguish complicated systems as separate from complex systems. I encourage you to investigate David Snowden's sensemaking model, which he calls the Cynefin framework.

A complicated system is one where an expert, using analysis, can understand causes and effects. An example of a complicated system and task is to disassemble and then reassemble an automobile. A knowledgeable mechanic (an expert) could perform the task but a layperson could not. Another example would be open-heart surgery.

Some environments for strategy issues involve complicated systems, such as a highly constrained industry where there is a very bounded domain, for example one in which there's an extensive and intrusive set of government policies and regulations. The solution used in a complicated system very much depends upon the expert's personal preferences.

The preeminent characteristic of a complex system is emergence, where the causes of a presently observed effect can only be seen in retrospect. Examples of complex systems are battlefields, markets, ecosystems, and organizational cultures. No one expert can have the answer, so the preferred approach to respond to complex systems is to assemble a panel of experts and encourage them to collaborate, with the expectation that some novel idea or practice will provide the solution.

An essential activity of strategy in complex systems is the use of probes, which are efforts designed to capture information from the external environment. An early-stage venture investment is an example of a probe.

Microskills of Strategic Thinking

THIS LISTING PROVIDES GENERAL DESCRIPTIONS of the 20 microskills covered in this book. (The reader can find more detail about each microskill in the designated chapters.)

Abductive reasoning – The practice of inferring possible causes or consequences of an observation, similar to educated guessing. Abductive reasoning yields hypotheses that can be tested with evidence. (Chapter 6)

Ambition – Motivation to make an impact for oneself or for others. Desire to express oneself, to achieve, to pursue excellence. (Chapter 4)

Analogous reasoning – Imagining the similarities and dissimilarities in objects, events, and ideas. A tool for characterizing relationships and expanding creativity. (Chapter 4)

Anticipation –The recognition and use of anticipatory assumptions, which is the way that we contemplate the future in the present moment. The three general approaches to anticipation are planning, preparation, and discovery. (Chapter 7)

Conceptual mapping – The making and using of maps that explain the relationships of concepts. A map is helpful for orientation and for navigation. (Chapter 4)

Contrarianism – Choosing actions that are opposite the majority's choices or conventional thought. (Chapter 5)

Courage – A choice to act despite one's anxieties. It is a manifestation of one's integrity and perspective. The opposite of courage is conformity. (Chapter 13)

Curiosity – An individual's thirst for knowledge about people, about how things work, and about the implications of weak signals. A choice to be in learning mode. (Chapter 4)

Devalorization – Using imagination to take away value and worthiness from an otherwise venerated idea. Willingness to make the profane sacred and make the sacred profane. (Chapter 5)

Empathy – The ability to discern the mental state of others: their emotions, their logic, their intentions. (Chapter 4)

High-quality questions – Strategic thinkers ask more and better questions. This microskill is the ability to formulate and ask questions that uncover nuanced and deeper truths. (Chapter 6)

Meta-cognition – Awareness of your own knowledge, skills, and thoughts; awareness of cognitive bias. Includes the ability to regulate your thinking, feelings, and behavior toward your preferences. (Chapter 11)

Open mental stance – A mental attitude that is receptive to novelty and recognizes that others have differing points of view. A tool of broad framing. (Chapter 4)

Personal resilience – The ability of the individual to bounce back from adversity or bounce forward into the future. *Grit* is a synonym. Displayed in a person's willingness to be inventive and innovative. (Chapter 4)

Pragmatism – A person who is guided by pragmatism desires to solve problems by applying an understanding of how the world works. (Chapter 4)

Reflection – This microskill is sharpness applied to one's own experiences, values, and preferences. It's an essential part of learning. (Chapter 4)

Reframing – Uses the imagination to synthesize new frames by deleting, strengthening, or weakening anchors. Four lenses for reframing are narrative, abstraction, projection, and partitioning (NAPP). Reframing increases the probability that you'll generate insights. (Chapter 9)

Sharpness – A person's attentiveness to and sensemaking of nuance. It implies that the person is open minded, but also skeptical, about the importance of a weak signal. A strategic thinker has a sharp mind in touch with the situation. (Chapter 4)

Skepticism – This microskill helps individuals to avoid belief in the faulty claims of others and to pursue truth. (Chapter 4)

Storytelling – An important microskill related to leadership, insights, and culture. The strategy of an organization follows a narrative arc that involves characters, situations, tensions, and resolution. (Chapter 4)

Manifesto for Strategic Thinking

A MANIFESTO IS a person's or group's public expression of intentions, motives, and reasoning. A recent example is the Agile Manifesto published by a group of software developers who were seeking better ways for developing software. The Agile Manifesto is a bland statement of values: for example, "we value working software over documentation."

I believe that radical manifestos are more-interesting and more-useful tools. Two well-known examples of radical manifestos are the U.S. Declaration of Independence and Martin Luther King Jr.'s "Letter from a Birmingham Jail." These manifestos are radical in the sense that they reject the values of powerful and elite groups. In this book I've identified the dominance of operational thinking in the culture and stated that it crowds aside progress in strategic thinking. I've also described the microskill of devalorization as a technique for challenging the status quo and described the use of colonial thinking as an imposition of values by one culture upon another.

A radical manifesto has three elements. The first is a description of the current state. The second is a pronouncement that the status quo is unacceptable. The third is a call to action for reforming incumbent institutions or creating new ones.

Here is my Strategic Thinking Manifesto:

> Many organizations tolerate mediocre concepts of strategy and strategic thinking. When these mediocre concepts guide decisions and actions, it puts at risk the organization's relevance and future prosperity.
>
> Competent strategic thinking is an essential driver of a better future for organizations and for their communities. This strategic thinking originates with sharp-minded individuals who pay attention to the weak signals of their situation, confront the challenges, and develop novel and better logics for using their scarce resources.

Tzara's Formula for Radical Manifestos

In 1918, Dada artist Tristan Tzara provided a formula for writing a manifesto: You have to want ABC and fulminate against 123. The formula is straightforward: List three things that you want and three things that bother you.

The first paragraph of the above manifesto is the 123. It's a complaint about things that are bothersome and annoying, even outrageous. The more specific the description of the source and effects of the irritation the better. If you can find it outrageous it enhances your point of view. For the above, I judged as most bothersome the presence of mediocrity in strategy and strategic thinking.

The second paragraph describes the things desired and corresponds to the ABC of Tzara's formula, the things desired.

Landmarks on the Map of Strategic Thinking

THE FOLLOWING LIST of strategic thinking landmarks are useful in developing a more-personalized understanding of strategic thinking. I suggest that you copy each landmark onto a sticky note and arrange them on your own conceptual map.

You will find the microskill of conceptual mapping helpful, particularly the discussion of navigational beacons, orientation cues, associative cues, and boundaries (Chapter 4). Further, you might find the discussion of bridges helpful (Chapter 5). Imagine specific instances of them from your own experience, as described in the discussion of meaningful learning (Preface). Some of these landmarks also appear in Appendix E.

Anticipatory assumptions – Those assumptions that describe or inform beliefs about the future.

Chance – Luck is always a factor in success and failure. Chance is one of the X-factors of strategic thinking.

Coordination – The effort to adjust work and resource configuration to reach a goal.

Core challenge – The focal point for strategy, an answer to the question, What is the biggest problem this organization faces that it can do something about?

Creative thinking – Imagining novel ideas or combinations of ideas. It has similarities to strategic thinking in expanding the boundaries of inquiry and the willingness to break from traditions and orthodoxy.

Critical thinking – Use of evidence and reason in order to discover objective truth. It has similarities to strategic thinking in its quest to describe reality.

Design – Strategy is concerned with the fit of an organization's strategic resources and the external environment. There are many similarities between design thinking and strategic thinking.

Discontinuity, disruption – A discontinuity is an unexpected change in a pattern. Discontinuities are typically weak signals that are not readily apparent. A discontinuity can lead to disruption, which is a misfit of resource configuration with the external environment.

Dominating ideas – A set of ideas that anchors people's memories and intentions. They are more easily seen in comparing the past to the present. In imagining the future, we can expect a new and evolving set of dominating ideas, even if we can't predict them. Those ideas both describe the situation and express our normative expectations of what the future should become.

Drive – Individuals with high levels of drive have high amounts of energy and ambition. Drive is one of the X-factors of strategic thinking.

Emergence – In complex systems, novel elements emerge and change the direction and velocity of the system. Emergence is one of the X-factors of strategic thinking.

Endowment – Strategic resources that have been accumulated by an organization. Endowments from strategy are often "spent down" by laxity and inattention to the situation, rather than being reinvested into new strategy.

Ethical reasoning – A cognitive process involving principles and logics for determining what is right and wrong in a specific context. Ethical codes are narrowly bounded rules and are found on the operational thinking map.

Evolvement – The change and improvement of strategy from an initial insight.

Future – The time beyond the present. The three horizons of the future are the immediate future (Horizon 1 or H1), a qualitatively different distant future (Horizon 3 or H3), and a zone of transition (Horizon 2 or H2). Another useful concept for describing the future is Joseph Voris's future cone, which has six future descriptors: the projected future, the probable future, the potential future, the possible future, the preposterous future, and the preferred future. Pillar IV of the definition of strategic thinking is "success in the future." Futures literacy is one of the three literacies of strategic thinking.

Insights – An insight is the realization of a better story. The use of the microskill of reframing can increase the probability of having an insight. Insight is one of the X-factors of strategic thinking.

Issues – Problems to solve or opportunities to capture.

Leadership – Choices by individuals to serve others by using influencing skills. Like the map of operational thinking and the map of strategic thinking, the conceptual map of leadership contains significant landmarks such as the leadership zone, the comfort zone, integrity, influencing, reality, and service to others.

Interesting things – Patterns, anomalies, curiosities that are salient in some way. Interesting things are often weak signals.

Interests – Examples of organizational interests are things like social justice and environmentalism. One way to identify interests is to identify organizational stakeholders and then identify their expectations of the organization.

Judgment literacy – This involves awareness of limits of perception and decision making, including cognitive bias, fallacies, illusions, neglects. One of the three literacies of strategic thinking.

Metrics – The measurements that are relevant to a group and their context. On the strategic thinking map, we search for leading indicators of future performance.

Novelty – New things that are interesting. A characteristic of strategy formulated for new, emergent situations.

Legacy – A concern with those artifacts, resources, values, and capabilities provided by an earlier generation to a later generation.

Nuance – Awareness of distinctions between otherwise similar concepts.

Obstacles – Concepts that constrain commitments, actions, and thinking. Flexibility is increased by relaxing constraints and eliminating obstacles.

Perspective – Personality plus point of view.

Probes – Tools for gaining early information in complex systems. They could be experiments, questions, prototypes, or ventures.

Projects – Temporary, unique, work endeavors. Many projects are operational and support optimizing the existing business model. Some projects (and programs of projects) are strategic in that their purpose is to adjust the organization's resources so as to better fit with the external environment.

Power – Power enables the organization to make progress on its core challenge. The source of the power is in the arrangement of an organization's resources.

Restructuring – A significant reconfiguration of the organization's resources, including mergers, acquisitions, divestitures, and strategic alliances.

Resilience – System resilience is the capacity, within the system, for reemergence in a new form after experiencing chaos. Personal resilience, or grit, is the ability to overcome adversity and anxiety.

Obstacles – Conditions that impede someone's intentions. In set-based design, obstacles help to define the boundaries of the solution space.

Scale – The ability to gain efficiencies in organizational processes and resources, or possession of advantage by having gained scale through some prior strategy.

Strategic fit – The fit of the organization's configuration of resources with the external environment.

Strategic resources – Long-lasting organizational competencies and assets that provide power.

Strategy – A specialized tool for advancing the organization's interests by managing issues that have broad and long-term impact. Literacy with strategy is one of the three literacies of strategic thinking.

Systems thinking – Use of cognition to model relationships between stocks and flows. It is similar to strategic thinking in the use of models to understand behaviors and the impact of managerial policies.

Weak signals – Objects or activities that are not widely perceived. Curiosities, anomalies, and coincidences are examples. Weak signals become strong signals when they become more prevalent, more salient, or are otherwise assigned importance during sensemaking. Also, see entries for discontinuities, interesting things, and novelty.

Useful Terms

I PROVIDE THESE DEFINITIONS to help groups apply a common language. This is not a comprehensive glossary.

Back casting – A planning technique that first identifies a future state and then applies imagination to describe the sequence of intermediate states or steps.

Business model – A description of elements of a business. The Business Model Canvas is a good tool for describing nine elements of a business model.

Competence – The ability of an individual to understand the situation and take reasonable actions.

Core challenge – A description of the fundamental challenge facing an organization. The word *challenge* can mean problem, opportunity, or issue that affects the interests of the organization. The word *core* is used to suggest that the challenge is fundamental and central to long-term success. The articulation of the core challenge is a prerequisite and foundation for crafting strategy.

Culture – The shared learning of a group of people. Cultural change means unlearning things as well as learning new things.

Discontinuity – A change in expectations due to a weak signal that may or may not be disruptive to the status quo.

Emergence – The arising of novel states in complex systems. One of the X-factors of strategic thinking.

Fit, strategic – How well an organization's business model fits the external environment.

Fuzzy front end of strategy – The activities of probing the external and internal environments of the organization. The external environment is characterized by VUCA (volatility, uncertainty, complexity, and ambiguity).

Goal – An aspiration or target. Not the same thing as a strategy.

Horizons 1, 2, and 3 – Refers to time horizons. Horizon 1 (H1) is the short-term future. Horizon 3 (H3) is the distant future, where the things that are common now are uncommon. Horizon 2 (H2) is an intermediate stage.

Insight – A change from a mediocre story to a better story, caused by a change in story anchors (reframing). It's one of four X-factors of strategic thinking. Not the same thing as intuition.

Leadership, personal – A choice to grapple with the multi-faceted nature of reality and the courage to help other people do the same.

Operational thinking – A mindset that's focused on running the existing business within the confines of an existing business model. Works *in* the business rather than *on* the business. Contrasts with strategic thinking.

Plan, strategic – Programming of resources and actions to implement an already crafted strategy. See also tactical decision.

Pockets of the future in the present (PoF) – A low-prevalence item that has the potential, in the future, to be high prevalence. See also signal, weak.

Probe – The practice of exploring a poorly understood space to discover useful information. It involves asking open-ended questions to gain a deeper understanding of the interests and issues of the organization.

Program – A collection of projects and other things where the benefits of managing them as a program are greater than the benefits of managing them as individual projects.

Programming a strategy – As part of reaching a strategic decision, and afterwards, the organization programs its strategy with resources and guidance, allowing for tactical decisions.

Signal, weak – An object or concept that is of low salience or low prevalence that's perceived by only a few people. A weak signal can become a strong signal.

Solutioneering – Selecting a solution to a problem without having an adequate understanding of the context and the root causes of the problem.

Strategic initiative – An endeavor undertaken to achieve three inter-related outcomes: 1) a boundary-spanning vision or strategic intent, 2) realization of important benefits to "strategic" stakeholders, and 3) transformation of the organization.

Strategic thinking – An individual's capacity for – and practice of – using cognition to identify and organize factors that increase the probability of success in the future.

Strategy – 1) A specialized tool used to advance the interests of the organization by managing issues that have broad and long-term impact; 2) The integration of ways, means, and ends; 3) A good strategy has a diagnosis, guiding policy, and coherent action; 4) The smallest set of choices sufficient to guide all other choices.

Strategy, business – The focus of a business strategy is to provide superior value compared to competitors.

Strategy, corporate – The focus of a corporate strategy is the selection of a portfolio of businesses. Businesses are added to or removed from the portfolio.

Strategy, functional – Specialization of an internal activity such as human resources, engineering, product lines, manufacturing, development, technology, etc.

Structured back end of strategy – Activities in the crafting of strategy associated with making sense of weak signals and arriving at the core challenge.

Tactical decision – A decision that must adapt to another "more-strategic" decision.

Personal Branding as a Strategic Thinker

B RANDS ARE PROACTIVE EFFORTS to convey impressions of virtues and values. A personal brand is an individual asset. It is not your reputation (which is assigned by others and out of your control).

A good strategy is something that matches unique resources to the nuances of the situation. There are several similarities to personal branding in that unique resources are configured to achieve a result. The elements are coherent and reinforce a message of excellence.

The following list provides a few suggestions for incorporating *competent strategic thinker* as part of your personal brand:

- **Perspective.** As defined in Chapter 10, *perspective* is personality plus point of view. Your personal brand is unique and original. Foremost, it reflects your experiences. Use the microskill of reflection to identify times when you have noticed and used a landmark on the strategic thinking map, as well as when you've applied each of the microskills. You want to be more aware of your use of reasoning and strategic logic. Develop opinions about organizations and their strategies, and enhance them with stories and examples from your experience.

It's also a good idea to anticipate questions that challenge your perspective. A personal brand is more than an aspiration. It needs to be backed up by proof. Who might challenge you and aspects of your character and experience?

- **Social media.** I encourage you to have a presence on social media and to use that presence to share your interest in strategy. Take the time to curate articles and postings that are of interest to you and thoughtfully comment on them.

  Review your lists of followers and those you follow on social media. Are they strategic thinkers?

- **Thought leadership.** I recommend that you develop a speaking and writing platform showing your research, original ideas, criticisms, and opinions on strategy and strategic thinking. Many conferences and symposia are looking for panel members, session speakers, and keynotes. There are also many opportunities to write on the topic in books, magazines, and blogs.

  I believe that it's better to communicate for engagement with the audience rather than communicate to create an impression. (As an example, review the "About the Author" section in the preface.)

- **Elevator speech.** An elevator speech is a short descriptive statement of yourself and the benefits you deliver to others. Ideally, when others hear it, they reply, "That's very interesting to me. Tell me more."

- **Reflect on significant projects and other accomplishments.** I've seen time and again that people's memories of their accomplishments tend to fade. There's a strategic-thinking narrative in many projects and lessons to share. As with the above comment on perspective, recall and describe for others the specific examples of your relevant experience.

- **Does your resumé reflect your personal brand?** I have reviewed many resumés, and most of them are boring, bullet-pointed lists of activities. Instead, consider listing significant accomplishments and explain how your ability to think strategically contributed to those accomplishments. What awards have you earned? When has someone publicly complimented your work?

- **Daily examples.** Through your daily interactions with others and your practice of leadership, show others your ability to think strategically. You can demonstrate the 20 microskills of strategic thinking discussed in this book.

- **Write trip reports.** I encourage you to write and share your learning experiences with your colleagues. Do this every time you attend a conference, visit a client or supplier, or participate in a meeting with an external stakeholder.

   Weak signals and pockets of the future are all around us. Identify them and consider their implications. Provide specific recommendations if appropriate.

To better distinguish your strategic thinking competency as a distinct brand, consider the messages and promises implied by a personal brand of operational excellence. Because operational excellence is different from excellence in strategy, the contrast will help you to sharpen your strategic thinking messages.

NOTES

PREFACE

xvii. **The premise of meaningful learning:** For more on meaningful learning and the scaffolding of learning and memory, see the writings of psychologist David Ausubel. http://www.davidausubel.org/index.html.

CHAPTER 1

1. **An example of ambiguity:** This 1915 picture, by William Ely Hill, is known as "My Wife and My Mother-In-Law." For more about this, see Esther Inglis Arkett, "The World's Most Famous – And Ambiguious – Illusion," *Gizmodo*, October 16, 2014. http://io9.gizmodo.com/the-worlds-most-famous-and-ambiguous-illusion- 1646895274. Also see "Perceptual Ambiguity," IllusionWorks LLC, 1997. http://psylux.psych.tu-dresden.de/i1/kaw/diverses%20Material/www.illusionworks.com/html/perceptual_ambiguity.html.

7. **Competent individuals:** A court of law would define a competent person (in the context of participating in a legal proceeding) as one who has "the ability to understand a situation and act reasonably."

11. **"Conceptually, we define":** See Robert H. Dorff, "A Primer in Strategic Development," in Joseph R. Cerami and James F. Holcomb Jr., eds., *U.S. Army War College Guide to Strategy* (Carlisle, PA: U.S. Army War College Press, 2017). http://www.au.af.mil/au/awc/awcgate/army-usawc/strategy/02dorff.pdf.

12. **"There is a die-hard attitude":** See Jerry Rhodes, *Conceptual Toolmaking* (Hoboken, NJ: Blackwell, 1991), 21.

15–16. **They developed a new set of dominating ideas:** See Richard Normann, *Reframing Business: When the Map Changes the Landscape* (Hoboken, NJ: John Wiley & Sons, 2001), 3.

16. **Oakland's strategic logic:** See Michael Lewis, *Moneyball: The Art of Winning an Unfair Game* (New York: W. W. Norton & Company, 2003), 124.

CHAPTER 2

25. **"Our strategy is to":** Put these phrases into a search engine and you'll find verification: *CEO* and *Our strategy is.*

25. **"in and of themselves"**: See Louis V. Gerstner Jr., *Who Says Elephants Can't Dance* (New York: HarperBusiness, 2002), 223.

31. **"The real challenge"**: See Henry Mintzberg, "Crafting Strategy," *Harvard Business Review* (July 1987).

34. **Karl Weick and Kathleen Sutcliffe**: See Karl E. Weick and Kathleen M. Sutcliffe, *Managing the Unexpected* (San Francisco: Jossey-Bass, 2005), 43; emphasis added.

35. **Ed Murphy was advising us**: For more, see Corinne Purtill, "Murphy's Law is Totally Misunderstood and Is In Fact a Call to Excellence," *Quartz*, May 16, 2017. https://qz.com/984181/murphys-law-is-totally-misunderstood-and-is-in-fact-a-call-to-excellence/.

37. **Bad strategy is:** See Richard Rumelt, *Good Strategy, Bad Strategy: The Difference and Why it Matters* (New York: Currency, 2011), 42.

40. **"improve the ability to identify"**: See Daniel Kahneman, *Thinking Fast and Slow* (New York: Farrar, Straus and Giroux, 2011), 5, or loc. 40 of 9397, Kindle.

40. **Futures literacy is:** For an introduction to futures literacy, see Riel Miller, ed., *Transforming the Future: Anticipation in the 21st Century* (London: Routledge, 2018). https://www.taylorfrancis.com/books/e/9781351047999. Miller's concept of futures literacy has influenced much of my thinking on the topic. I use the phrase *futures literacy* a little more narrowly than he does.

CHAPTER 3

43. **Christopher Columbus is one of the most significant people:** *Time* magazine ranked Columbus #20 in a list of world history's most significant people.

43. **Christopher Columbus was born:** Much of the Columbus narrative was drawn from the Wikipedia entry, along with and augmented by Phillips and Lyon (noted below).

44. **The 30-year span from 1462 to 1492:** See William D. Phillips Jr. and Carla Rahn Phillips, *The Worlds of Christopher Columbus* (Cambridge, U.K.: Cambridge University Press, 1991).

45. **Some scholars refer:** Some scholars have actually termed Columbus's voyage as the "Toscanelli project." For example, see Mark Burdman, "The 'Toscanelli Project' Factor in the Christopher Columbus Story." *EIR* 14, no. 12 (March 20, 1987). http://www.larouchepub.com/eiw/public/1987/eirv14n12-19870320/eirv14n12-19870320_048-the_toscanelli_project_factor_in.pdf.

46. **"drop down south"**: The quote about Columbus's most significant insight is from Eugene Lyon, "The Search for Columbus, An In-Depth Analysis of the Genealogy of Christopher Columbus," *National Geographic* 181, no. 1 (January 1992).

47. **Columbus pivoted again:** The pivot toward the African trading model was described by William D. Phillips Jr. and Carla Rahn Phillips. (Page 12 tells you that Columbus acknowledged by the fourth voyage that he had not found the Asia that he expected and page 158 explains the new trading model).

47. **We can identify some of Columbus's criteria:** See "1492: An Ongoing Voyage," Library of Congress. https://www.loc.gov/exhibits/1492/columbus.html.

50. **"struggle against the limitations":** The full quote is from Norman Wiener: "The world of the future will be an ever more demanding struggle against the limitations of our intelligence, not a comfortable hammock in which we can lie down to be waited upon by our robot slaves."

52. **DICE:** Thanks to William Hoang for noticing the DICE acronym for the four X-factors.

52. **In a survey of 250 CEOs:** See Del Jones, "CEOs Show How Cheating Death Can Change Your Life," *ABC News* (March 11, 2009). https://abcnews.go.com/Technology/story?id=7057064&page=1.

54. **Its author, Michael Lewis:** Lewis related this story in his 2012 commencement speech at Princeton, titled, "Don't Eat Fortune's Cookie." See https://singjupost.com/michael-lewis-2012-commencement-speech-to-princeton-full-transcript/.

55. **"Luck plays a large role":** See Daniel Kahneman, *Thinking Fast and Slow* (New York: Farrar, Straus and Giroux 2011), 9, or loc. 144, Kindle.

56. **"the arising of novel":** See Wikipedia, s.v. "Emergence." https://en.wikipedia.org/wiki/Emergence. Economist Jeffrey Goldstein provided a current definition of emergence in the journal *Emergence*.

58. **"Neither Bill Gates":** See Paul Graham, "Frightenly Ambitious Startup Ideas," PaulGraham.com. http://www.paulgraham.com/ambitious.html.

CHAPTER 4

59. **several distinctive, developable microskills:** I borrowed the idea of macro-abilities and microskills from Richard Paul, "Strategies: Thirty-Five Dimensions of Critical Thinking," in A. J. A. Binker, *Critical Thinking: What Every Person Needs to Survive in a Rapidly Changing World* (Rohnert Park, CA: Foundation for Critical Thinking, 1991). http://www.criticalthinking.org/data/pages/93/2dc1156cb915ed5e2d4de94d2bfe79e9513644fd4c683.pdf.

60. **"They tend to question everything":** See Adam Bryant, "How to Be a CEO, from a Decades Worth of Them," *New York Times* (October 27, 2017). https://www.nytimes.com/2017/10/27/business/how-to-be-a-ceo.html?rref=collection%2Fcolumn%2Fcorner-office&action=click&contentCollection=business&region=stream&module=stream_unit&version=latest&contentPlacement=1&pgtype=collection.

61. **"impracticality in pursuit of ideas"**: The definition here is adapted from the Wikipedia description.

64. **People need to feel that the story is credible:** Many people know that movie adaptations differ from books. The movie *Moneyball* took several liberties in its telling. For example, the character of Peter Brand bore little resemblance to the real-life Paul DePodesta.

64. **"he faces tests"**: See Gideon Lichfield, "The Science of Near-Death Experiences," *The Atlantic* (April 2015). https://www.theatlantic.com/magazine/archive/2015/04/the-science-of-near-death-experiences/386231/.

67. **"Strategy must rank as"**: See David Barry and Michael Elmes, "Strategy Retold: Toward a Narrative View of Strategic Discourse," *Academy of Management Review* 22, no. 2: 429–52.

69. **"The power of authoritative knowledge"**: A quote from Brigitte Jordan in Kathy Levine's "Resilience as Authoritative Knowledge," *Journal of the Association of Research on Mothering* 10, no. 1: 133–45, in the context of explaining different birth practices in different cultures. See https://jarm.journals.yorku.ca/index.php/jarm/article/viewFile/16339/15198.

70. **Will Taylor's model of learning:** See Alan Chapman, "Conscious Competence Learning Model," Businessballs.com. https://www.businessballs.com/self-awareness/conscious-competence-learning-model-63/.

72. **Several years ago, I interviewed:** See Greg Githens, "The Pizza Turnaround," *Visions Magazine* (December 2010).

73–74. **An important task of strategic thinking:** See Wayne Michael Hall, *The Power of Will in International Conflict: How to Think Critically in Complex Environments* (Santa Barbara, CA: Praeger Security International, 2018).

75. **many executives are lost:** Simon Wardley provides a remarkably honest story about his early floundering as a CEO in Chapter One of his online book, *Wardley Maps*. https://medium.com/wardleymaps/on-being-lost-2ef5f05eb1ec.

76. **Besides navigational beacons:** See Edgar Chan, Oliver Baumann, Mark A Bellgrove, and Jason B Mattingley, "From Objects to Landmarks: The Function of Visual Location Information in Spatial Navigation," *Frontiers in Psychology* (August 27, 2012). https://www.ncbi.nlm.nih.gov/pmc/articles/PMC3427909/.

CHAPTER 5

81. **The operational thinking map is a separate map:** The military often uses the phrase *operational level* as a contrast to a *strategic level*. I'm not equating operational thinking with the military use of the words *operations* or *operational level*.

89. **"The word *process*"**: I searched for the phrase *Vice President Process* on LinkedIn and found over 34 thousand results in job titles and over 4,000 job postings containing the words.

89. **Regardless of the preferences of managers:** For more on the distinctions between process, practice, and art, see Michael Grieves, *Product Lifecycle Management: Driving the Next Generation of Lean Thinking* (New York: McGraw Hill, 2006).

94. **Jerry Weinberg explains:** See Gerald M. Weinberg, *The Secrets of Consulting: A Guide to Giving and Getting Advice Successfully* (New York: Dorset House Publishing, 1985).

95. **"industrial mutation":** Schumpeter quoted from this source: "Creative Destruction," Investopedia.com. https://www.investopedia.com/terms/c/creativedestruction. asp.

CHAPTER 6

99. **The fuzzy front end of strategy:** The phrase *fuzzy front end* is common in new product development environments. It refers to a phase where the innovator searches for opportunities in an uncertain space marked by unpredictable market demand, technical feasibility, and rivals with disguised intentions. The fuzziness contrasts with the relatively more-structured and more-formal back end, which involves designing specific offerings, developing marketing plans, producing the offering, launching it into the market, and transitioning to ongoing product management activities. Product developers argue that the quality of activities in the front end determines innovation success.

99. **The individual is noticing interesting things:** The words *curiosities, coincidences,* and *anomalies* are terms used by Gary Klein in *Seeing What Others Don't: The Remarkable Way We Gain Insights* (New York: Public Affairs, 2013). Their value in sparking insights is explored in Chapter 9.

101. **"You don't trade markets":** See Van K. Tharp, "The Psychology of Trading." http:// www.vantharp.com/tharp-concepts/psychology.asp.

103. **gemba visits:** *Gemba* is a Japanese word that roughly means to "go into the field and observe the truth." It is an observational technique widely used in new product development and quality improvement.

103. **The practice of set-based design:** An excellent introduction to set-based design is provided by Preston Smith in Chapter 5 of *Flexible Product Development: Building Agility for Changing Markets* (San Francisco: Jossey Bass, 2007). Smith published a revised edition in 2018.

106. **Steven French writes:** See Steven French, "Re-framing Strategic Thinking: The Research – Aims and Outcomes," *Journal of Management Development* 38, no. 3 (March 20, 2009). https://www.deepdyve.com/lp/emerald-publishing/re-framing-strategic-thinking-the-research-aims-and-outcomes-F0T0gh5Kjx?arti cleList=%2Fsearch%3Fquery%3Dsteven%2Bfrench%2Bstrategic%2Bthinking.

106. **"Moonshots don't begin":** Listen to Derek Thompson, "Inside Google's Moonshot Factory," *The Atlantic* (November 2017). https://soundcloud.com/user-154380542/inside-googles-moonshot-factory-the-atlantic-derek-thompson.

109. **Interestingly, research shows that asking for advice:** See Alison Wood Brooks, Francesca Gino, and Maurice E. Schweitzer, "Smart People Ask for (My) Advice: Seeking Advice Boosts Perceptions of Competence," *Management Science* (June 2015). https://www.hbs.edu/faculty/Publication%20Files/Advice%20Seeking_59ad2c42-54d6-4b32-8517-a99eeae0a45c.pdf.

110. **John Sowa defines:** See John F. Sowa, "The Challenge of Knowledge Soup." www.jfsowa.com/pubs/challenge.pdf.

112. **Abductive reasoning is used:** For example, see Amy C. Edmudson and Paul J. Verdin, "Your Strategy Should Be a Hypothesis You Constantly Adjust," *Harvard Business Review* (November 9, 2017). https://hbr.org/2017/11/your-strategy-should-be-a-hypothesis-you-constantly-adjust.

112. **Hypothesis Testing:** A few of those biases are briefly listed in Chris Bradley, Martin Hirt, and Sven Smit, "Have You Tested Your Strategy Lately?" *McKinsey Quarterly* (January 2011). https://www.mckinsey.com/business-functions/strategy-and-corporate-finance/our-insights/have-you-tested-your-strategy-lately.

112. **The simplest and easiest approach:** I drew these three levels from John F. Sowa's article, "Crystallizing Theories out of Knowledge Soup." http://www.jfsowa.com/pubs/crystal.htm.

114. **"We can't be sure":** See Martin A. Schwartz, "The Importance of Stupidity in Scientific Research," *Journal of Cell Science* 121 (2008): 1771.

CHAPTER 7

118. **William Gibson remarked:** William Gibson said during a 1999 interview on National Public Radio, "The future is already here – it's just not very evenly distributed." Some interesting background on the quote is provided at https://quoteinvestigator.com/2012/01/24/future-has-arrived/.

118. **The Three Horizons:** See Andrew Curry and Anthony Hodgson, "Seeing in Multiple Horizons: Connecting Futures to Strategy," *Journal of Futures Studies* (August 2008). http://jfsdigital.org/wp-content/uploads/2014/01/131-A01.pdf

121. **"The right lessons from Kodak":** See Scott D. Anthony, "Kodak's Downfall Wasn't about Technology," *Harvard Business Review* (July 15, 2016). https://hbr.org/2016/07/kodaks-downfall-wasnt-about-technology.

128. **There are three different kinds of anticipation:** This discussion on anticipation was influenced by Riel Miller, *The Future Now: Understanding Anticipatory Systems* (Chicago: World Future Society, July 16, 2009). http://www.leadingfuturists.biz/wp-content/The_Future_Now_v0.9_WFS_July_17_2009.pdf.

CHAPTER 8

136. **"The most important thing"**: See Louis V. Gerstner Jr., *Who Says Elephants Can't Dance: Leading a Great Organization Through Dramatic Change* (New York: Harper Business, 2002), 2.

136. **"For customers"**: Gerstner, 115.

136. **"After UNIX cracked"**: Gerstner, 119.

139. **"There was little true strategic"**: Gerstner, 46. Gerstner writes that he found the meeting exhausting and confusing.

140. **"He was disaggregating IBM"**: Gerstner, 119.

140. **IBM is too big**: Richard Rumelt made this observation about the importance of a changed diagnosis, which completely changed the guiding policy. The revised diagnosis noticed that IBM was different and held advantages. Its task was to improve internal coordination and agility. See Richard Rumelt, *Good Strategy, Bad Strategy: The Difference and Why It Matters* (New York: Currency, 2011), 83.

141. **"I can't tell you"**: Gerstner, 57.

144. **This results in a meaningless distinction**: See Roger L Martin, "The Execution Trap," *Harvard Business Review* (July-August 2010).

144. **Sometimes those lower-level decisions**: See Bill Vlasic, "Volkswagen Engineer Gets Prison in Diesel Cheating Case," *New York Times* (August 25, 2017). https://www.nytimes.com/2017/08/25/business/volkswagen-engineer-prison-diesel-cheating.html.

144. **"the most important decision"**: Gerstner, 61.

144. **The first essential characteristic of a strategic decision**: This section draws from the reasoning by Eric Van den Steen of Harvard. He defines strategy as the smallest set of choices sufficient to guide all other choices. Van den Steen says: "A strategy is not (1) a detailed plan of action or (2) a comprehensive set of choices and decisions; it is a plan of action boiled down to its most essential choices and decisions." See Eric Van den Steen, *A Theory of Explicitly Formulated Strategy*, Harvard Business School Strategy Unit Working Paper No. 12-102 (May 3, 2012).

146. **Policy describes a pattern of decisions**: Richard Rumelt explains this as "guiding policy" in *Good Strategy, Bad Strategy*.

147. **"bone-jarringly difficult"**: Gerstner, 153.

147. **Empowerment is a function**: For more, see William Nel, ed., *Management for Engineers, Technologists and Scientists* (Cape Town, South Africa: Juta and Company, 2006).

148. *Accountability* **is defined as:** See Greg Githens, "Accountability is the Willingness to Have Your Performance Measured," *Leading Strategic Initiatives*, 2013. https://leadingstrategicinitiatives.com/2013/05/08/accountability-is-the-willingness-to-have-your-performance-measured/.

148. **"The saga would pivot":** Gerstner, 121.

148. **"I believed very strongly":** Gerstner, 123.

149. **"All of this":** Gerstner, 127.

150. **"We were going":** Gerstner, 107.

CHAPTER 9

151. **Gerstner counts a meeting with Dennie Welsh:** See Louis V. Gerstner Jr., *Who Says Elephants Can't Dance? Leading a Great Enterprise Through Dramatic Change* (New York: HarperBusiness, 2002), 129–30.

152. **Gary Klein explains:** See Gary Klein, *Seeing What Others Don't: The Remarkable Ways We Gain Insights* (New York: PublicAffairs, 2013). I drew the definitional ideas for creating better stories from Chapter 2 and the three pathways from Chapter 8.

155. **Their logic is this:** This list paraphrases Rick Ross in Peter M. Senge et al., *The Fifth Discipline Fieldbook* (New York: Crown Business, 1994).

156. **"tremendous strengths":** Gerstner, 214.

156. **"so that it was viewed":** Gerstner, 130.

156. **The ladder of inference:** See Chris Argyris, *Action Science: Concepts, Methods, and Skills for Research and Intervention* (San Francisco: Jossey-Bass, 1985).

159. **Imagine a garden:** Gary Klein defines a garden-path story as when "someone adopts an erroneous frame and tenaciously preserves it despite mounting evidence to the contrary." See Klein, 238.

159. **A garden-path sentence:** See Brandon Specktor, "7 Simple Sentences That Drive English Speakers Crazy," *Reader's Digest*. You can find this and other examples at https://www.rd.com/culture/garden-path-sentences/.

160. **Gary Klein explains:** Gary Klein used the word *mediocre* sparingly in his book, writing that "shifts were discontinuous discoveries – unexpected transitions from a mediocre story to a better one" (Klein, 23), and about a "mediocre frame" (Klein, 75).

161. **The following four concepts:** The concepts of narration, abstraction, partitioning, and projection are described in Alan M. Davis, *Software Requirements: Objects, Functions, & States* (Upper Saddle River, NJ: Prentice Hall, 1993).

162. **Themes also serve:** The ideas in these paragraphs originated in a paper by David Barry and Michael Elmes, "Strategy Retold: Toward a Narrative View of Strategic Discourse," *Academy of Management Review* 22, no. 2: 429–52.

162. **"For IBM the lesson":** Gerstner, 175.

162. **"Our strategic moves":** Gerstner, 257.

165. **It's based on Richard Normann's advice:** This upframing technique is described in Richard Normann, *Reframing Business: When the Map Changes the Landscape* (Hoboken, NJ: John Wiley & Sons, 2001).

168. **"IBM's unique":** Gerstner, 130.

CHAPTER 10

179. **His habits of mind:** For more discussion of the quantitative mindset and how it can hinder strategic thinking, see Matthew J. Schmidt, "A Science of Context: The Qualitative Approach as Fundamental to Strategic Thought," in U.S. Government, *Exploring Strategic Thinking: Insights to Assess, Develop, and Retain Army Strategic Thinkers* (Progressive Management, 2014). https://ssl.armywarcollege.edu/dclm/pubs/Developing%20Army%20Strategic%20Thinkers.pdf.

179. **A difficult conversation:** See Douglas Stone, Bruce Patton, and Sheila Heen, *Difficult Conversations: How to Discuss What Matters Most* (New York: Penguin Books, 1999).

183. **"Character is both developed:"** See Rick Warren, *The Purpose-Driven Life: What on Earth Am I Here For?* (Grand Rapids, MI: Zondervan, 2002).

186. **To him it was common sense:** His remarks, including the quote that opens this chapter, can be reviewed in the video Jensen Huang, *Vision Versus Perspective*, 2009. https://ecorner.stanford.edu/video/vision-versus-perspective/.

CHAPTER 11

189. **"Unfortunately, the world":** See Eugene Soltes, "The Psychology of White Collar Criminals," *The Atlantic* (December 14, 2016). https://www.theatlantic.com/business/archive/2016/12/pyschology-white-collar-criminal/503408/. Also see Eugene Soltes, *Why They Do It, Inside the Mind of the White-Collar Criminal* (New York: PublicAffairs, 2016).

190. **Many people opine:** The "fundamental attribution error" is people's tendency, when judging the behaviors of others, to put more emphasis on personal characteristics and ignore situational factors.

190. **"expended surprisingly little effort":** See Soltes, *Atlantic*, and Soltes, PublicAffairs.

191. **"Success breeds complacency":** See Andrew Grove, *Only the Paranoid Survive* (New York: Doubleday, 1996).

192. **Metacognition is:** This definition is drawn from Lauren Scharff, "What Do We Mean by 'Metacognitive Instruction'?" *Improve with Metacognition* (March 21, 2015). http://www.improvewithmetacognition.com/what-do-we-mean-by-metacognitive-instruction/.

195–96. **I use the acronym DAYRT:** I drew these factors from Sylvia Boorstein, *It's Easier Than You Think: The Buddhist Way to Happiness* (HarperSanFrancisco, 1995). I replaced Boorstein's description of lust with yearning.

198. **"that's where the light is brightest":** This is known as the streetlight effect. An interesting look at its history is found at "'Did You Lose the Keys Here?' 'No, But the Light Is Much Better Here,'" Quote Investigator. https://quoteinvestigator.com/2013/04/11/better-light/.

198. **The availability heuristic:** See Daniel Kahneman, *Thinking Fast and Slow* (New York: Farrar, Straus and Giroux, 2011).

199. **The illusion of nostalgia:** For more, see Stephanie Coontz, *The Way We Never Were: American Families and the Nostalgia Trap* (New York: Basic Books, 2016).

199–200. **"The company's golden age":** See Louis V. Gerstner Jr., *Who Says Elephants Can't Dance? Leading a Great Enterprise Through Dramatic Change* (New York: HarperBusiness, 2002), 212. Also see Gerstner endnotes in previous chapters.

200. **Expertise, in this fast-changing world:** For more, see Karl E. Weick and Kathleen M. Sutcliffe, *Managing the Unexpected: Assuring High Performance in an Age of Complexity* (San Francisco: Jossey-Bass, 2001), 109. The authors suggest that the decision-making work should migrate to persons or teams who have expertise in the choice-problem combination.

200. **The planning fallacy:** The phrase *planning fallacy* was first used to describe the reasoning errors for optimistic project duration estimates. It's now in broader use for expressing any planning, including strategic plans. For more, see Daniel Kahneman's answer to an interview question. You can see the full text at Gallup, "The Truth About How We Think," *Gallup Business Journal* (March 20, 2012). http://www.gallup.com/businessjournal/153062/truth-think.aspx.

201. **"What do you get when":** Adapted from a joke in Scott Adams, *How's that Underling Thing Working for You?* (Kansas City, MO: Andrews McMeel Publishing, 2011).

201. **Bernhard Gunther:** See Bernhard Gunther, "A Case Study in Combating Bias," *McKinsey Quarterly* (May 2017). https://www.mckinsey.com/business-functions/organization/our-insights/a-case-study-in-combating-bias.

CHAPTER 12

208. **These three questions:** I learned these three questions from John Arnold, *Shooting the Executive Rapids* (New York: McGraw Hill, 1981).

211. **I encourage you:** See Peter M. Senge, *The Fifth Discipline Fieldbook* (New York: Crown Business, 1994). It offers a readable explanation of the ladder of inference, with further examples and related tools.

216. **Barry Johnson's five types of decisions:** See Barry Johnson, *Polarity Management: Identifying and Managing Unsolvable Problems* (Amherst, MA: HRD Press, 1992).

CHAPTER 13

221. **"We are called upon":** See Rollo May, *The Courage to Create* (New York: W.W. Norton & Company, 1975).

222. **Leadership is a choice:** Similar ideas have been attributed to Warren Bennis, Seneca, Dan Goleman, and others.

222. **I find it helpful to define a "leadership zone":** The concept of leadership described in this chapter is a paraphrasing of Susan J. Ashford and D. Scott DeRue, "Developing as a Leader: The Power of Mindful Engagement," *Organizational Dynamics* 41, no. 2 (2012): 146–54. http://webuser.bus.umich.edu/sja/pdf/DevAsLeader.pdf.

223. **I find the BALD framework:** These four forces are described in Paul Lawrence and Nitin Nohria, *Driven: How Human Nature Shapes our Choices* (San Francisco: Jossey-Bass, 2002).

226. **The opposite of bravery is cowardice:** The contrast of courage and conformity is suggested by this Jim Hightower quote: "The opposite for courage is not cowardice, it is conformity. Even a dead fish can go with the flow."

227. **Jerry B. Harvey suggests:** The source of these four questions is Jerry B. Harvey, *The Abilene Paradox and Other Meditations on Management* (San Francisco: Jossey-Bass, 1988), 120.

228. *Extra*-**ordinary Leadership:** I believed for a while that I had originated the idea of extra-ordinary leadership, but later I discovered quite a few references connecting Ralph Stacey and the topic.

228. **"Ordinary leadership involves":** The earliest citation for the contrast of perfecting the known versus imperfectly seizing the unknown is Kevin Kelly, "New Rules for the New Economy," *Wired* (September 1997). https://www.wired.com/1997/09/newrules/.

231. **Consider asking *questions in the service of the asked*:** I learned about this idea from Tim Doherty, "Lessons from the Believing Game," *The Journal of the Assembly for Expanded Perspectives on Learning* 15 (2009). https://trace.tennessee.edu/jaepl/vol15/iss1/5.

232. **"Hard work is about risk":** See Seth Godin, *Whatcha Gonna Do With That Duck? And Other Provocations, 2006–2012* (New York: Portfolio, 2012).

232. **Increasing purposefulness:** See Heike Bruch and Sumatra Ghoshal, "Beware the Busy Manager," *Harvard Business Review* (February 2002).

233. **"You really have to understand":** See H. Anna Suh, ed., *Van Gogh's Letters: The Mind of the Artist in Paintings, Drawings, and Words, 1875–1890* (New York: Black Dog and Leventhal, 2010).

234. **The concept of ambiguity:** There has been little attention given to ambiguity in the mainstream of leadership thinking. My evidence for this claim includes a sampling of leadership books on my personal bookshelf (I didn't find a single index entry about ambiguity), a search of several of the top-ranked leadership books on Amazon (only the occasional citation), and some conversations with colleagues who teach leadership seminars (not a firm grasp of what a leader should do about ambiguity). Using the search phrase *leadership and ambiguity*, I discovered a small handful of management books that featured ambiguity, notably David J. Wilkinson, *The Ambiguity Advantage: What Great Leaders are Great At* (Basingstoke, U.K.: Palgrave Macmillan, 2006), and Paul Culmsee and Kailash Awati, *The Heretic's Guide to Management: The Art of Harnessing Ambiguity* (Marsfield NSW, Australia: Heretics Guide Press, 2016).

235. **Research shows that humility is linked:** See Michael W. Austin, "Humility," *Psychology Today* (June 27, 2012). https://www.psychologytoday.com/blog/ethics-everyone/201206/humility.

235. **Humble CEOs:** See "It's Hard to Find a Humble CEO. Here's Why," *The Conversation* (August 21, 2017). https://theconversation.com/its-hard-to-find-a-humble-ceo-heres-why-81951.

236. **When you feel gratitude:** See Robert H. Frank, *Success and Luck: Good Fortune and the Myth of Meritocracy* (Princeton: Princeton University Press, 2016).

APPENDIX C

246. **In 1918, Dada artist Tristan Tzara:** See Tristan Tzara, "Data Manafesto," *391.org* (March 23, 1918). http://391.org/manifestos/1918-dada-manifesto-tristan-tzara.html#.WvrwfogvyM8.

ACKNOWLEDGEMENTS

No one can become proficient at their craft without help. I am indebted to those who taught me and worked with me over the years. Some were teachers, some were mentors, some were colleagues, some were clients, and some were my students. They are too numerous to mention, but not forgotten.

I received valuable critiques and suggestions for improvement on my early drafts and manuscript from John Watson, Jack Duggal, Sue Smedinghoff, Gary Hamby, Robert Beatty, Rita Northrup, Gerald Lowe, Kristina Brown, Jeff Wolfe, and Justin Bushko. A special shout out goes to Jennifer Vincent and Robert Presley for their generous investment of time.

A picture is worth a thousand words. I appreciate the illustrations by Tanja Russita (Figure 1-3, Figure 5-1, and Figure 9-1) and Doan Trang (Figure 7-1 and Figure 12-1). Each creatively translated my vague ideas into concrete images.

And finally, I am grateful to Jim Pennypacker and Deborah Weiss at Maven House Press for their invaluable support and professional guidance during the manuscript development, editing, and production.

Thank you all!

INDEX

ABOUT THE AUTHOR

Greg Githens is an executive coach, seminar leader, keynote speaker, and management consultant with work experience on six continents. His audiences and clients include Essilor of America, Ecom Group, VR Systems, United Illuminating, Weber-Stephens, PetSmart, United Healthcare, The University of Toledo, Sauder Woodworking, SSOE, The Andersons, Bryan Healthcare, the American Red Cross, 3M, IBM, and the United States Air Force.

The most important tool is the one between your ears is an idea that informs much of his teaching, writing, and advice. He has authored numerous articles on strategic thinking, strategic initiatives, innovation, program delivery, and new product development. He holds a master's degree in business administration from Bowling Green State University, a master's degree from Miami University, and a bachelor's degree from The Ohio State University. He holds the Project Management Professional (PMP) certification.

CPSIA information can be obtained
at www.ICGtesting.com
Printed in the USA
LVHW091105040619
620087LV00002B/6/P